Mapping Populism

Taking Politics to the People

John Agnew
University of California, Los Angeles

Michael Shin
University of California, Los Angeles

ROWMAN & LITTLEFIELD
Lanham • Boulder • New York • London

Executive Editor: Susan McEachern
Editorial Assistant: Katelyn Turner
Senior Marketing Manager: Amy Whitaker

Credits and acknowledgments for material borrowed from other sources, and reproduced with permission, appear on the appropriate page within the text.

Published by Rowman & Littlefield
An imprint of The Rowman & Littlefield Publishing Group, Inc.
4501 Forbes Boulevard, Suite 200, Lanham, Maryland 20706
www.rowman.com

6 Tinworth Street, London SE11 5AL, United Kingdom

British Library Cataloguing in Publication Information Available

Library of Congress Cataloging-in-Publication Data Available

ISBN 978-1-5381-2401-7 (cloth)
ISBN 978-1-5381-2402-4 (pbk.)
ISBN 978-1-5381-2403-1 (electronic)

Contents

List of Figures and Maps   v

Preface   vii

1   Introduction: The "Wave" of Populism   1

2   Mapping Populism   19

3   Should We Stay or Should We Go? European Immigration, Globalization, and Brexit   47

4   Reality Bites: The Unexpected Victory of Donald Trump   67

5   Two Steps Forward, One Step Back? Marine Le Pen and the National Front in France   91

6   When in Rome . . . Populism and the Five Star Movement in Italy   113

7   Conclusion   137

References   147

Index   165

Figures and Maps

FIGURES

Figure 2.1	Embrace the world or protect ourselves?	24
Figure 2.2	Left behind.	37
Figure 2.3	Turnout decline across democracies, 1950–2016.	41
Figure 2.4	Peak populism?	45
Figure 3.1	How Britain voted.	53
Figure 3.2	Voting by age group.	58
Figure 3.3	Trust in Cameron and Johnson.	63
Figure 3.4	Key issues surrounding Brexit.	65
Figure 4.1	Dimensions of polarization in the United States, 1994–2017.	75
Figure 4.2	Change in voter turnout by race in selected states, 2012–2016.	84

MAPS

Map 2.1	Populism across the European Union.	30
Map 3.1	Geography of Brexit.	51
Map 3.2	Brexit turnout.	59
Map 4.1	2016 presidential election margin versus 2012 presidential election margin, by US congressional district.	79
Map 4.2	Red state, blue state—electoral college winner by state, 2016.	80

Map 4.3	Estimated voter turnout by county, 2016.	82
Map 5.1	The geography of Round 1 results.	98
Map 5.2(a)	Le Pen vote share, Round 1.	99
Map 5.2(b)	Fillon vote share, Round 1.	100
Map 5.3(a)	Voter turnout, Round 1.	104
Map 5.3(b)	Voter turnout, Round 2.	104
Map 5.3(c)	Voter turnout differential, Round 1 versus Round 2.	105
Map 5.3(d)	Null vote, Round 2.	105
Map 5.4	Geographic age distribution in France, 20–59.	106
Map 6.1(a)	Geography of Forza Italia, 2018.	124
Map 6.1(b)	Geography of Democratic Party, 2018.	125
Map 6.1(c)	Geography of League, 2018.	126
Map 6.1(d)	Geography of Five Star Movement (M5S), 2018.	127
Map 6.2(a)	Change in Forza Italia, 2018–2013.	128
Map 6.2(b)	Change in Democratic Party, 2018–2013.	129
Map 6.2(c)	Change in League, 2018–2013.	130
Map 6.2(d)	Change in Five Star Movement (M5S), 2018–2013.	131
Map 6.3	Geography of 2018 voter turnout.	132
Map 6.4	Geography of youth unemployment, 2016.	135

Preface

King Canute, the Danish-born king of England in the early eleventh century, apparently rebuked his courtiers for their public flattery of him that he could control the tides. History has in fact recorded the opposite: that Canute was arrogant enough to believe that he was powerful enough to do so. In this regard Canute has become something of a poster king for a politics in which a single leader or movement can move the earth by sheer strength of will. Contemporary populism across the United States and Europe cannot be entirely reduced to this simple story. But it certainly has this aspect to it. The nostalgia for immediate and complete territorial sovereignty as a solution to all problems is based on a narrative that completely oversimplifies the actual history of the powers exercised by national governments in relation to both one another and to other actors (Agnew 2018a).

A sleight of hand is often involved in identifying the "people" to whom "control" will be "returned." "The people" is supposedly the entire body of residents or citizens, but usually the actual people implied is a founding ethnic or regional group whose centrality is now in question. What we call "postmodern" populism uses ambiguous signaling about the identity of the people and the recognition they deserve rather than offering much by way of a set of consistent policy measures even as it recruits those disillusioned with existing politics and institutions in support of leaders and slogans that promise a better tomorrow. Some of this undoubtedly reflects grievances over recent economic travails, but, in our view, the form of contemporary populism is shaped much more by concerns over status anxiety in the face of a rapidly shrinking and changing world.

This book explores the recent explosion of populism across the United States and western Europe, specifically, the United Kingdom, France, and Italy. We use a geographical perspective to test the main tenet of populism that a politics unmediated by geographical differences and institutional practices is possible in redeeming the territorial state for the people. This is populism's alternative to what has become "normal" electoral politics exercised through political parties with distinctive demographic and geographical constituencies. This may seem to be a "hard" test. Contemporary populism, however, seeks to break substantially with conventional mediated politics by emphasizing a direct connection between leader and populace, the use of new social media to do so, and the excoriation of established media of communication and the political "caste" that the media are seen as enabling. This is the "populist illusion" that Pierre-André Taguieff (2002) speaks of. As Jan-Werner Müller (2016, 35) puts it, "Populists always want to cut out the middleman, so to speak, and to rely as little as possible on complex party organizations as intermediaries between citizens and politicians."

More specifically, we also emphasize the breakdown in conventional representational politics in the hands of established political parties, leading to increased nonvoting and deliberate abstention from electoral contests and the importance of the new social media in mobilizing voters for populist movements, leaders, and claims. The current wave of populist outbreaks is not therefore a simple reiteration of a historic and unchanging "populism" directly inherited from the past but an adaptation to new material and symbolic circumstances triggered by a sense of "crisis" (a favorite word of populists worldwide) in conventional politics and the availability of new means of political communication (Moffitt 2016).

The book is organized into seven chapters. The first chapter lays out the three central issues—the meaningfulness of the very term "populism," the distinctive character of contemporary populism, and the notion of "the people" that lies behind it—as well as the mapping approach that we take in looking at four specific cases. The mapping approach draws loosely on a previous paper published in 2017 (Agnew and Shin 2017). The second chapter provides a more detailed discussion of our perspective on populism, drawing particularly on the writing of Benjamin Moffitt (2016), Rogers Brubaker (2017), John Judis (2016), and Luca Ricolfi (2017), among others. None of these writers is responsible for what we have done with their important contributions to the debate over the political sociology of contemporary populism. We spend considerable energy discussing the history of populism to show how much the recent explosion has important historical roots and precursors, yet is also different in crucial ways.

The subsequent four chapters deal chronologically, from 2016 through 2018, with the most recent electoral manifestations of populism as defined in Chapter 2. Chapter 3 addresses the UK referendum on leaving the European Union, Chapter 4 details the election of Donald Trump to the presidency of the United States in the same year, Chapter 5 examines the French presidential election of 2017 and the case of the National Front, and Chapter 6 describes the rise of the Five Star Movement in Italy in the 2018 national election and how its electoral success relates to other populist movements in the present (the League) and in the recent past. In each of these chapters we follow basically the same methodological format, using electoral analysis, reports on opinion surveys, and mapping of electoral outcomes, primarily in visual terms, to show overall outcomes. We draw attention to three specific facets that we claim help us understand the recent rise of populism: nonvoting and electoral turnouts, the role of leaders, and the significance of new social media. The final chapter provides a brief summary of the cases, the main conclusions that can be drawn from comparing the four cases, and a set of observations about the current situation of populist movements in the four countries, as well as populism's general impact on politics more generally in the future.

A number of people have helped bring this book to fruition. We would particularly like to thank Susan McEachern at Rowman & Littlefield for her patience and enthusiasm, Felicity Nussbaum for offering considerable editorial assistance, and Benjamin Forest for encouraging us to venture into a comparative endeavor. As with our 2008 book, *Berlusconi's Italy*, we are convinced also with regard to this project on populism that *unus vir nullus vir* (two heads are better than one).

John Agnew
Michael Shin
January 12, 2019

1

Introduction

The "Wave" of Populism

Since 2016 a "wave" of populism has swept over a broad swathe of countries with fateful consequences. The wave has included such events as the decision to leave the European Union on the part of the UK electorate (Brexit), the election of the reality-TV celebrity Donald Trump to the US presidency, and the creation of a populist-based government in Italy. It also involves the more widespread emergence of a new approach to politics across an array of countries that often demonizes immigrants, frequently finds favor with authoritarian-nationalist dictators, such as Russia's Vladimir Putin, who are seen as both "strong" and "decisive" compared to dithering regular democratic politicians, and that invariably looks for a renewed emphasis on national solutions in the face of an overpowering globalization and too much interference in "our" business from supranational alliances and organizations such as the North Atlantic Treaty Organization, the North American Free Trade Agreement, and the European Union.

The current wave also extends well beyond Europe and North America to cover populisms of various genres in the Philippines, Bangladesh, India, Turkey, Brazil, and elsewhere. The end of the Cold War and the questioning of economic globalization provide the overall geopolitical frame for this tendency for populations to turn inward.

In this book we cannot address all these elements in empirical detail, even though many of the general considerations apply across all the cases mentioned. That populism as a phenomenon is worldwide, however, is important to note. Populism is not just an issue for so-called liberal democracies. Rather, it signifies the end of the optimism about the spread of liberal democracy that was based in large part on multiparty elections and the institutionalization of the rule of law that characterized the 1990s.

The election of Donald Trump has been particularly consequential in that the United States has not been, at least until now, just another country. Crucially, then, populism can have consequences well beyond the borders of those who would like to reinforce theirs when the country in question is a powerful and influential one. Trump's success is an inspiration to right-wing populists worldwide (Rachman 2018). Trump's "America First" slogan, borrowed seemingly unconsciously from 1930s US isolationist/pro-Nazi usage, signifies a clear rhetorical retreat from US sponsorship of both globalization and liberal democracy. Some who support Trump might well think that it also means no more US military interventions around the world. That remains to be seen. But it also indicates how much populism involves recycling slogans from prior times of populist explosion.

The current movements are not, however, simply a revival of older varieties of populism. They also suggest that much of what now qualifies as populism is in fact a reaction to the cultural changes that have accompanied the changing world order over the past fifty years. Trump's base of supporters, like those voting "leave" in the Brexit referendum, those voting for Marine Le Pen in France in 2017, and some of the Italian populists elected in 2018, are all engaged in an unlikely revolt against the "globalist hegemony" that dates from the late 1960s. That the globalization of this epoch has its roots more in technological change and in the strategies of multinational businesses searching for ways to overcome the limits to their profitability imposed by remaining national in orientation escapes much notice. The focus is usually on the cosmopolitan "ideology" of urban-living cultural elites rather than the practices of big business.

Contemporary right-wing populism also argues against what, in shorthand, we might call "1968": the civil rights and antiwar rebellions of that year (Betz 2018). The culture wars that began at that time, associated in particular with women's and minority rights but critical of traditional cultural norms tout court, are a powerful part of contemporary populism's political target. Yet populism borrows from that era in its disdain for technical expertise, meritocracy, and parliamentary compromises. Above all, it is also against the cosmopolitanism and the "world that knows no boundaries"—motifs that it associates with the aid given to foreigners and fuzzy border enforcement that have undermined governmental prioritization of "our" people.

WHY NOW?

The term "populism" is by no means new, and its use is a contentious one across a relatively wide range of political movements that have differences as well as similarities in organization and outlook. If Brexit arose because of a split within the UK Conservative Party, and Trump's ascendancy has involved the capture of the US Republican Party, elsewhere populism is the result of distinctive political movements founded outside the bounds of established parties. In much writing about contemporary populism, the presumption is that it is a relatively sudden phenomenon arising spontaneously from the efforts of those "left behind" economically in the recent great economic recession beginning in 2007–2008 and/or in response to immigration, particularly that involving refugees and undocumented immigrants, as a major political issue (for the former, see, e.g., McQuarrie 2017 and Essletzbichler et al. 2018; in both regards, see, e.g., Hobolt 2016).

There is little doubt that these factors have been of importance in stimulating the spread of support for populist politicians in recent years. Globalization and its consequences, such as the declining power of labor unions, stagnating working-class incomes, austerity budgets, and increased anxiety about the future, provide the backdrop to recent political change (e.g., Cowie 2010; Rydgren 2006; Spruyt et al. 2016; Streeck 2017). For the post–World War II baby boomer generation looking backward, there is enormous nostalgia for a world seemingly lost but whose guarantees were often less certain than are now supposed (e.g., Webber and Rigby 1996). The ending of the Cold War in 1991 both removed the sense of geopolitical stasis that had prevailed for forty-five years and undermined the political parties on the left and the right that had become somewhat oriented to its ideological division. Some, such as the Communist parties in Italy and France and the Christian Democrats in Italy, disappeared from the scene. Others scrambled to give themselves new meaning.

It is our contention, however, that today's populism is a style of political mobilization and communication based on the identity and language of "ordinary people" versus a commanding political "elite." It reflects a blistering critique of established mechanisms of politics, such as traditional political parties, state bureaucracies, professional politicians, and technocratic expertise, more than a set of settled policy positions about this or that "issue" (Moffitt and Tormey 2014). Indeed, its proponents appeal emotionally to voter identities as much as or more than to reasoned preferences or opinions about specific problems (e.g., Sides et al. 2018; Davies 2018a; Norris and Inglehart 2019). They criticize "establishment politicians" for being too focused on specifics and empirics and not addressing the overriding questions of the day (immigration, job security, future economic prospects, status uncertainty, terrorism, etc.) that they believe require dramatic gestures and the disruption of conventional norms. This version of populism is antagonistic to and belittling of its "foes" rather than agonistic, in the sense of accepting a degree of accommodation with political adversaries in order to resolve different policy issues.

"Crisis" is the constant refrain of populists, reflecting the fact that populism is more about triggering a break with the past, politically and constitutionally, by invoking crises about this and that danger or threat rather than presenting a straightforward response to an external crisis such as recession or austerity (Moffitt 2015). In other words, it is rhetorical, opportunistic, and, above all, oppositional in character; it is devoted not to defining clear programs of action but to emphasizing the negatives of the present that only total change (i.e., election of its proponents) can resolve. Indeed, policies are often made up "on the fly" and dropped if they do not rouse much popular enthusiasm. It is about triggering identity crises, not addressing material interests, per se.

ARE POPULISTS EVERYWHERE AND NOWHERE?

This book is not primarily a treatise in political theory concerned to refine or refute a definition of populism (see, e.g., Abromeit 2017). The focus is much more on the trajectory of political actors and events labeled as "populist" across a limited number of countries—Italy, France, the United Kingdom, and the United States—to show how well the appeals of these actors have fared in terms of support from voters across the length and breadth of the countries in question. Our purpose is to show how the lived experience of voters of different generations in different places combines with the way elections are organized (such as referenda on Brexit or the electoral college in US presidential elections) to produce electoral outcomes for populist actors. In so doing the argument confronts one of the central claims of all those labeled as populist: that politics does not require any sort of geographical or institutional mediation but can be organized on a purely national basis through emphasis on the singular role of the "leader" or the technological possibilities of media such as television and internet platforms, including websites, Twitter, and Facebook. Contemporary populism, therefore, in distinction from establishment politics in the form of conservative, liberal, and socialist parties, should be relatively invariant in its appeal across the national territory, without social class or other bias, simply because it represents the spirit and purpose of "the people" as a whole. This view claims to be based in "popular sovereignty" rather than to reflect the various demographic and economic segments conventionally attached to establishment parties.

As we proceed through our case studies, we attempt to retain a high degree of objectivity in our effort at understanding the basis of support for the different populist movements. But this should not be confused with neutrality (on the distinction between objectivity and neutrality, see, e.g., Haskell 1998). As citizens of two of the countries at hand, we cannot but examine the various movements in a critical light. Thus, at the same time that we present considerable empirical evidence to describe the roots of populist sentiment, usually in the visual form of maps and graphs, we also must necessarily refer to the rhetorical excess and overclaims that are the all-too-frequent stock-in-trade of contemporary populism. Not to do so would be a dereliction of scholarly duty. Seeking to understand does not require a commitment to excuse.

As one example of the confusion, we would point to an article by Mark Lilla (2018) that finds some evidence for environmentalism and communitarianism, as opposed to just xenophobia and jingoism, in a faction within the French Far Right. That faction adopts, he argues, a Gramscian strategy of changing society (thus follows in the footsteps of Italian Communist Antonio Gramsci), but Lilla fails to point out how overwhelmingly reactionary this faction still is (McAuley 2019a). Another example would be the book by Matthew Goodwin and Roger Eatwell (2018) that, while based in empirical data from the United Kingdom and United States and scattered information from elsewhere, tends to the apologetic in completely overstating, for example, the crucial role of multiethnic and working-class support for Brexit and

Trump. The fact that only a minority of the eligible population actually voted for either is occluded in favor of an emphasis on how much "multiculturalism" and left-wing identity politics have paved the way for populism. The authors miss the fact that dissatisfaction with liberal democracy need not take such reactionary forms. The line between "understanding" and "apology" is often a narrow one.

In this chapter we provide a brief overview of populism as it relates to European and US contexts today in comparison to past eras. We then turn to the question of "the people" that is central to a discussion of populism. In describing our approach to "placing" or mapping populism, we lay out the main thesis of the book: that the politics without geographical and institutional mediation that populism promises is clearly unrealizable while democratic elections remain the modus operandi of political life. This requires us to show the ways in which geography affects collective electoral expression. Finally, the chapter concludes with a summary of the general approach and organization of the book.

WHAT IS POPULISM?

The word "populism" is increasingly capacious (e.g., Brubaker 2017; Hubé and Truan 2017). At one time it referred specifically to political movements geared toward diminishing the political influence of economic elites and pushing for redistribution of incomes to "the people" at large. This was the meaning populism had in US politics at the turn of the twentieth century. This version was entirely left-wing in the sense of verging on or overlapping with socialism, at least of the parliamentary or electoral varieties. This type of populism still has political mileage: witness the success of Bernie Sanders in the 2016 US Democratic Party presidential primaries and caucuses and of Podemos in Spain and Syriza in Greece. Radical politics at the local level across the United States can also lay claim to the term "populism" (e.g., Grattan 2016).

Increasingly, however, particularly in Europe and North America, populism is now right-wing and overtly nationalist rather than leftist and weakly nationalist or localist (e.g., Bonikowski 2017). It is fervently disruptive, looking for totalistic change in the status quo. The compromises and pork barrel exchanges that typically make politics work across socially and geographically heterogeneous countries are decried as deceptive and corrupt. Dark conspiracies, once confined to the nutcase fringes of politics, are posited openly. "There's something going on" provides a rhetorical vacuum into which listeners can give their own answer with whatever threat or fear of challenge or difference from immigrants, Jews, Muslims, Islamist terrorists, the European Union, Chinese economic competition, and so on they care to choose (e.g., Knight 2002; Angelos 2017; Evans 2018). The collective memory of where this conspiratorial mind-set took the world in the 1930s has been lost (Ganesh 2018).

Oppositional demagoguery, rather than much in the way of constructive policy proposals that could actually be followed once government were achieved, tends to be the leitmotif of much contemporary populism, including the often central claim to be "overcoming" the historic distinction between Left and Right. Clearly, however, in response to what they claim established parties have failed to do, most contemporary populist movements promise their potential supporters *protection* in the face of fear and danger (Ricolfi 2017). Likewise, sense of loss more than potential for the future tends to be the overwhelming refrain: "taking back the country" rather than discussing what that might actually involve (e.g., Stephens 2018). The campaign in Britain to leave the European Union in 2016 had all these features. Nostalgia for a world that had been lost after joining the EU in 1972 was its leitmotif. There was no plan for what to do next if the referendum were successful.

Yet the French National Front, the American Trump, the Hungarian Victor Orban, and the Spanish Podemos are all labeled populist, although the first three are avowedly nationalist and the last is clearly radical-socialist. This leads some commentators to wonder if the term has lost any continuing analytical meaning in reference to an identifiable "people," its original point of origin. Attacks on vaguely specified "special interests" and claims to represent "the people against the politicians" are all that most movements designated as populist have in common. The term "populism" now serves only a propaganda purpose: to normalize "center" politics by exiling political movements critical of contemporary economic and social trends, particularly the neoliberal capitalism associated with economic globalization, to the populist extremes by labeling them as "populist" (D'Eramo 2013).

In other words, globalist elites use the term to deny the victims of globalization their role as victims. The rise of contemporary populism certainly correlates with the stagnating incomes, increased income inequality, and declining life opportunities for many in countries that experienced high economic growth and increasing incomes from the 1950s through the 1980s. Populism is directed at the political parties that sponsored the technocratic "there is no alternative" trade agreements, supranational institutions, and austerity budgets in the years since (e.g., Roberts 2010; Crouch 2011; Blyth 2013). Given that populism can be a response to real material circumstances and not simply the revenge of historic prejudices, the term "populist" is currently in danger of becoming one entirely of polemical abuse. It can, in normative formulation, provide the means for constructing a "real" people in a counterhegemony against the dominance of oligarchy or technocracy (as in Ernesto Laclau's essays in Howarth 2015, for example). This was one of the main inspirations for Podemos in Spain (Errejón and Mouffe 2016). Laclau's experience with Latin American populism, particularly Peronism in Argentina, led him to carefully explore the ways in which a leftist populism could be built but also to identify the ways in which it could drift into authoritarianism (Tarragoni 2017). Unfortunately, this sort of thoughtful articulation of goals and policies is not at all typical of most movements labeled as populist.

Whatever the truth to this claim that populism is an increasingly meaningless term, we think that it exaggerates the idea that supporters of this or that populism are simply rational actors pursuing their interests, for in many regards they are responding to emotional triggers pulled by demagogic politicians. In fact there are typologies of populism to help distinguish the range of meanings the term has now acquired. Perhaps the two constants that serve to make the term of some continuing analytic use lie in (1) the idea of "taking politics to the people" by means of limiting and undermining the dominant political caste or establishment of existing political parties, which are seen as unresponsive to popular demands and the public interest and as increasingly captured and corrupted by private interests, and (2) the framing of "the people" in the entirely territorial sense of a founding or native group, particularly the "ordinary people" in it, increasingly threatened by foreign and/or domestic invaders, migrants, or cultural influences. Bringing back "sovereignty" to these people is the refrain, when in fact sovereignty in the sense of a totally contained and territorialized statehood has never ever been absolute (Agnew 2018a). Like magic, however, all their worldly problems will be resolved once all powers elsewhere are repatriated homeward. This is the fantasy of "sovereign populism" (Taguieff 2007; Feltri 2018).

TYPES OF POPULISM

The major differences among "types" of populism involve relative emphasis on the role of the leader/inciter-in-chief, the nation as opposed to the people (making it indistinguishable from ethnic nationalism), the promise of a "new beginning" versus rotation between essentially centrist/status quo parties, the identification of a past golden age, dismissiveness toward the arguments and evidence of intellectuals and scientists, and desire to wreck the current state apparatus or "deep state" and bureaucracies that service "undeserving" groups. Other important elements of difference among the types include appeals to the "common sense" of ordinary people, the role of a foreign or domestic threat (a minority group, foreigners, immigrants, or external enemy), pursuit of a religious agenda in response to economic and cultural changes emanating from domestic "cultural elites" and beyond national shores, and regime change in the sense of challenging current constitutional arrangements to get around separation of powers and limits on majority rule.

Though populist movements do differ, then, in terms of their organization and content, they all reflect the increasing conflict between what can be called popular "common sense" and the knowledge claims of so-called elites. On the one side are arrayed those who understand the world in terms of "natural" racial hierarchies and civilizational claims, and on the other are those who welcome a world of relatively open borders and cross-cultural influences. At least that is the framing of the conflict offered by the "organic intellectuals" of populism such as Steve Bannon in the United States and Beppe Grillo in Italy. A large part of this seems due to a sense of collective invisibility in which other, less deserving groups get "welfare" at their expense (this sentiment is particularly strong in the United States [Mettler 2018; Badger 2018]); a profound suspicion of existing politics and politicians, including those of governing institutions; and a lack of trust in "business as usual" but an inability to situate this in a broader critique of the contradictions of capitalism and liberal democracy, including the fact that it was their lauded national states that enabled the very globalization that they now rail against (e.g., Crehan 2016; Schiavone 2013; Rosanvallon 1992; Slobodian 2018).

There is obvious overlap on the part of many populisms with nationalist and fascist movements, although if the term "populist movement" is to mean anything it should lack the overt orientation to imperialism and territorial expansion, explicit repudiation of the entire current constitutional regime, and redemption for irredentist brethren or ethnic cleansing that tend to characterize the other two. As with fascism and associated authoritarianisms in 1920s and 1930s Europe, contemporary populist movements do feed off one another (e.g., Hall 2018). In this regard, and in the focus on enemies at the gates, contemporary incidences of populism are the inheritors of fascism (Finchelstein 2017). But they are not the same (e.g., Riley 2018; Beard et al. 2018). In our view, therefore, to the extent that the term has utility, populism best refers to a general discursive frame applied by observers to political movements of a specific style and strategy—taking politics to the people—rather than an ideology with a clear or coherent kernel of complaints and proposals beyond the two shared general characteristics mentioned previously (e.g., Aslanidis 2015; Tarchi 2015).

"THE PEOPLE" AND POPULISM

Given the definition of populism as involving taking "politics to the people," a brief discussion of "the people" and the overall understanding of politics to which populism putatively refers is in order. This requires discussing something about the nature of "the people" and how they are served by transcending conventional political parties and routines through the role of the leader.

First off, the question "What is a people?" is a normative one. As Kevin Olson (2016, 107) puts it, "We think of peoples as having powers, and we accord them a significance not shared by other collectivities." In much political and social theory, "the people" ties a group of people to the state by means of the claim to sovereignty. This understanding, despite its myriad deficiencies in missing how much, for example, the term (and affiliates such as "the popular") has had derogatory overtones (the "common people," a devalued social identity), draws attention to the central claim of populism of "going to the people" for its legitimacy. Of course, it is precisely the derogatory sense that inspires much analysis of populism: from the self-exclusion from regular politics of marginalized groups to how "'the people' becomes a people" (Olson 2016, 112) and how peoples are created through acts of collective imagination and performance. There is no neat mapping of sovereignty onto *the* people all in one go. One's people is privileged by endowing "it" with historic roots in an ancient or eternal past and by associating it with a homeland that the group has occupied throughout that past time as with a nation. The claim to territorial sovereignty by the people gives spatial form to "the idea of a democratically self-regulating people, one in which the subjects of law are also its authors. 'The power of the people,' by extension, is a product of a particular way of imagining politics" (Olson 2016, 1239). This could be the people as the demos or sovereign people. It is in this way that the concept of "the people" can be co-opted for populism by invoking the connection to sovereignty particularly by reclaiming it from foreign influences and external contamination.

But beyond the spatial-temporal definition of "the people" as the purpose and instrument of politics, movements of all stripes typically labeled as populist also tend to emphasize hostility to "normal" political parties and professional politicians as instruments of narrow sectorial interests (business, unions, churches, etc.). This is in contrast to the notion of the people as a whole and the positive role of a rhetorically dynamic and decisive leader whose performance and command over mass media provide a common locus for an otherwise diffuse and disorganized "base" in the people. In the first regard, of hostility to politics-as-usual, a "pure people" is contrasted with a "corrupt elite" whose allegiance is to party and self rather than to the people (e.g., Mudde 2004; Canovan 2002; Anselmi 2017; Diamanti and Lazar 2018). The "spirit of party," to borrow a turn of phrase from Simone Weil (2013), is seen as undermining more than facilitating the true representation of the people. An "oligarchy of insatiable Brahmins" (Rizzo and Stella 2009, 7) sucks the lifeblood out of the people. In the face of this refusal of a mediating institutional role for parties, the leader takes on an outsize role.

In the second regard, therefore, populism typically requires a mechanism such as a leader who will stand in for parties in linking the people together across the territory. The leader-people connection personalizes representation at the same time that it short-circuits the political parties and undermines the cleavages among the people that the parties typically mobilize for their own benefit (Calise 2016). Rhetoric is crucial. Take the example of Donald Trump. His rhetoric is central to his political success. He tells stories, frequently without any empirical basis, onto which his audience can hang their grievances. He does so in rallies of supporters where there is no prospect of any sort of disputation of his questionable claims. This may be "bullshit," in the sense of the term used by Harry Frankfurt (2005) to refer to talk that is about things the speaker doesn't actually know much if anything about, but the defense can be that politics is all about opinions anyway and that all politicians lie. At least this guy tells us lies we like. As William Connolly (2017, 12–13) puts it,

> His style is not designed first and foremost to articulate a policy agenda. It draws energy from the anger of his audience as it channels it. It draws into a collage dispersed anxieties and resentments about deindustrialization, race, border issues, immigration, working-class insecurities, trade policies, pluralizing drives, the new place of the United States in the global economy, and tacit uncertainty about the shaky place of a neoliberal culture on this planet. The speech montages then transfigure these anxieties into anger as they identify convenient targets of outlet for that anger. Trump's animated gestures, facial expressions, finger pointing, strutting, signature phrase clusters, and recurrent

twirls around the stage to call out the roaring acclaim of the audience amplify the words he recites. They incite and direct anxiety into anger as they recall a time in America in which white triumphalism felt secure. Each element in a Trump performance flows and folds into the others until an aggressive resonance machine is formed that is more intense than its parts.

In particular, as Marco Tarchi (2015, 279) has noted, "the charisma of the outsider" is vital to this rhetorical role. The leader should preferably come from outside the commonly referenced political world to save the people from the disaster of party government by mobilizing an "antipolitical" political movement even as he creates his own party or takes over an existing one. Even though Trump, for example, has spent his adult life advertising and branding himself as a deal maker and TV celebrity, he is a wealthy man who has also spent much time and money lobbying and hobnobbing with politicians. He mobilizes his famous "base" through "insider signaling": rhetorically embracing the cause of those now claiming they are excluded from their historic centrality to the polity. This can range from so-called dog whistle appeals—notoriously using certain turns of phrase that stand in for a stigmatized group, such as African Americans, whose recent political successes will be overturned—to explicit support for political positions hitherto outside the frame of reference of existing political parties (e.g., leaving international organizations, abandoning treaties, praising violent extremist groups, attacking Muslims and the disabled).

This melding of leader with cause usually takes the form of what has been called "tabloid realism," taking up the claims, frequently false or unverifiable, about the suffering imposed by others (elites, foreigners, and so on) on the people as characterized by popular media outlets such as newspapers and television that appeal to mass audiences. Classic examples would be Fox News in the United States and the British tabloid newspapers, such as the *Sun* and the *Daily Mail*. If at one time people shared the same news sources, such as the nightly news on a limited number of TV channels and hometown newspapers, increasingly they live in polarized media bubbles of cable news and politically affiliated internet news sites that they choose in order to reinforce their prejudices rather than find out anything fresh (e.g., Mayer 2019; Starr 2019). Spreading stories about enemies via social media has also emerged as a do-it-yourself approach for populists, sometimes with the help of foreign intelligence services interested in disrupting established democratic politics, as in the Russian hacking to influence the 2016 US presidential election on behalf of Donald Trump.

Attacking the "mainstream media" (particularly so-called quality newspapers and television news that report in a fact-driven rather than ideological way) is important in establishing the prophetic role of the leader. The media must be discredited to discredit the empirical truth in which they claim to trade. Steve Bannon, Trump's house theoretician, insists that the imperative is to dominate the conversation, not to engage in a battle of ideas: "The Democrats don't matter," he says. "The real opposition is the media, and the way to deal with them is to flood the zone with shit" (quoted in Thornhill 2018). Intertwined with populism in this regard can be both patrimonialism (in which the leader literally stands in for the people) and prebendialism (where the leader promises to reward followers materially for their devotion).

Populism is always in danger of going in these directions when the leader is not checked in some way, perhaps by the mass media or the judiciary (e.g., Szelenyi 2015; Calise 2016). Privileging certain media as reliable and others as "fake" and undermining the independence of the judiciary become important strategies for populist leaders in pushing on from initial electoral success. In the spirit of Aurelio Lippo Brandolini (2009), the fifteenth-century Florentine political theorist who argued for the essential instability of republics compared to monarchies, it could be said that with leaders "going to the people" without mediation, the people usually become the agent of the leader rather than vice versa.

PLACING POPULISM

Whatever specific form it takes, populism must necessarily operate across a given national-popular territory and reflect the different identities and interests of people as they are scattered from one place to another. All elections are also typically organized on a geographical basis. Political action is still presumably sited differentially across a national territory because "the people" are geographically differentiated by interests and identities that emerge from both local contexts and differences in their connectivity to national and global economies despite claims to "the people's" national singularity (e.g., Agnew 1987, 2002; Nicholls 2009). Likewise, spatial imaginations about the nature of the people as a collectivity are shaped around placed interests and identities (e.g., Wills 2013; Wendel 2015). After saying something about this geographical perspective on political representation, we turn to a brief discussion of the main features of populism that we explore in subsequent chapters about specific instances of the phenomenon, from the election of Donald Trump and the Brexit referendum to the National Front in France and the strands of populism in Italy, particularly that associated with the Five Star Movement. These features—spatial demography and voter participation in elections, the role of particular leaders, and the significance of political communication—are examined at greater length in Chapter 2.

Places and the Shaping of Political Attitudes

A commonplace of social psychology is that people's attitudes are shaped by where they are. In everyday life people exploit a small set of repeatedly visited locations (Alessandretti et al. 2018). Situational factors enter into interpersonal interactions, the attribution of trust and knowledge, judgments about ethics, and consumption decisions. From this viewpoint, there is no such thing as discrete individuals. The boundaries of the "self" are fluid. As a result, decisions, choices, and actions are all inspired by links with others. Terms such as "social networks" and "the social logic of action" have been coined to describe these interdependencies (Zuckerman 2005). "Network effects" are well established: people can and often do change preferences simply on the basis of what others say and do. Face-to-face relationships are absolutely central to the development of selves. From parental and household influences to friendship and acquaintanceship circles, people are social beings whose lives and behavior circulate around well-worn paths and routines. These are anchored to the sites in which social situations are located. Social media have changed none of this (Dunbar 2016; Dunbar et al. 2015; Stephens and Poorthuis 2015; Spiro et al. 2016; Lengyel et al. 2015).

Numerous studies have shown that the social contexts in which people develop their attitudes are spatially defined (e.g., Zuckerman 2005). The social heuristics or rules of thumb that we come to rely on to make decisions are the result of social interaction conditioned by where we work, play, worship, and learn. This does not mean that everyone in a given place agrees on everything—far from it. Rather, whatever attitudes people exhibit emanate from the experience of anchored social networks. But different people have different experiences that reflect their command over resources, their relative social power, and restrictions on the range of their sites of social interaction. Hence, though some common orientations can be expected, there is absolutely no expectation of complete uniformity in attitudes and subsequent behavior. Nevertheless, places do differ systematically in their economic bases, social structures, and sociodemographic characteristics. Indeed, there is evidence that as a result of selective migration, places can become increasingly homogeneous in various sociodemographic respects (e.g., Johnston et al. 2016).

The social spaces arising in different places, therefore, are most at stake in defining how political attitudes and behavior arise and change. But the relative presence of different types of sites or locales for interaction ultimately conditions how interpersonal and communal influences really operate. The "background geography" of places underpins the social spaces of interaction (e.g., Newburger et al. 2011; Sampson 2012). Some places have big factories; others do not. Some places have many peasants; others do not. Some places are dominated by agribusiness; others are not. Some places have long-standing cultural and recreation activities tied to churches; others do not. Some places are heavily urbanized; others are not. Some places are well tied into transportation and communication networks; others are not. Some places have been affected by natural calamities; others have not. Some places have very specialized economies (and equally narrow elites); others do not. Some places are magnets for immigrants; others are not. And so on. There are systematic correlations between these different types of place and the sorts of political attitudes and behavior that they encourage (Agnew 1987).

Places, the settings for sites of social interaction, structure the ways in which political attitudes and organization develop. In Italy, for example, a number of obvious historic geographical features lie behind the more dynamic churning of the economy and society to produce the basic template of geographical differences. These would include, for example, the long-established political division of the peninsula before final unification into one state only in 1870, the settlement system with its lack of a single dominant city and its orientation fundamentally affected by the long coastline and long mountainous spine of the Apennines, and the more successful history of large-scale industrialization in the country's northwest. Other elements of geographical differences include the diffuse urbanization that has characterized large parts of central and northeastern Italy since the 1970s, notwithstanding major efforts at redistributing industry and supplementing incomes in most southern regions that lag behind the north in terms of economic growth, and the peculiar geography of Catholic Italy, with practice reflecting the prior political divisions of the peninsula and attendant views of the church as much as the relative pace of secularization (e.g., Coppola 1997; Cartocci 2011; Cozzo 2011). Other countries have their own, if very distinctive, repertoires of such differences. In that regard, Italy is by no means unique.

The Decline of Thinking Geographically about Politics

This way of thinking about politics is by no means new, even though the ideas of social psychology that inform it could sound unfamiliar to many current students of politics. Indeed, down until the 1950s in the United States and elsewhere, the social logic and social geography of politics was everywhere predominant. Political sociology retained an emphasis on "territorial" or geographical cleavages and the impact of "neighborhood effects" on voting behavior for even longer. Italian Fascism, for example was widely understood as a movement that had its roots in the towns of the Po Valley and among the middle classes of areas with a powerful socialist presence (e.g., Agnew 1987). The US South was the dominion of the Democratic Party until the 1960s when the passage of the federal Civil Rights Act of 1964 led many southern whites to turn against the party whose president, Lyndon Johnson, introduced the legislation (e.g., Kuziemko and Washington 2018).

Two trends in social science since the 1960s have obscured this heritage of geographical thinking about politics and made writing about "place and politics" appear more novel or exotic than is actually the case. The first was the borrowing from microeconomics, arguably the most "scientific" of the social sciences in terms of its reliance on a nineteenth-century model of physics, of an ontology of action focused on autonomous individual actors engaged in rational calculation about political goals (often called "methodological individualism"). From this viewpoint, social environments are solely sources of informational and material constraints, not the identities, interests, and preferences associated with the individuals themselves. Recently, however, the more sociological view has undergone something of a revival, suggesting, for example, that prejudices as much as reasons underpin motivations and that social influences cannot be reduced to the effects of separate individuals simply bumping up against one another (Massey 2012). In one particularly evocative discussion, Didier Eribon (2013, 45) points out how much people in working-class communities in northern France in the 1960s voted Communist not out of any sense of the global political economy and a conscious commitment to class struggle but "as a form of protest, and not a political project inspired by a global perspective. You considered what was right around you, not what was far off, either in time or space."

The second was the presumed victory of the nation-hyphen-state as the sole focus of political activity. This has had two implications. One is the focus on national electoral politics as a sort of sporting event or horse race in which national-level majorities are all that is of much interest. The actual "making" of such majorities might involve political operatives with detailed local knowledge, but academic students of politics need to know only how to predict the overall outcome, not how to explain how it comes about. The other is to collect national-level survey data that gives you the traits and opinions of individual voters divorced from any concern about social context, other than the national. The presumption is that as long as you sample sufficiently across demographic characteristics (age, sex, race, ethnicity, class, etc.), you can know enough to predict results.

Yet multivariate statistical analysis using such population characteristics in relation to right-wing populist movements has proved disappointing partly because of the difficulty of selecting census indicators that match the actual factors of interest but also because it fails to model the process whereby people actually make their voting decisions (e.g., Amengay and Stockemer 2018). As a result, we should be "skeptical of deterministic explanations of political change" (Rydgren 2006, 121) that search for a single "smoking gun" based on national-level variables rather than more complex scenarios. Part of the problem is that not only local and regional differences but also influences emanating from beyond national borders make the presumption of national-level containment of political determinants open to doubt (Veltri 2010). But the combination of methodological individualism and "methodological nationalism" has undoubtedly become the "common sense" of political studies just about everywhere.

Whether it represents "good sense" is another question entirely. The increased complexity of political offerings, rising electoral abstentionism and nonvoting, and the emergence of place-specific political movements (such as regionalist and separatist movements in Spain and the United Kingdom) have made it less and less useful in its own terms. The paradigm is in trouble. In the words of Ilvo Diamanti (2012a, 103), after he offered a similar diagnosis to ours, "It is therefore difficult to understand what is happening in politics without taking account of the everyday life, of the common sense of the territory; without profoundly exploring the places where the parties, the institutions, and democracy find the roots to their legitimation and their consensus."

To this should be added the fact that electoral contests are usually organized on a geographical basis in the sense that votes are cast for representatives by areal constituencies (and sometimes for multimembers by proportional representation, sometimes for single-member majoritarian constituencies or a combination thereof, and, occasionally, in two-turn elections in which the second round is between the top vote getters in the first), referendum votes are aggregated by locality and region, and votes for some offices, such as that of president in the United States, are organized indirectly through mechanisms such as the electoral college, whereby the cumulative vote by state and not the overall national vote determines the result. In the United States the mechanics of electoral choice have increasingly produced electoral outcomes in which a single party dominates in some places and faces inevitable defeat elsewhere, and the number of "battleground" places where voters have a "real" choice has shrunken (e.g., Hopkins 2017). In US congressional elections, gerrymandering and primary elections that rely on the turnout of few but often extreme voters have polarized electoral districts to the extent that incumbents are usually elected without much challenge from other parties, and there is a massive bias in favor of rural areas.

In the elections to the US House of Representatives between 2012 and 2016, for example, the bias was such that it took fully 21 percent more votes on average for the Democrats to win a seat than for Republicans. The indirect election of the president has also produced two recent elections (2000 and 2016) when the candidate with fewer votes nationwide has been elected. Certain states, because they are more competitive, become crucial in the outcome. As the American comedian Stephen Colbert joked on the night of the 2012 presidential election, "A nation votes, Ohio decides." As is well known, Donald Trump is president of the United States because of the electoral college. His winning of the 2016 presidential election by small margins in Michigan, Pennsylvania, and Wisconsin was more important than his loss of California by over 3 million votes.

HOW TO MAP POPULISM

How do these considerations about the geography of political choice and the spatial organization of elections intersect with mapping populism? We would identify a number of indicators that allow us to examine individual cases, yet also have a common template for making comparisons across different cases. First we turn to what can be considered perhaps the most important preliminary sign of the turn to populism: increased nonvoting for the established political parties. Declining involvement in national politics is an important feature of many liberal democracies. Significant decreases in voting in recent years perhaps can be interpreted, at least in part, as suggesting a population increasingly available for populist alternatives to conventional political parties. This reflects in large part the declining capacity of traditional parties and affiliated organizations, from church-related to secular ones, to mediate between society and state. The aging of cohorts more attached to established parties and the coming of age of new generations available for new affiliations are part of this shift. But differential turnout by age group tends to enhance the importance of older voters. In some places they can be the agents of populism more than the young. But declining overall turnout is also the result of the increased role of personalities and the mass media in political life in reducing the sense of the importance of political articulation and aggregation through conventional political parties.

The second facet of contemporary populism is the central role of the leader in populist upheavals. Ironically, given the emphasis on the people as the arbiter of political virtue, populism typically involves a leader as the untrammeled patriarch, like Moses of old, who will lead the people to the Promised Land. In these cases we focus on such figures as Beppe Grillo, Donald Trump, Marine Le Pen, and Boris Johnson, all of whom exhibit clear symptoms of populism in leadership style. The dramatic role of television and internet-based social media organized around distinctive populist themes is the third facet considered. The leading public face of the Italian Five Star Movement, Beppe Grillo, a well-known comedian, is another example of the leader-populism connection. But the Five Star Movement is much more innovative in terms of its populism than simply with respect to the role of its leader. It disavows traditional grounded organization for the use of the World Wide Web. This is populism for the twenty-first century. But does it in fact augur a post-place politics in which there is unmediated connection between people, leader, and government?

What runs across the three facets of contemporary populism is a fairly constant refrain of suspicion of institutional mediation of the "will of the people" through highly organized parties and rejection of a class of specialized politicians (e.g., Urbinati 2012). Beyond these commonalities, there are significant differences across and within populist movements in, for example, attitudes toward continuing membership in the European Union, whether or not to retain the euro, immigration controls, and so on. Yet a more general theoretical question is raised by all the cases. This is that, from Jean-Jacques Rousseau's *The Social Contract* (2002 [1762]) onward, the question of how to organize the democratic general will of a people without various means of mediating between central state institutions, on the hand, and the mass of the people, on the other, has been a vital issue in defining the nature of democracy in modern nation-states (Badiou et al. 2016). So, by examining the three facets of populism spatially, we can say something about the central theoretical conundrum of how populism can address the general will, and, more specifically, we can use a spatial lens to show how much, if at all, mediation through place still works to produce not voting/abstention, how different levels and intensities of support for populist leaders and their movements are spread geographically, and whether seemingly placeless populist platforms such as that of the Five Star Movement's internet yield spatially uneven patterns of support. How much have the various populisms started to realize Rousseau's dream?

APPROACH AND ORGANIZATION OF THE BOOK

The next chapter explores the recent history of populism in Europe and the United States in more detail. In so doing it provides an overarching narrative for the rest of the book. Emphasis is placed on the range of movements in terms of their substantive and stylistic differences as well as their similarities. Nevertheless the overall thrust is to suggest that the populisms that have sprung up in recent years have not come out of nowhere but have roots in past periods in which populism flourished and thus provide recycled tropes and memes for present use. They connect to recent broad historical events typically discussed in relation to globalization, the decline of established parties (particularly on the center-left), and the polarization of populations within countries between economically dynamic and declining regions.

Attention then turns to developing the three empirical features of populism described above: spatial demography/turnout and the pool of potential voters for populism, leadership, and communication technologies and the promise of easy participation. The choice of the four cases in relation to the overall universe of populist movements and moments is then raised in terms of what each has to offer to a broader understanding of populism. Four subsequent chapters take up the four cases that are central to the book: the United Kingdom and the 2016 Brexit referendum, the 2016 election of Donald Trump in the United States, the 2017 electoral performance of the National Front in France, and the rise of the Five Star Movement in Italy in 2018 in the context of the various populisms in that country since the 1990s.

The book ends with a final chapter that draws some provisional conclusions about the four examples and the overall condition of populism. We also revisit some of the criticism of the term "populism" and consider whether other language might better describe the varied phenomena we encounter in the book. Finally, we discuss how mapping populism rather than engaging in polemical debate about the word offers a more skeptical perspective on its limited prospects as long as votes are cast in relatively free electoral contests. Populism simply presupposes a degree of uniformity or homogeneity across the territories it claims for its sovereign people that those very people in their variety and agency can never be expected to deliver. So much the better for them and for democracy, you could say. If it does succeed, however, it may mark the coming apart of the very combination of liberal democracy and capitalism that has marked the United States and much of Europe for the past sixty years.

2

Mapping Populism

Despite the increased reference to populism in politics, it has no essential meaning. Rather, as noted previously, populism is concerned with opposing the politics of accommodation. As it spreads, it sucks in establishment politicians who then adopt much of its language and attitude by appealing directly to "the people" and declaring that, as newly minted "antipoliticians," they will "refound" the political system. Matteo Renzi in Italy and Emmanuel Macron in France both took this tack in confronting more "authentic" populists. Of course, that does not make them "genuine" populists. They remain committed to the politics of accommodation.

Historically, populism has been about the rejection of "the powers that be" on behalf of "the people." US agrarian populism of the 1880s and 1890s, manifested above all in the People's Party, called for the end of nationwide banking, free silver, an eight-hour workday, and nationalization of the railroads. The clear policy focus of this 1890s US populism stands in contrast to more recent iterations of populism that underscore increased detachment from the materialist-rationalist narratives that once informed both liberalism and socialism and the rise of a politics that is apparently more about arousing emotions and identities than about pursuing material interests. In this regard they borrow somewhat more from the authoritarian nationalism and fascism that characterized the European 1920s and 1930s.

Emphasis is now placed on identifying the political caste and parties that always betray us—the people. The impact of external forces and foreign influences, particularly immigrants, is identified as specific aspects of the failure of the powers that be. But it is the blurring and fusion of such political issues and entertainment through mass and social media—from TV to Facebook and Twitter—that appeals to certain segments of the population at the core of contemporary populist movements. Even the so-called leftist populism of Podemos in Spain emphasizes the process of politics and uses television to that effect rather than offering many detailed policy prescriptions. In conjunction with an effective charismatic leader, media technologies, in what we could refer to as postmodern populism, are presumed to offer the mediation that replaces place-based social influences. This book, taken as a whole, shows that in fact they do not. Populism will begin to retreat only when this reality dawns.

In this chapter we propose and defend the use of populism as an analytic category in understanding the recent "wave" of populism in Europe and the United States. We place this wave in the long history of "populist moments" across the twentieth century and down to the present day. Consideration then turns to how to explain the current "populist conjuncture." The electoral decline of mainstream parties is given particular attention. Following on, we propose three elements of what we term "mapping populism" to provide a framework for comparing the four cases that are central to the book. The chapter ends with a justification for the four cases related to other possibilities, with a brief description of the overall situation of populism across Europe and North America.

WHY POPULISM?

There are all sorts of populism, which is why the term itself is so contested. Does it make sense to sweep a relatively disparate set of movements across multiple countries into a single category? Too often the term is used, as we alleged in the introduction, to dismiss certain selected movements as extremist and dangerous that arise as a result, in part at least, of the deficiencies of existing political parties as transmission belts and aggregators of the desires and demands of significant numbers of people. Even more profoundly one can point to their genesis in serious institutional failures on the part of governmental systems: think of the slow-motion breakdown of the separation of powers between branches of government in the United States long before the appearance of Donald Trump, with an increasingly ineffective legislative branch in particular (e.g., Lazare 1996; Agnew 2005, Chapter 5; Mann and Ornstein 2012). Other important factors include the corrosive role of "big money" in funding election campaigns and the way that dramatic increases in income and wealth inequality, plus the costs of election campaigns, has corrupted government (e.g., Mayer 2016). Additional elements involve the increasing acceptance of a common menu of neoliberal economic precepts about the virtues of markets and the privatization of hitherto public services on the part of center-left parties in Europe (including an increasingly neoliberal European Union) to the extent that the differences between Left and Right have all but dissolved (in the economic substance preached by parties labeled as either) (e.g., Judis 2016; Ricolfi 2017; Goodhart 2017). Growing income, wealth, and health inequalities within countries since the 1980s have coincided with the globalization of production and increased financialization of economies worldwide. The difficulties governments have had in adequately responding to these developments suggest how much there is a material basis to protest movements wanting to go back to a golden age or close the door to the world at large (Ricolfi 2017; Piketty 2018).

Debating Populism

Some scholars have attempted to argue that a singular logic can explain the appearance and form of populist movements. Manuel Anselmi (2017, 51–57) makes a good case for dividing the social science literature on the phenomenon according to three types of populism: as a political ideology, as a political style, or as a political strategy. The differences between them result in part from which actors and which methods are used to investigate the varied populisms. The emphasis falls in the first case on leaders and their policy statements, in the second on the internal logic of speeches and public discourses, and in the third on the links between parties and their leaders. None seems to provide the purchase on populism in its complexity that is required. This sort of "smoking gun" social science, in which one factor or cause is seen as being entirely sufficient across all cases and in all aspects, does not seem to match very well the appearance and workings of the populisms in question.

Very clearly, there are deep differences in the issues that seemingly inspire the instances of populism represented by the Sweden Democrats, the French National Front, the Dutch Party of Freedom, the Alternative for Germany, the Lega and Five Star Movement in Italy, the pro-Brexit United Kingdom Independence Party (UKIP) and Conservatives in the United Kingdom, and the Freedom Caucus and Trump supporters within the US Republican Party. Some are self-confessedly illiberal, such as Victor Orban's populist-nationalist Fidesz regime in Hungary. Others are more xenophobic and/or racist in their hostility to refugees and immigrants, as with the Italian Lega, the Alternative for Germany, and Trump, even while they tend to favor national business more than interventions on the side of their voters in fiscal and monetary affairs. At the same time opposition to the European Union and/or to globalization inspire others in a number of different ways, such as with Podemos in Spain, Syriza in Greece, and the left wing of the Labour Party in the United Kingdom. Ironically, given their self-confessed focus on "their" people alone, the various groups do collaborate, ironically again in settings like the European Parliament, and offer support for one another in publicity. For example, consider the joint appearances between Victor Orban and various other populist leaders; the joint witch hunt against George Soros, the Hungarian-born billionaire, for his support of various innocuous open-society groups in central Europe and the Central European University by the Fidesz government of Hungary and right-wing organizations affiliated with the US Republican Party, like Judicial Watch; and the common funding for the National Front in France and the League in Italy from sketchy Russian sources linked to Vladimir Putin. Given the divergent characters of the different countries, with their different population sizes, distinctive economic structures (for example, dependence on exports), varying reliance on the EU for funding, and different experiences with immigrants and refugees, it is not clear that a shared ideology about the exceptionalism of "their" individual peoples will be enough to maintain any sort of *Internationale* of nationalist-populists such as that envisaged by Steve Bannon, the chief ideologist of Trump's populism (e.g., Gosling 2018; Scheuermann 2018; Veronese 2018).

The Elements of Contemporary Populism

Rogers Brubaker (2017) fruitfully suggests that what conjoins all these movements is a "family resemblance," to borrow a phrase from Ludwig Wittgenstein, in the ways in which they combine and display a set of elements of a political "repertoire." None of these elements taken individually is uniquely populist. It is the combination that makes them populist. Moreover, the populist repertoire is always present but only deployed under certain determinative conditions such as those prevailing over the past few years. Umberto Eco (1995) first made these points in his discussion of what he called "ur-fascism," or the profound differences but also important similarities among all so-called fascist movements (Italian Fascists, German Nazis, Spanish Falangists, and so on) that made calling them "fascist" meaningful. You can thus outline a set of features that are typical of "eternal fascism" or ur-fascism "even though these features cannot be organized into a system; many of them contradict each other, and are also typical of other kinds of despotism or fanaticism." Eco then identifies fourteen features of the political repertoire of fascism, including the cult of tradition, disagreement as treason, irrationalism, obsession with plots, machismo, action for action's sake, and so on.

To Brubaker (2017), the central element of populism is the claim to speak and act in the name of "the people." As suggested in the introduction, this is quite a feat given the fact that the concept can apply to a nation, a demos, stigmatized ordinary folk, or just plain folk in the sense of individual persons. An audience hears what it wants from this list of possibilities. That is part of the beauty of populism. It is about not logical deduction but emotional resonance. But beyond this is the opposition drawn between a "pure" people and a "corrupt elite." This is the second element that Cas Mudde (2004, 543) has emphasized in his influential writing on populism. Of course, the elite are also seen in some versions of populism as having allies in those spongers and irresponsible people who soak up resources and are unjustly privileged by elites in all too many public policies (Müller 2016, 23). This misses, though, a third element that is frequently present, if with different intensities, in all types of populism: an emphasis on outside forces and groups that disadvantage the territory and/or places occupied by the people. These can be specific groups: Mexican immigrants for Trump; bureaucracies, such as the European Commission in Brussels for supporters of Brexit; or anonymous forces such as unregulated globalization for many others. What they share is a focus on a sharply drawn *us* inside and *them* outside (Goodhart 2017).

If these are the three foundational elements of the discursive and stylistic repertoire of populism, Brubaker (2017) identifies five other elements that show up differentially across the various populisms. The first is a politicizing of what has been depoliticized, or, in other words, bringing back into discussion what seemed to have been settled. Above all, this means calling into question technocratic positions that rely solely on empirical evidence and notions that "there is no alternative" to, for example, neoliberal economic policies. Healthy skepticism about technocracy can easily mutate into know-nothingism or a cult of ignorance. The second is a radical majoritarianism, or assertion of the rights of most ordinary people, or "the silent majority," against the claims of minorities. This is particularly characteristic of the more nationalistic and racist groups. A third element is anti-institutionalism, or a sense that procedural democracy involving oppositional parties and political accommodation works against the people. Suspicion of professional politicians and their parties is key to this element. It is broadly shared across populisms of various ideological stripes.

We would see the two final elements as key in distinguishing contemporary populism most clearly from other political styles. Fourth is an emphasis on protection, as we emphasized in the introduction. This involves protecting the people from threats coming from elites and minorities and, above all, foreign influences and dangers. In this context, the rhetoric of perpetual crisis is important in mobilizing supporters, who are then invited to observe symbolic acts such as building walls, restricting immigrants, rounding up miscreants, rewriting immigration laws, and so on (Moffitt 2015, 2016). By way of illustration, when asked in an opinion survey whether they would prefer to protect themselves or embrace the different, populist supporters respond much more positively to the former than to the latter (see Figure 2.1). The choice at hand is "Which do you prefer: 'Our lives are threatened by terrorists, criminals and immigrants and our priority should be to protect ourselves' or 'It's a big beautiful world, mostly full of good people, and we must find a way to embrace each other and not allow ourselves to become isolated.'"

Fifth and finally, Brubaker (2017) observes how important a clear shift in the character of political communication is to populism. In particular, he notes that there is a "populist style" that opposes "popular common sense" and "plain speaking" to "politically correct" and polite speech and bodily behavior. In a brilliant riff on Trump's capacity to lie shamelessly without losing his audience—indeed, while commanding it more seriously—Emily Ogden (2018) says, "Even if Mr. Trump's audience retains a suspicion that he himself might be a swindler, that doesn't necessarily work to his disadvantage. The attacks on his truthfulness have an alarming tendency to reinforce his message that he's a master of the deceptive arts. In a treacherous world, you need a treacherous ally—treacherous, at least, to your mutual enemies. So become Mr. Trump's apprentice!" As we said in the introduction in referring to Trump's rallies, exactly this aspect necessarily integrates the other elements, when they are present, into a compelling approach to storytelling that appeals to significant chunks of national populations. The stories may vary but the messages and mode of telling have much in common (Salmon 2014; Moffitt and Tormey 2014).

Embrace	Protect	
11%	89%	**Front National ●** (FN, France)
12%	88%	**Alternative fur Deutschland ●** (AfD, Germany)
19%	81%	**Lega Nord ●** (LN, Italy)
24%	76%	***Trump Voters ●**
29%	69%	**Kukiz'15 ●** (Poland)
31%	89%	**UK Independence Party ●** (UKIP, UK)
33%	67%	**Prawo i Sprawiedliwość ●** (PiS, Poland)
34%	66%	**Les Républicains** (LR, France)
42%	58%	***Brexit Voters ●**
44%	56%	**Movimento 5 Stelle** (M5S, Italy)
51%	49%	**Christlich Demokratische Union** (CDU/CSU, Germany)
56%	44%	**Conservative Party** (UK)
58%	42%	**Soziademokratische Parti Deutschlands** (SPD, Germany)
59%	41%	**Partido Popular** (PP, Spain)
59%	41%	**Parti Socialiste** (PS, France)
62%	38%	**.Nowoczesna** (.N, Poland)
66%	34%	**Partito Democratico** (PD, Spain)
69%	31%	**Labour Party** (UK)
72%	28%	**Partido Socialista Obrero Espanol** (PSOE, Spain)
79%	21%	**Unidos Podemos** (UP, Spain)

selected right-wing populist movements ●

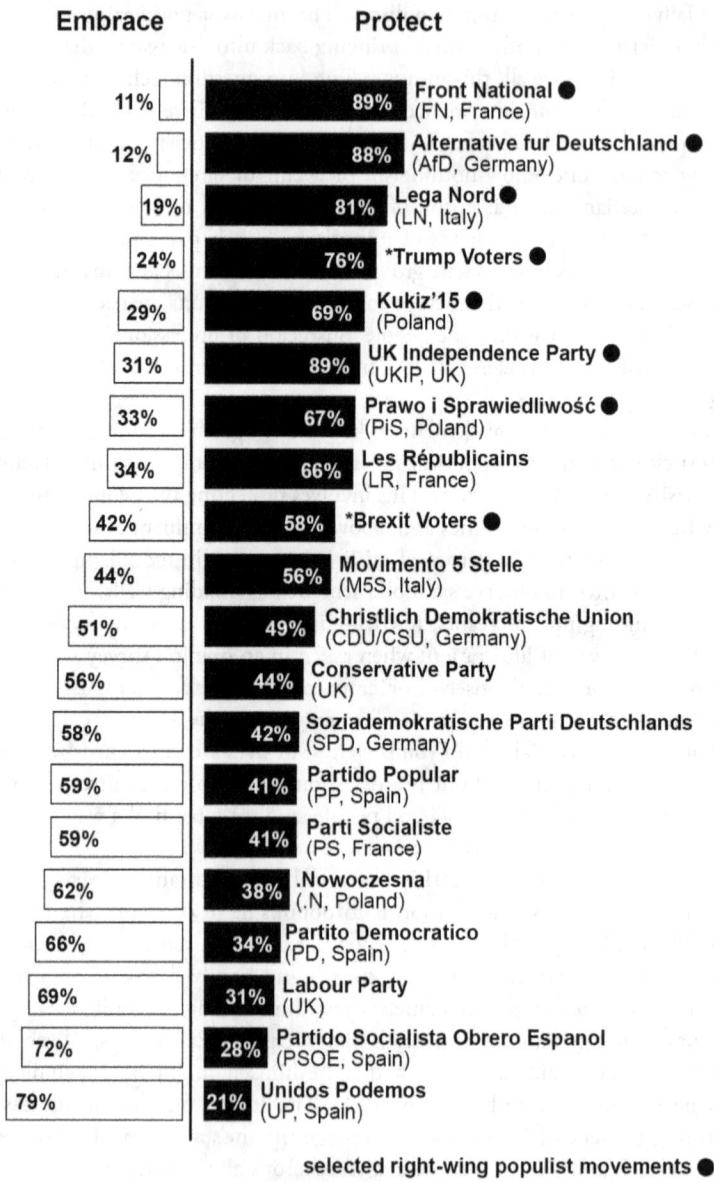

Figure 2.1. Embrace the world or protect ourselves?
Source: Adapted from https://daliaresearch.com/right-wing-populism-the-european-world-view-divide.

POPULISMS OLD AND NEW

As defined above, populism is not new in many respects. It has mutated from earlier beginnings. All its manifestations today are based in deep strands of strongman authoritarianism privileging a historic people against its enemies, external and internal (King 2017). Most important for present purposes is to understand something of its history and, above all, why it has undergone such a revival recently. The term itself is an American creation with roots going back to the American Revolution and the presidency of Andrew Jackson. The anti-immigrant Know Nothing movement of the 1840s made "nativism" a national phenomenon (Bennett 1988). In fact, recent right-wing populism in the United States has much more in common with this outburst of antiforeign and anti-immigrant sentiment than it does with the party that introduced the term "populism" to the world at large in the 1890s. It took on its most organized shape in the People's Party of the 1890s. Organized explicitly as a party against the power of national banks and their political allies, this party originated in the long economic depression at the close of the nineteenth century. It foundered on the divergent views of its western and southern elements toward civil rights for African Americans and women and its absorption into the Democratic Party. It was never a party that claimed to be for the people, as such (Müller 2016, 90). It was rooted in agrarian dissent. Nevertheless, it set the stage for subsequent outbursts of populism, from right and left, typically then captured and disciplined by the two ramshackle political parties that have long institutionalized themselves in the United States. This two-party dominance reflects the workings of a congressional electoral system that is based on single-member districts and majoritarian votes. This discourages third-party candidacies.

US Populist History

In US politics a high degree of consensus has often prevailed about a range of issues for long periods, punctuated historically by two distinctive types of change (Judis 2016, 20–21). The first involves realigning elections in which the center of gravity of politics shifts wholesale in response to major events such as depression and economic crisis but within the bounds of conventional party politics. This happened, for example, with the elections of 1932 and 1936 and the New Deal policies that followed and again in 1980 with the election of Ronald Reagan and the neoliberal changes in national economic policy this then entailed. In each of these cases populist impulses were also involved but were seemingly tamed by the establishment parties relatively quickly. In the Reagan case, however, his antigovernment rhetoric and opposition to the public welfare and civil rights legacies of the New Deal helped soften up the Republican Party and the country at large for the later emergence of Trump. The Richard Nixon years and the effort of the Republican Party to recruit disaffected white southerners to the party had already led to an emphasis on identifying the so-called silent majority opposed to the street politics of 1968 and seeing the federal government in a hostile rather than a favorable light (King and Anderson 1971). Howard Phillips, for example, worked with the Conservative Caucus in the 1970s and 1980s to channel the bitterness and alienation that many white Americans felt in the face of the desegregation struggles on the part of African Americans and the bureaucratic overreach of the federal government that they thought had followed (e.g., Frank 2009).

One of the peculiarities of Trump's populism, compared to the European ones and some older US ones, has hence been his focus on pushing back against the so-called administrative state, rolling back taxes on higher-income groups and removing environmental and financial regulation, rather than using it to actively serve his constituency. This has led to the charge that his is a "pluto-populism" (plutocracy + populism), favoring the business elite, of which he is a member, while manipulating identity issues relating to race and immigration to garner greater popular support (Norris and Inglehart 2019).

The second type of shift in the political zeitgeist involves insurgencies in which "catalytic populists" emerge to challenge the status quo (Judis 2016, 21). Examples here would include the People's Party campaign against laissez-faire capitalism in the 1890s, Huey Long's Share Our Wealth program in Louisiana in the early 1930s, Father Charles Coughlin's Far Right radio populism in the 1930s, and the presidential campaigns of George Wallace in 1968 and 1972 that helped destroy the New Deal coalition between northern and southern Democrats. They created the "middle American radicalism" (Warren 1976) that then migrated to the Republican Party and lay the groundwork for Donald Trump's takeover of the party in 2016. Bernie Sanders's effort to capture the Democratic nomination in 2016 can be seen in many respects as an attempt to return to the New Deal and even aspects of the People's Party campaign. Unlike for Trump with the Wallace effect and the capture of the Republican Party by so-called Tea Party activists from 2008 onward, there was simply insufficient groundwork in the shape of political allies within the Democratic Party for Sanders to build an instantaneous populist upsurge. Arguably, his "style" was also insufficiently attuned to the sound bite politics mastered by Trump in that he staked out clear policy positions rather than based his appeal on demonizing opponents and stigmatizing segments of the population. His "analytic" as opposed to Trump's "intuitive" approach to his audience proved telling in the end, suggesting how important the latter now is to successful populist politics (e.g., Pennycook and Rand 2018).

Sanders and Trump did not simply appear out of nowhere then. In addition to having the existing precursors mentioned above, they also followed in the footsteps of more recent presidential candidacies and protest movements from the 1990s onward. Figures such as Pat Buchanan and Ross Perot ran presidential campaigns that covered some of the same ground and appealed to many of the same types of people as did Trump twenty years later. Though a businessman, Perot arguably campaigned in policy terms more to the center-left than to the right, even if he shared the populist style of the outsider riding to the rescue of the people. Trump likewise combines positions on issues such as trade and international organizations that are fundamentally the opposite of those that have been the norm in the Republican Party for many years. In the aftermath of the financial crisis of 2007–2008 and the election of the first African American president in 2008, Occupy Wall Street and the Tea Party faction in the Republican Party provided the activists and the issues that later inspired, respectively, the campaigns of Sanders and Trump in 2016.

The Tea Party, more a congeries of local groups than an organized enterprise, though it did lead to the Freedom Caucus of right-wing "populist" Republicans in the US House of Representatives, was particularly important for Trump's later success. He readily seized on its unremitting hostility to any and all initiatives of the Barack Obama administration, such as the Affordable Care Act ("Obamacare"), its efforts at delegitimizing Obama by claiming he was born in Kenya ("birtherism"), of which Trump was a major proponent, and its association of government spending and size of government with undeserved handouts to minorities and the undeserving. When he descended the escalator in New York's Trump Tower to announce his candidacy for the US presidency, he excoriated Mexicans as a threat to the security of the country, which he promised would end with the construction of a "beautiful wall" between the United States and Mexico (paid for by Mexico). Meanwhile, Trump kept the paymasters of the Republican Party on side by promising huge tax cuts favorable to them once he was elected. His populist audience swallowed the idea that what was good for business would "trickle down" to them. This "pluto-populism" does not travel that well to Europe.

European Precursors

There is some danger, then, in seeing the contemporary surge of populism through an entirely US-centered lens. It is not as if other populisms are simply imports from the United States. Other historical sources beyond the peculiarities of the American experience range from the Narodnichestvo of late czarist Russia, with its peasant-communitarian commitment to maintaining a way of life increasingly compromised by the spread of industrial capitalism; to the "national populisms" of Latin America from the 1930s to the 1950s, particularly Peronism in Argentina; to mid-twentieth-century fascism and authoritarianism, such as the Fronte dell'Uomo Qualunque in the years immediately after the collapse of Italian Fascism and French Poujadism (Union et fraternité française) in the mid-1950s. Most of these expressed such sentiments as hostility to regular forms of political representation in parliaments, defense of the small people against the powerful, rejection of class struggle as a political motif, defense of national territories and local places and associated traditions, critique of elites, exaltation of the people and its common sense, and opposition to the greed and corruption of politicians (Ricolfi 2017, 125–26).

Populist groups never entirely disappeared from the European political spectrum. They merely moved off center stage. The openness to new parties of the proportional-representation, multimember district electoral systems that prevail in much of

Europe (though not in the United Kingdom) is part of the story. Beginning in the 1970s a number of groups became increasingly active and achieved some support across a range of European countries. The earliest were in Scandinavia, especially Denmark, where the Progress Party received 16 percent of the national vote in 1973, and Norway, where a party of the same name entered parliament in the same year with 5 percent of the vote. In 1972 Jean-Marie Le Pen, previously a Poujadiste deputy in the French parliament, founded the National Front in France, which by 1984 had acquired 11.2 percent of the vote and ten seats in the election to the European Parliament. Thereafter, a proliferation of populist movements across Europe lasted more or less down until 2008. These included the British National Party (1982) and UKIP (1993) in the United Kingdom, both of them xenophobic, racist, and hostile to the EU, but with different constituencies across the country. UKIP was founded as an anti-EU rather than an anti-immigrant party. Others, such as the Republicans in Germany (1989), New Democrats in Sweden (early 1990s), and Flemish Bloc in Belgium (peaking in 2007), came and went. The strange "libertarian-populist" parties of Pim Fortuyn (assassinated in 2002) and Geert Wilders in the Netherlands had somewhat more staying power.

The same could be said for the Northern League in Italy, which originally came out of a set of local parties oriented toward the secession of northern Italy from Italy. It became increasingly oriented to anti-immigrant and racist themes to the extent that since 2016 it has renamed itself "the League" and become an avowedly anti-immigrant populist-nationalist party. An interesting example of a proto-Trump populism also comes from Italy, something of a laboratory for populism down the years. This is the party created from scratch in 1994 by the media tycoon Silvio Berlusconi, which he called Forza Italia, after the chant for the national soccer team. This was as much a personal as it was a populist party, devoted to protecting Berlusconi's media and other business interests as much as his "people." The collapse of the Italian party system in 1992 following a massive corruption scandal that ensnared the governing Christian Democratic and Socialist parties, followed by the breakup of the Communist Party as the Cold War ended, created an opening for a party such as Berlusconi's. His approach was to demonize Communists, even though they were disappearing, and to flirt with anti-immigrant and anti-EU positions. More especially, Berlusconi's populism was redolent of postwar Italian *qualunquismo* in its attacks on professional politicians and institutions such as the judicial system and in its praise for strong rulers. He was an early admirer of Vladimir Putin.

At the same time, three other trends were to reach fruition only after 2008 (Ricolfi 2017, 129–31). The first was the increasing success of the Progress Party in Norway and the National Front in France. The latter reached an amazing success in 2002 when its candidate, Jean-Marie Le Pen, received more votes in the first round of the presidential election than the Socialist Lionel Jospin and went to the runoff with Jacques Chirac, the candidate of the traditional Right. The second was the transformation of a number of previously nonpopulist parties into fully fledged populist ones. The main examples here are the Freedom Party in Austria and the Swiss Democratic Union of the Centre (UDC) or People's Party. Originally liberal in orientation, these parties converted into anti-EU and anti-immigrant parties. Euroskepticism increased across western Europe in tandem with new initiatives beginning in the 1990s that turned the EU into a stronger set of institutions, particularly in relation to the Schengen zone for free movement and the arrival of the euro as a common currency for some of its members (e.g., Berezin 2009). The third trend was the clamorous success of populist-authoritarian parties in central and eastern Europe following the collapse of the Soviet Union and in reaction to the rampant corruption and cronyism of the period right after the collapse. Vladimir Zirinovsky's Liberal Democratic Party in Russia, Orban's Fidesz in Hungary, and Law and Justice in Poland are the best known, with the latter two becoming increasingly prominent after 2008. But most European countries had at least one populist movement by the end of the period.

So, it is since 2008 that the constellation of populist movements has come to acquire its greatest scope, often with votes in national elections in excess of 10 percent of the total and in European elections, given lower turnout on the part of supporters of conventional parties, above 20 percent. Indeed, by 2018 the two main populist parties in Italy, the League and the Five Star Movement, had acquired more than 50 percent of the total vote in the national election and created a government. The National Front in France has become the second most important political force in the country, and populist parties like the UDC in Switzerland, the Progress Party in Norway, and the Freedom Party in Austria are now government and not simply opposition parties. UKIP in the UK managed to produce the Brexit referendum by the threat that the Conservative Party leader and then prime minister David Cameron thought they posed to his party. In trying to exorcise the anti-EU elements from his party, he fell into a trap that UKIP had arguably created through its relentless focus on trying to extract the United Kingdom from the EU. Now several newer groups, such as the Sweden Democrats and the Alternative for Germany, have appeared to spread the specter of populism far and wide across the continent. Several "anomalous populisms," particularly Podemos in Spain and Syriza in Greece, represent somewhat different movements than the others coming out of the street politics of the extreme Left in the face of austerity budgets and the depredations visited on countries such as Greece as a result of the eurozone crisis beginning in 2012 (see, e.g., Ramiro and Gomez 2017 on Podemos). Unlike the other populists, these tend to emphasize class struggle and the need to define the people in less national-exclusivist terms than is the case with the others. As of 2016–2017, populist movements of various stripes had become vital actors across the length and breadth of Europe (Map 2.1).

The Recent Efflorescence of Populism

This leads us to ask what has happened to bring about this recent efflorescence of populism across so many countries? In the next section we will examine in a little detail how much the breakdown of other parties, particularly those on the center-left, has created an opening for populist movements. Here we identify the overall

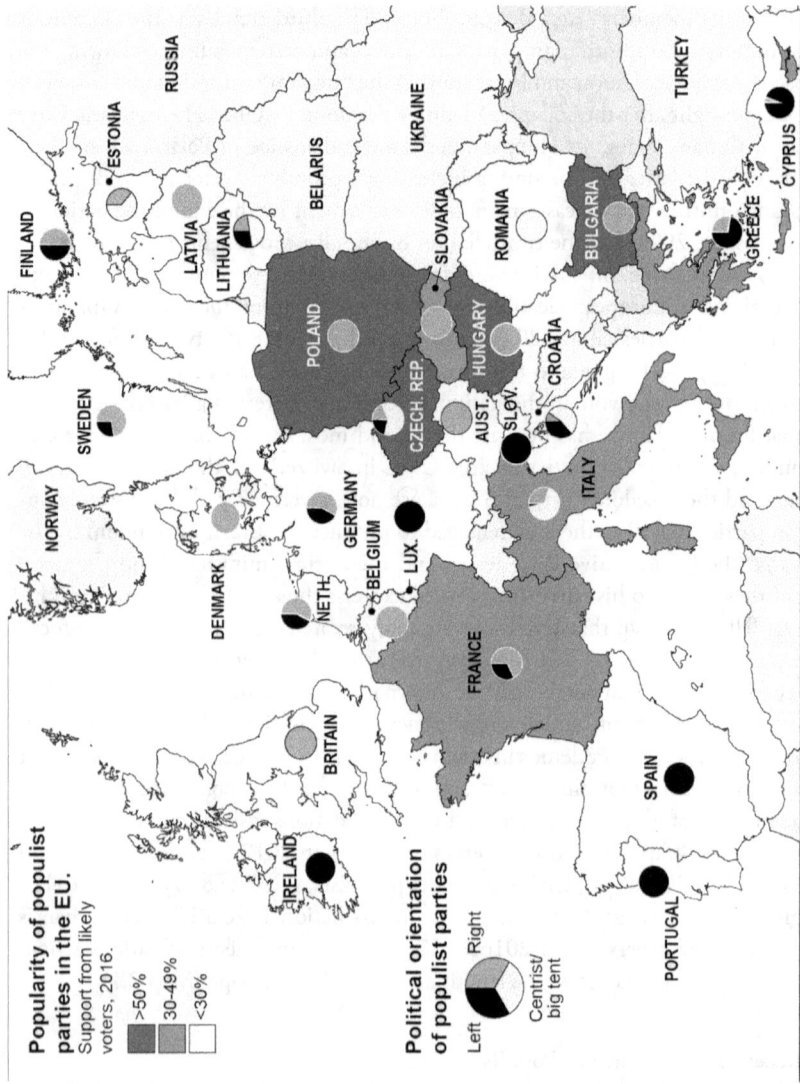

Map 2.1. Populism across the European Union.

Source: Adapted from Foundation for European Progressive Studies (https://www.feps-europe.eu)

contextual forces that have helped bring about what Brubaker (2017) calls the "populist conjuncture." The purpose is not to explain particular events, such as the votes for Brexit or Trump, but to ask how various historical-social trends have come together to produce the very possibility of outcomes such as the election of a Trump or a populist government in Italy. We would identify, following in the footsteps of Rogers Brubaker (2017), Luca Ricolfi (2017), and John Judis (2016), two structural trends and a couple of crises that have triggered sudden boosts for populist movements. The two trends are the decline in the efficacy of political institutions and the rising popular demand for protection. The crises, conceived as such by the populists, are the financial crisis (and the eurozone crisis that followed) and the immigration/ refugee panics associated with Islamic terrorism and the vast influx of refugees into Europe in the summer of 2015. The crises serve as focal points for the broader trends that suggest to voters the importance of making electoral choices that they might in "cooler circumstances" otherwise be reticent to make.

As we will argue in more detail in the next section, political parties have become increasingly detached from their traditional electorates in many countries. This reflects in part the growing numerical dominance of the middle classes in countries such as the United States, the United Kingdom, France, and Italy, along with the decline in manufacturing employment and increased numbers of university graduates who have become the main targets of all parties (e.g., Ford and Goodwin 2017). The "subcultures" that once underpinned support—for example, the Italian Communist and Christian Democratic parties and the British Labour and Conservative parties— have eroded in the face of the "mediatization" of politics and the increasing similarity in policy proposals emanating from hitherto "opposite" sides of the Left/Right political divide. This trend long predates the "crises" that engulfed the parties in the 2000s. The end of the Cold War was crucial in bringing this trend to a head if only because the Left-Right division on a global level was reproduced to a certain degree within countries as well, not least in France and Italy, where Communist parties were long entrenched but disappeared as the Cold War ended between 1990 and 1992.

Perhaps of even greater significance than the erosion of stable subcultures based in distinct social classes and groups with ancillary institutions (such as trade unions and co-ops) is the increasingly technocratic and less ideological outlook of many traditional parties to the extent that politics itself is held hostage to expert opinion. This is typically less true on the center-right, as with the US Republicans, who have become increasingly ideological and suspicious of any sort of expert knowledge about anything, than with the center-left parties, such as the Democrats, who have become increasingly both a party of group interests and technocrats (Grossman and Hopkins 2016). Trump and his minions widely mocked Hillary Clinton's command of policy positions and the numbers that justified them during the 2016 US presidential election campaign. The massive failure of US and UK national intelligence agencies in the run-up to the invasion of Iraq in 2003, in particular the false claim that the then government of Iraq had "weapons of mass destruction," and the disastrous reliance on experts predicting that all would be well before the 2007–2008 financial collapse finally ruined blind faith in a technocracy that was already under challenge (e.g., Nichols 2017; Zimring 1996). This, plus failure to bring criminal charges against bank executives who had precipitated the Great Recession, aided the cause of those populists who wanted to change the narrative about the crisis from the failings of the banks to the public costs of providing support for the undeserving (Tooze 2018).

"Party government," in the sense of different parties representing segments or sections of society, has thereby declined as technocracy and populism challenge its premises on behalf, respectively, of expert knowledge and the people (e.g., Rydgren 2006). Political pluralism and the articulation of loyal opposition are thus sacrificed at the competing altars of "the people" and superior knowledge (e.g., Caramani 2017). Powerful institutions are also more distant and sometimes more inadequate than in the past. One reason for much of the hostility to the EU is the opacity and democratic deficit associated popularly with its operations. Concurrently, institutional failures, such as legislatures' lack of responsiveness to constituents and their collusion with lobbyists and those they should regulate at arm's length, so to speak, encourages disenchantment with politics as normal.

If this were not enough, large-scale immigration from beyond the borders of Europe and the United States and the inability of governments to deal adequately with the economic and social dilemmas facing ordinary people have made the whole question of "Who is the people?" a more urgent one. "Protection" from the world takes on a whole new significance when the world seems out of control with social, economic, and cultural changes that call into question many of the certainties on which people have built their lives. The relative prosperity that many people remembered experiencing in the postwar decades across Europe and the United States is now a distant memory replaced by decreased rates of labor force participation (particularly among men), high levels of youth unemployment, the prospect that children will be poorer than their parents, huge increases in income inequality, and the feeling that if globalization might deliver cheaper consumer goods, it has also produced an increasing dearth of jobs for the less skilled back in what used to be the world's industrial societies (Agnew 2005, Chapters 7 and 8; Piketty 2018). But although recent income declines experienced by average working-class people are emphasized in some accounts as encouraging voting for populists, economic growth itself does not correlate highly over the course of the past ten years with voting behavior (all governments are now subject to ejection irrespective of the rate of economic growth while they have been in office) (*Economist* 2017c). It is much more a question of a sense of relative deprivation relative to minorities on the part of the relatively affluent whites that is behind much populist voting (Mols and Jetten 2017; Mutz 2018; Jardina 2019).

Concurrently, a host of cultural changes linked to what Brubaker (2017) calls "emancipatory liberalism"—from multiculturalism and speech codes to women's rights to careers, LGBT rights, gay marriage, and so on—and sponsored by cultural "elites" with Hollywood and Manhattan as their homelands have been driven into every nook and cranny of the often culturally conservative provinces. At the same time, "the guns and religion" culture of the boondocks, as it is labeled in America, may be found scattered around Europe too. It is portrayed in the mainstream media in almost entirely negative terms. Foreign governments, particularly that led by Russia's Vladimir Putin, long popular with US religious conservatives and right-wing groups across Europe for his own open but cynical appeals to homophobia and "family values," stoke the divisions from afar using social media and lobbying to play up the sense of cultural endangerment. Populism feeds off the resentments and bitterness that results (Norris and Inglehart 2019).

Yet there would be no guarantee that these structural shifts would produce any sort of populist moment if not for two recent crises that populists have masterfully exploited to their advantage. The first of these was the financial crash and Great Recession, followed, particularly in southern Europe, by the eurozone crisis. This managed to bring a combined focus on how much the national welfare had been sacrificed to the supranational and global interests and identities of elites and on the failures of established parties and politicians to address the real problems facing their populations. The widespread popular sense of socioeconomic insecurity that followed 2008, based as much on anxiety about preserving one's status as on actual loss of incomes and wealth, was readily tapped into by populists. The austerity budgets forced on the governments of countries such as Italy, Ireland, Portugal, Spain, and Greece and chosen by the United Kingdom became particularly important fodder for populist complaints about how much democratic politics had been undermined by technocratic insistence by the EU, the European Central Bank, and the International Monetary Fund that there was no alternative. Yet, of course, the main problem was in fact Germany's massive balance-of-payments surplus with other countries in the eurozone without any acknowledgment that monetary unification, as with the euro, requires a high degree of fiscal consolidation. Anti-German government attitudes thus became an important part of populist politics in countries such as Greece.

In the second crisis, a rush of refugees drew attention to an older and bigger question about the necessity for and impact of foreign immigration. Many right-wing organizations in the United States and Europe have long lobbied about the economic and cultural dangers of immigration, particularly from countries with racial and religious differences from their currently dominant white and nominally Christian populations. But declining birthrates among such populations, the demand for unskilled labor in occupations that people of European ancestry are loath to fill (washing dishes in restaurants, picking field crops, caring for infants and the elderly, etc.), and the increased knowledge about such possibilities on the part of Africans and Latin Americans have provided a huge demand-side stimulus to migration. At the same time, the regulation of migration has become increasingly arbitrary, and legal migration itself is now increasingly arduous. Terrorist incidents, from those of 9/11 in the United States to the 2015 Bataclan attacks in Paris, have also been important in drawing the threat to traditional cultural homogeneity of culturally distinctive immigrants/refugees together with the threat to personal security posed by foreign difference. Tying terrorism to immigration, notwithstanding the fact that most terrorists are homegrown or, as in the United States, admitted on visas issued by US consulates in allied countries such as Saudi Arabia, has been a vitally important part of the appeal of populist figures such as Marine Le Pen in France and Geert Wilders in the Netherlands.

The problem, so to speak, has come into focus with the situation of refugees, many of them from wars in which the United States and its European allies have played more than marginal roles, as in El Salvador and Guatemala, Afghanistan, Iraq, and Syria. Many of refugees from the latter three had been trapped in surrounding countries such as Lebanon, Turkey, and Jordan. Suddenly, in 2015 about 1 million of them left Turkey in a massive movement across the Aegean Sea into Greece and through the Balkans to western Europe, particularly Germany. The German government's decision in September 2015 to open its borders to asylum-seeking refugees and the agreement of Swedish and other governments to also take a share of the total number became a great issue for populists Europe-wide. It not only jump-started the explosion of support for Alternative for Germany but also became an issue for Victor Orban in Hungary, who justified building a border fence by saying that he was in fact saving Europe from its "suicidal liberalism" (Brubaker 2017). Refugees from narcogangs and systematic violence in Central America have come to symbolize the same conundrum along the southern US border for Trump and his supporters.

Yet the overall number of migrants is down in both Europe and the United States. Asylum seeking is subject to international law and is not the same as illegal immigration for economic purposes. Trump regularly connects the recent refugee buildup with the activities of a criminal gang, MS-13, founded in Los Angeles in the 1980s by an older round of refugees. In this case they were refugees from a war in El Salvador in which the United States was an active participant. Not a word about that from Trump. Beyond this specific instance of fearmongering, the systematic occlusion of the distinction between refugees and economic migrants has been vital to populists in using refugee crises to excite enthusiasm about a broader crisis of "uncontrolled immigration."

PARTIES AND POPULISM

The decline of electoral support for conventional parties has served to provide a particularly important opening to populism across a number of countries. So, beyond its specific contribution to the current populist moment, the decline in support is worth considering for its contribution not just to the explosion of populism but also to the prospects of reestablishing some sort of "normal" party politics if and when this moment passes. Over the past thirty years, established center-left and center-right parties have all lost electoral support across a wide range of countries. This has been tempered in the case of countries with majoritarian electoral systems, such as the United States and United Kingdom, by the difficulties facing third parties without pools of voters in specific places. Some of this is down to reforms that have curbed the ability of parties to finance themselves and control the doors to electoral candidacy. Together, these changes, mainly since the 1970s and often as responses to scandals, have encouraged the rise of powerful interest groups and wealthy individuals as alternative political "sponsors" to what had been party functions. Everywhere, too, there has been a net downward drift in electoral turnouts, particularly marked in central Europe and in countries such as Italy, where turnouts were historically quite high. The United States has long had much lower turnouts than other liberal democracies in part because of barriers to registering to vote but also because even many people who do register then do not vote. As the role of parties as mediators has weakened, so have party identification and electoral turnout.

Party Decline

Scholars have drawn attention to several aspects of the decline of parties and the role it has played in opening up politics to populist movements and their distinctive approach to reframing issues and drawing in hitherto inactive voters as much as or more than "converting" existing voters to their cause. Four aspects have been proffered as explaining entirely or in part the relationship between the decline of established parties, on the one hand, and the rise of populist movements and their ideas, on the other. In our view, all of these speak to the overall context in which populism has arisen anew. It is not a question of one versus the others. The first is the increased similarity in the "electoral offerings" of orthodox parties and the decline of the Left/Right polarity on issues of inequality and states versus markets that this has entailed. The second is the mismatch between what parties offer and what their electorates demand on issues such as economic competition and immigration. Third is the difficulty established parties face now that the massive expansion of direct communication through television and social media has sidelined organization on the ground, so to speak, one of their historic advantages in political mediation. Fourth and finally, national populations are increasingly polarized in values and interests to the extent that each side sees the other as completely beyond the accommodation and loyal opposition that characterized much of politics during the long period from the 1950s to the 1970s. This last one more closely fits the United States than it does most of the other countries with recent populist explosions. But even in countries such as Italy and France with strongly ideological cleavages between parties, there was between the 1950s and the 1970s considerable scope for cross-party agreement.

The Left-Right distinction between political forces and the ideas they represent goes back at least to the French Revolution. It is still the most familiar way in which observers try to make sense of electoral politics tout court (Bobbio 1996). Today, it is not just that many populists challenge this distinction in favor of inside and outside (or closed versus open) as the guiding motif for politics, as alleged earlier, but that actual parties have increasingly drifted away from the signifier even as it still has meaning for many people relative to the issues of the time, such as income inequality, the role of the state, managing trade, and so on. As early as 1979 Nicos Poulantzas (1979) noted that new social movements engaged in struggles over specific issues increasingly bypassed established political parties in preference for direct action and open denigration of parliamentary politics. At much the same time, existing parties, particularly on the left, became increasingly centrist in policy orientation so as to appeal to burgeoning middle classes as manual workers declined in number.

As numerous commentators have noted, this trend toward occluding the Left and the Right has been particularly prevalent among historically leftist or center-left parties, which since the 1980s have come to share views indistinguishable from those of the Center-Right about social equality and the role of states versus markets in economic life (e.g., Ricolfi 2017). With the decline in trade union memberships and the increased role of business cash in funding elections, all parties came increasingly to rely on quid pro quo financial support (e.g., Cagé 2018). This has clearly encouraged something of a neoliberal drift on the part of the center-left parties.

The so-called Third Way, associated with such putatively center-left politicians as Tony Blair in the United Kingdom and Bill Clinton in the United States, was in fact nothing of the sort. It was rather the full-fledged adoption of the programs of Margaret Thatcher and Ronald Reagan, respectively, that had arisen in the 1980s to respond to the macroeconomic crises and burgeoning globalization of that time. They accepted the view that there was no alternative to the increasing competitiveness of economic life, increased income inequality, and the importance of adjusting to the new global economic order. The year 2008 was to prove their Waterloo. They justified their viewpoint in technocratic terms reflecting their educational credentials as experts who could be relied on to get things right. They also respected the role of institutional constraints, such as the independence of central banks, and the importance of social norms, such as repaying sovereign debt. Yet, of course, when things went poorly, their expertise and respect for institutions and norms proved problematic to their voters (Guiso et al. 2017). Even after 2008 this track proved attractive for a while. Later mutations of this process of going beyond Left and Right would include Matteo Renzi's efforts at turning the Italian Democratic Party into a centrist party and Emmanuel Macron's centrist-conservative invention in France: En Marche. The electoral offerings of social democratic and other center-left parties from 1990 until 2014 or so were increasingly indistinguishable from those on the center-right. They have paid the price in electoral terms. Their votes collapsed (Figure 2.2).

Increasingly, however, parties of all ideological hues took policy positions that were out of sync with their historic electorates. They were increasingly alike in political-economic terms, therefore, but also increasingly irrelevant in the eyes of many of their erstwhile voters. The preoccupations of significant numbers of people and those of all politicians no longer matched. On the left, so to speak, social questions relating to the rights of stigmatized groups became more important than political/economic concerns that were increasingly ceded to the hidden hand of the market. This was particularly the case with the Democratic Party in the United States, as

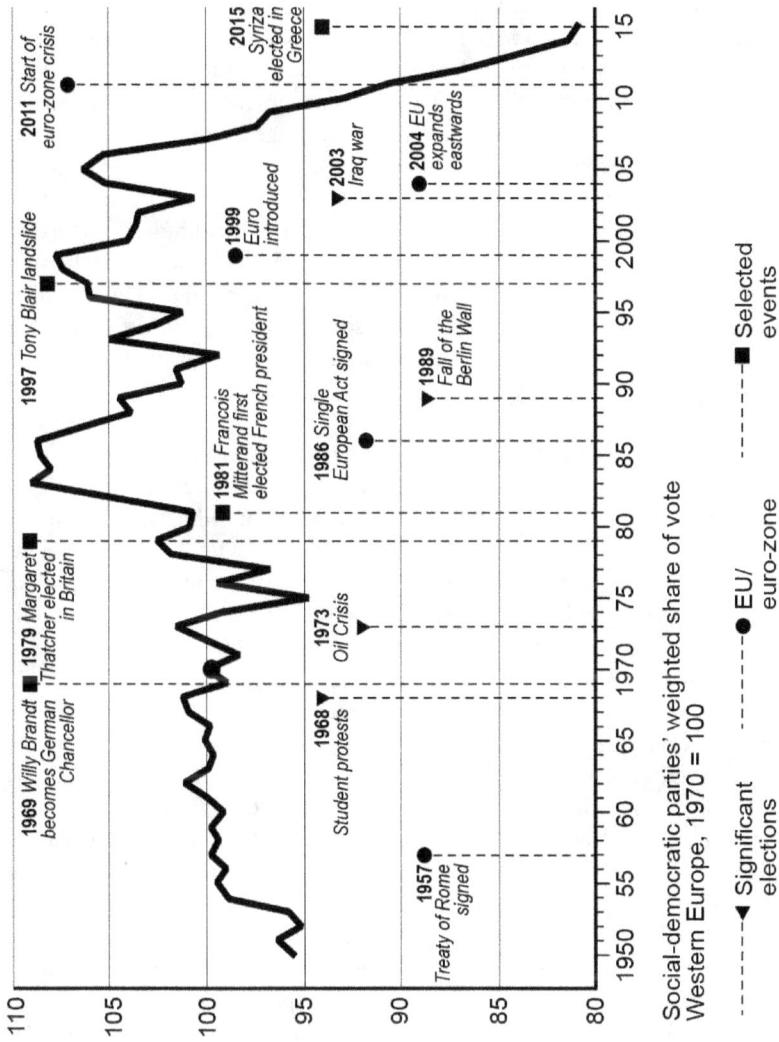

Social-democratic parties' weighted share of vote
Western Europe, 1970 = 100

Labels on chart:

1957 Treaty of Rome signed

1968 Student protests

1969 Willy Brandt becomes German Chancellor

1973 Oil Crisis

1979 Margaret Thatcher elected in Britain

1981 Francois Mitterand first elected French president

1986 Single European Act signed

1989 Fall of the Berlin Wall

1997 Tony Blair landslide

1999 Euro introduced

2003 Iraq war

2004 EU expands eastwards

2011 Start of euro-zone crisis

2015 Syriza elected in Greece

Legend:
▼ Significant elections
●------- EU/ euro-zone
■------- Selected events

Figure 2.2. Left behind.
Source: Adapted from https://www.economist.com/briefing/2016/04/02/rose-thou-art-sick.

it became the party of the urban middle class and minorities more than the party of the white working class. But it was also characteristic of center-left parties more generally, including the Labour Party in the United Kingdom, the Socialist Party in France, the Democratic Party in Italy, and social democratic parties in the Netherlands and Scandinavia. Ricolfi (2017, 179) identifies the kernel of the problem when he writes, "The distance between the problems (and ethical dilemmas) that animate progressive culture and the everyday problems of common folk became too large." Even as parties reform themselves, such as the British Labour Party since 2015 with a new left-wing leader, they remain internally divided on crucial issues, such as Brexit, simply because they can no longer channel a single message for a coherent electorate.

But it was not just the Center-Left alone that drifted into the political ditch. Even though the more conservative parties have retained voters better than have the center-left parties, they too have seemed ever more out of sorts with their electorates. As the main architects of "there is no alternative," they have had to adjust the balance of globalist and nationalist themes to match changing public opinion. Their hostility to territorial politics in terms of appealing to distinctive place-based constituencies, long a staple of center-right and center-left parties alike, meant abandoning the possibilities of geographically targeted public policies at precisely the moment that globalization began hollowing out some places even as it rewarded others. Denigrated as "pork barrel" politics or as exchange voting, ideological nationalization was the only option that the Right now had on offer. Reacting to electoral pressures from right-wing populists by adopting some of their positions, they then had to keep upping the ante as the pressures escalated. Margaret Thatcher and Ronald Reagan both managed to serve equally global and national masters (recall that both London's financial "big bang" and the neocolonialist Falklands/Malvinas War occurred while she was UK prime minister). This has become an increasingly difficult balancing act. Brexit in the United Kingdom and the ascendancy of Trump in the United States reflect fissures in the dominant right-wing parties, Conservative and Republican, respectively, because of the contradictions underlying both. Neither can continue to square the circle of being open for business and nationalist at the same time.

The older parties remain largely dependent on a model of organization grounded in territory. They have local branches and organize events on a local basis. Here too, however, the parties have largely abandoned their local activism for national organizations and campaigns that do not connect with increasingly disconnected electorates (Shea 1999; Applebaum 2019). As we argue in the introduction and in subsequent chapters, it is not that voters are no longer grounded. Far from it: everyday life and social networks are still very grounded in specific place settings. Parties, however, no longer have the unchallenged reach into places that they once had. Political messaging and mobilization are more and more based in modes of information gathering and processing that are independent of the mediation of political parties and feedback from local constituencies. They remain modern enterprises in postmodern times. At one time television was a unifying medium when there were few channels and each tried to situate itself in terms of capturing the maximum audience.

With cable and satellite television coming into their own in the 1990s, this model was replaced by a niche/customized approach in which different channels defined distinctive demographic and political audiences for their broadcasts. Politically affiliated newspapers provided the example for the new model, leaving behind the idea of providing an objective rendering of the news of the day for one based on clear partisan affiliations. Rupert Murdoch was a pioneer of this translation as he moved into cable news, creating Fox News in 1996 to challenge the "centrist" news provided by the main US networks. Others followed suit in the United States and elsewhere. The Italian media tycoon Silvio Berlusconi was skilled at combining a daily visual diet of soap operas and so-called reality shows with a style of presenting news that focused on the scandalous and ephemeral. News was now designed to appeal to the existing opinions and prejudices of viewers rather than to provide unfiltered, factual information.

Opinion Polarization

The net effect was to encourage a polarization of opinions as people heard only an echo-chamber version of events (e.g., Benkler et al. 2018; Mayer 2019). Outrage and anger became important registers for how news was presented. Celebrities, famous for being famous rather than for having any obvious talent, became part of the regular mix of what was increasingly infotainment. The boundary between news and entertainment was breached. Even though the party affiliations of the new outlets were often clear, they nevertheless stretched and often broke the constraints of simply representing established party positions on this or that issue (e.g. Starr 2019). In other words, they led rather than followed. With the development of social media such as Facebook and Twitter, the decentralization of information sources has continued apace.

Populist movements have been adept at moving into this environment even as older political parties have played catch-up. In Italy the populist Five Star Movement has organized itself almost entirely through the internet (Loucaides 2019). This trend extends well beyond the one movement. Populism today is very much a creature of television and, above all, the web. If television is the main medium for older people, the internet is the force behind the mobilization of younger people for populism. As Alessandro Dal Lago (2017, 103) puts it, referring to the 1940s-era ur-populist from Argentina, Juan Peron, "Little Perons grow across the net." The infotainment and reality shows of cable television and the new digital media have softened up populations with ever more labile political affiliations in a world of communication with fewer and fewer mediators and buffers. Conspiracy theories and wacko ideas about vaccinations and the flatness of the earth now circulate without fear of disputation in circles among which wild ideas have much allure (e.g., *Economist* 2018f). Existing parties have little chance.

Finally, the relatively new partisan niches of television and social media draw attention to what lies behind them: the increased polarization of populations on the basis of cultural values and economic interests reflecting the geographical polarization of countries on the basis of the costs and benefits of globalization. In the United States the polarization owes much to the shift of the parties toward distinctive and nonoverlapping constituencies. The conversion of white southerners to the Republican Party since the 1970s has been a frequently noted aspect of this trend. The social base of the party has thus changed profoundly. Many traditional Republicans from the Northeast and California have found themselves designated as "RINOS" (Republicans in name only) as the party has become culturally conservative in ways it never had been previously. The party has aligned itself closely with what has been called "White Christian America," a declining demographic but one that can be relied on to turn out for Republican candidates (Jones 2016). At the same time the Democratic Party has become increasingly and contradictorily the party of the middle class in major metropolitan areas, in the coastal states of the Northeast and West, and with the growing demographic of minority groups. In Congress this outcome has led to less and less collaboration across what is an ideological, not simply a party, divide. Yet, particularly for many right-wing Republican activists, their party has remained a work in progress. Until the arrival of Trump in 2015, they remained disaffected from their party even as they voted for it. Indeed, as of mid-2015, "27% of Republican Party identifiers held unfavorable views of the Republican Party. Only 11% of Democrats had unfavorable impressions of their party" (Campbell 2016, 194). Burrowed deeply within the Republican Party, these were populists awaiting their messiah.

The peculiar features of the US party system—its institutionalizing of two parties and the centrality of specific cultural issues to political polarization within it (status anxieties of men no longer able to be sole providers for their households, gay rights, abortion, etc.)—should not distract from the recognition that political polarization on the basis of economic interests and cultural attitudes has been an ongoing feature of politics in other countries too. In particular, rural-urban, metropolitan-hinterland, and growing-shrinking/dynamic-stagnating distinctions are important for understanding the ways in which populists can insert themselves into existing electorates to their advantage. In France, for example, support for the National Front was once particularly embedded in places such as southeastern France that have concentrations of returned settlers from colonies, such as Algeria, but has increasingly spread to declining industrial regions and to the wider countryside. The Brexit vote in the United Kingdom was fairly evenly spread across the country as a whole but was higher in rural/middle-class England and among some older people in declining industrial areas in northern England than it was elsewhere. Finally, in Italy the Five Star Movement has more support in the underdeveloped South, even as its 2018 partner in national government, the League, receives most of its vote in the small towns and countryside of the North. Sociogeographical polarization is an important part of the story of how populist movements have moved in on the established parties and stolen their votes.

THREE FACETS OF TODAY'S POPULISM

Our method for mapping populism in the four cases involves a focus on three facets of populism today. To the best of our ability, we use empirical evidence from election returns and survey research in a number of visual formats to construct the ways in which the elections turned out geographically and then how each of the analytic facets helps to explain the outcomes. In this regard we are inspired by the graphical approach used by the *Financial Times* reflecting the view of John Tukey, the mathematician and devotee of charts, that "the greatest value of a picture is when it forces us to notice what we never expected to see" (Smith 2018).

The first facet is the availability of supporters and voters disaffected from politics-as-usual. The way of getting at this population is to examine the increased nonvoting for established parties. The logic is to presume that unaffiliated and discouraged potential voters constitute a reservoir from which populist movements can grow and potentially conquer office. Electoral participation in national elections has declined recently in most liberal democracies (for Europe, see Figure 2.3). Until the 1980s, average voter turnout in national elections hovered around 80 percent. Since then it has gone down to around 70 percent (Blais 2010). In Italy, turnout decline is even more dramatic, from over 90 percent in the late 1970s to 70 percent in 2013. Nearly one-third of the potential Italian electorate did not vote in 2018. Across three US presidential elections (2008, 2012, and 2016), fully 45 percent of those eligible to

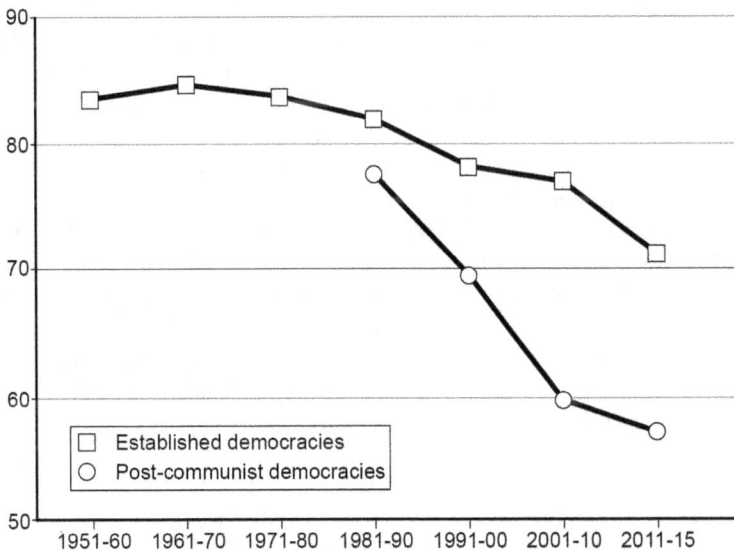

Figure 2.3. Turnout decline across democracies, 1950–2016.
Source: Institute for Democracy and Electoral Assistance (https://www.idea.int/data-tools/data/voter-turnout).

vote did not. Moreover, voter turnout differentials can have major consequences. In the 2016 British referendum on leaving the European Union, voters aged eighteen to twenty-four had a turnout of 36 percent, whereas those over sixty-four had a turnout of 83 percent. Given the overall tendency of the younger age group to have voted to remain and the older group to have voted to leave, who voted and who did not was a critical factor in determining the outcome. Of course, if voters and nonvoters are not demographically or attitudinally distinctive, voting might not matter much beyond meeting a civic duty.

Reasons not to vote are varied. People often assume that their one vote does not matter, particularly if local votes are skewed to an incumbent or candidate who cannot be easily outvoted. People also have other priorities and responsibilities, like work, family, or vacation, on Election Day. Why are so many more people now not voting? There is no stock model of electoral turnout (Stockemer 2017). We contend that people might be choosing not to vote because they do not like the available options or are alienated from the system of traditional parties through which voting typically finds its expression. More than simple nonvoting, this is abstentionism: a positive and conscious decision not to participate in elections (Van Reybrouck 2015). Two distinctive explanations have been proposed to account for increased nonvoting. The context or competition school posits that less competitive elections and lower voting ages have produced an increasingly large pool of nonvoters. The generation school argues that potential voters today, as opposed to previous generations of voters, are increasingly disaffected from organized party politics for reasons such as detachment from parties and overall lack of interest in politics (e.g., Blais and Rubenson 2013).

The first argument may well fit the US and UK cases, but across all the cases at hand, the second has wider relevance. Our attention therefore turns to the generation argument. Generational experiences arguably affect the relative propensity to vote by reflecting both life cycle and cohort effects. If the former relate more to individual experience, the latter are a feature of collective experience associated with different times and places. By way of example for the former, income security becomes more important than income growth with age. As an example of the latter, people who came to political maturity in Italy in terms of discovering politics as teenagers during Fascism will thereafter have different attitudes to political participation and affiliation than those who came to political maturity in the late 1960s. Napoleon Bonaparte was apparently of the opinion that "to understand a person, you must understand what the world looked like when he was twenty" (Lanchester 2018, 7). There is empirical evidence from the United States and the United Kingdom that people tend to adopt political identities in their late teenage years that stick with them across their lifetimes (Ghitza and Gelman 2014; Ford and Goodwin 2014). Sometimes growing populism, therefore, is associated with a youthful vote, given both its lack of voting history and facility with the new technologies of communication. But it is clear from the United States with the Trump vote that the elderly can also go over to the wild side. Crucially, the experiences that together constitute generational effects can be expected to differ geographically.

The second focus is on the key role of the leader in populist upheavals. This is ironic, given populism's overall emphasis on the people as the centerpiece of political life, but it is an undeniable feature of populist movements. Populist movements that dismiss the mediating role of parties, institutional management, and geographical distinctions in interests and identities always seem to rely on a leader whose persona provides a focal point for the movement that would otherwise be absent. What, then, makes for a populist leader who is seen as the very personification of the movement itself? Some of the leaders arrive on the political scene at times of crisis in world or domestic politics. Silvio Berlusconi arrived suddenly on the Italian political scene at precisely that moment when the old party system died but a new one had not yet formed. Such moments are rare, yet provide the opportunity for ambitious and resourceful leaders to emerge outside the usual tracks of political recruitment to high office. Others inherit the position, as with Marine Le Pen in France, or use their celebrity, like Donald Trump in the United States and Beppe Grillo with the Five Star Movement in Italy, to move into leadership.

The new potential leader must, however, also demonstrate a capacity to appeal to people beyond the existing social and political cleavages exposed and exploited by established parties. Typically, the notion of charisma (a powerful charm and magnetism that engenders enthusiastic response) is invoked to account for this capacity (for an explicit comparison of Berlusconi with Trump as a populist leader, see Agnew and Shin 2016). The first aspect of charisma is an ability to stage or present the new personality as a credible leader. He or she must be presented to the public as having the background and skills needed for the task. Invidious comparisons with the "existing political class," allied to success in the business world or entertainment as an antidote to the endless self-serving and "mere talk" of regular politicians, serve this purpose (Tarchi 2015). From this viewpoint, politics is no longer a profession but a mission. The leader is a savior who requires absolute authority but in return promises absolute love for the country. The rhetorical rationalism of policy proposals and evidence-based argument that was the source of authority for the mainstream parties is disavowed for a storytelling based on sound bites that exalt the leader as the singular voice of those "betrayed" by the parties. As Erving Goffman (1959) emphasized in his sociology of self-presentation, the potential leader must also convey a belief in the "part" he or she is playing in the political drama now underway. The performance is crucial. Driving engagement by means of provocation and hyperbole, not possession of governing skills, is what distinguishes populist leaders from their conventional adversaries (Da Empoli 2019). How does this play out in terms of electoral success across the national territory?

Third and finally, we examine how the means of communication have facilitated, complemented, and intensified the role of populist leaders and their movements. Running across contemporary populism is a deep suspicion of the institutional and geographical mediation of the "will of the people" through organized political parties and a rejection of a so-called political class. We explore how television tends to reinforce and mobilize voters who already share the perspectives they are absorbing.

These they tend to acquire by other means, including face-to-face social interaction. Television messages also must be interpreted in familiar terms. This is so much the case that, as Giovanni Sartori (1989, 189) said, television can encourage localism more than national homogenization because it takes attention off parties and puts it on politicians and their service to constituencies.

A second recent trend involves the increased significance of so-called social media organized in relation to the web and the associated technologies such as smart phones, laptop computers, and Skype. Politics need no longer have much if any grounding in place, as people can be mobilized for various political goals over differing time spans by social media such as Twitter and Facebook and by means of internet listserves and billboards (Gerbaudo 2018). Exhibit A for this phenomenon in Italy has been the recent success of the Five Star Movement (known also by the acronym M5S standing for Movimento Cinque Stelle in Italian) initially organized by comedian Beppe Grillo. In the 2012 local elections, it polled about 10 percent of the vote nationally and won several mayoral contests, including in Parma. In the 2013 national elections it polled the largest number of votes of any single "party," despite being outnumbered overall by the two main electoral alliances. In 2018 it went into a coalition government with the largest share of the vote in the national election, around 34 percent. The movement is organized almost entirely on the web. To what extent, however, do the various technologies of mass communication represent the real possibility of transcending mediation and thus realizing the dream of the general will as an unmediated politics?

THE FOUR EXAMPLES AND OTHERS

We would not wish to give the impression that the four cases we examine in subsequent chapters are a representative "sample" of types of populism. They come from four relatively large countries in terms of population, involve distinctive electoral systems, represent different metamorphoses of populism (inside and outside existing parties), and include regular elections as well as one referendum. They are the cases about which there has been the most discussion in academic literature and in popular debates inside and outside the countries in question. They are also influential insomuch as they represent particular mutations of populism in settings that have been differentially open to its growth. Thus, of the four cases, Italy has had the longest recent experience in concocting various types of populism, France has had the longest-running case of a populist party knocking on the doors of power (the National Front), and Brexit and the election of Donald Trump represent the most fateful effects of populism on the world at large. They are all current examples of populism as an important vote getter (Figure 2.4).

It is not that the Scandinavian/Nordic and Dutch populists, Fidesz in Hungary, and Alternative for Germany do not matter. They have their own distinctive trajectories. But they also share much in common with cases examined here. Several recent

United Kingdom
EU membership referendum:
Jun 23, 2016

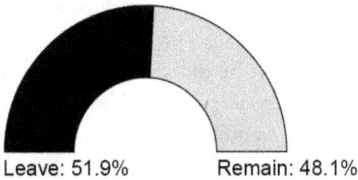

Leave: 51.9%   Remain: 48.1%

United States
Presidential election:
Nov 8, 2016

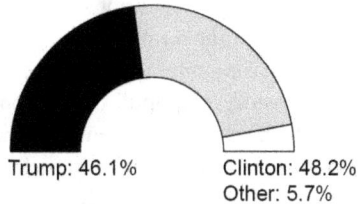

Trump: 46.1%   Clinton: 48.2%
                Other: 5.7%

Italy
Parliamentary election:
March 4, 2018

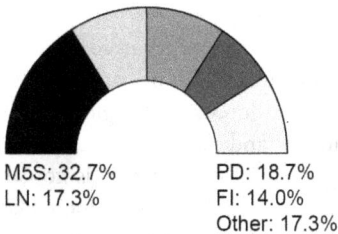

M5S: 32.7%   PD: 18.7%
LN: 17.3%   FI: 14.0%
              Other: 17.3%

France
Presidential election:
May 7, 2017

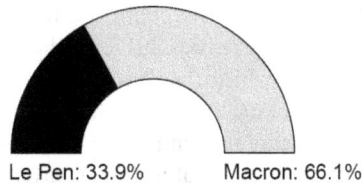

Le Pen: 33.9%   Macron: 66.1%

Figure 2.4.   Peak populism?
Source: Adapted from https://www.weforum.org/agenda/2017/05/has-populism-peaked-what-emmanuel-macrons-victory-tells-us.

comparative studies suggest that the features of populism we identified earlier—the emphasis on "protecting" the people, the difference between the people and the political elite or caste, economic protectionism and reestablishment of national sovereignty, and, above all, the modus operandi of the leadership—are widely shared even with the so-called leftist populisms (e.g., Ivaldi et al. 2017; Rooduijn 2018). Interestingly, in countries such as Spain and Portugal with a history of right-wing authoritarianism in power as recently as the 1970s, right-wing populists have had a more difficult time introducing themselves into the political system. The Spanish Far Right party Vox gained seats in the regional parliament of Andalusia in 2018 and is only slowing emerging as a national force. This limited success so far also reflects the existence of a range of regionalist as well as left-wing populist parties and perhaps a lesser amount of resentment toward immigrants than found elsewhere in Europe (e.g., Buck 2017; although see Stothard 2018). So the nationalist-populist wave is hardly universal across the democratic world. Beyond their specific characteristics, our examples are also used to establish the basis for whether the claim of populism to provide a geographically and institutionally unmediated politics actually lives up to its billing as long as at least a modicum of electoral democracy is operational.

CONCLUSION

Populism takes different forms at different times and in different places. But this does not mean that there is not something to the idea that all the groups and movements with which the term has become linked do not share a great deal in common. This chapter has pointed to how these similarities can be understood in relation to the overall history of populism in modern democratic polities. Notwithstanding the fact that most of the current movements with significant electoral support are conservative or even reactionary in their politics, it is important to bear in mind that these and also the few more inclusive, future-oriented populist groups have become of electoral significance because of the complacency and policy failures of existing parties. We have shown how much the rise of populism correlates with the hollowing out of existing parties, particularly, if not exclusively, on the center-left.

Two general conclusions follow from this argument. One is that populism is not simply a threat to party politics "as usual" but can also be a corrective to the existing parties (e.g., Stavrakakis 2017). If they are to have a future, they need to recognize the extent to which they have become redundant in the eyes of large parts of the overall electorate, including their former voters. Addressing the global political economy, including immigration, income inequality, and the stresses these have produced, is clearly central to this situation. The problem for the parties is not simply of their own making. Of course, populist movements can also become more like traditional parties if they become amenable to political accommodation and friendly to existing institutions. They have the potential to reform recalcitrant political systems.

The second conclusion is that this is a crucial time for the future of liberal democratic politics. The rise of populism is a symptom of the disintegration of the popular basis of the democratic capitalism that seemed so triumphant as recently as the 1990s and the end of the Cold War. The connection between liberalism and democracy is loosening as the demands of the former for open markets and so on conflict with the demands of increasingly illiberal electorates. Beyond the immediate electoral horizon, however, books such as those of Yascha Mounk (2018) and Steven Levitsky and Daniel Ziblatt (2018) draw attention more to the unraveling of the norms that underpin democratic politics as we have known it than to the straightforward transfer of votes to populist insurgents. As Mounk (2018) notes, the two main components of liberal democracy—individual rights and the popular will—are more and more at odds with one another. The outcome is uncertain across an increasing range of countries.

3

Should We Stay or Should We Go?

European Immigration, Globalization, and Brexit

On June 23, 2016, the United Kingdom's forty-four-year membership in the European Union came to an apparent end when, on a turnout of 72 percent of the electorate, the highest in any context since the national election of 1992, 51.9 percent voted to leave and 48.1 percent voted to remain. This outcome has been widely interpreted as a "populist moment." Not only did it involve a revolt against the official positions of the main political parties, Conservative and Labour, but it also represented a backlash against an organization (the EU) associated with relatively open borders and international cooperation in the face of promises to return to a classic nation-state that could makes its own way in the world and protect its population more adequately from the threats of immigration and distant rule makers.

But some of those who voted leave may also have seen voting to leave the EU as a surrogate for voting against the failures of party government and, given the rarity of referenda in the British political system, as an opportunity to vent a more generalized frustration and anger with the political-economic status quo (McKenzie 2017). It was not simply the revenge of the so-called left behind in the wake of recent job losses and welfare austerity acting to assuage their recent falling fortunes by opting to abandon the EU (Clarke et al. 2017; Gordon 2018). Many of the postindustrial parts of England, for example, where leave votes did outnumber remain ones, had been in economic decline since long before the United Kingdom even joined the EU. The poorest urban places in Scotland voted more heavily for remain than did many more affluent areas (Agnew 2018b). Missing in many accounts is the fact that much of Conservative "Middle England" voted to leave the EU by margins similar to or larger than many of the traditionally Labour industrial working-class areas. It was, after all, divisions in the Conservative Party, as we shall see, that brought about the referendum in the first place.

THE EUROPEAN UNION AND
THE UNITED KINGDOM'S "POPULIST MOMENT"

Compared to the United States, Italy, and France, the United Kingdom has long seemed relatively immune to the siren song of populist movements as described in previous pages. From 1945 until 1974, two parties dominated in a majoritarian electoral system in which third parties have difficulty gaining entry and seats commensurate with their national vote totals. From 1974 until 2010, third parties, particularly the Liberal Democrats (and then the Scottish National Party [SNP] in Scotland alone), challenged the others by capturing around a quarter of the votes in national elections and becoming first or second party with a substantial number of seats. Beginning in the 1990s several new movements on the far right did arise to challenge the status quo. The most important of these in electoral terms after 2010 was the United Kingdom Independence Party (UKIP), founded explicitly in the early 1990s to campaign for the country's withdrawal from the European Union. Though it never succeeded in winning a single seat in a national election, it did meet with some success in elections to the European Parliament. This reflects the fact that those elections are conducted under proportional representation in multimember constituencies. Votes there translated more fairly into seats than they did in the majoritarian system. With 26.6 percent of the vote in the 2014 European election, UKIP eclipsed both of the major parties. This finally persuaded Conservative prime minister David Cameron to call the referendum in order to quiet anti-EU sentiment in his own party and outflank the electoral threat from UKIP. The decision was reinforced when the Conservatives acquired a smaller-than-anticipated majority in the 2015 national election and the expanded vote of UKIP in that election suggested the need to clear the air. Expecting a vote of "remain," Cameron thus made one of the great political miscalculations of modern British history.

Initially, the genesis of UKIP and more widely shared skepticism about the EU can be viewed as a direct response to the Single Market and Maastricht agreements of the late 1980s that deepened the political-economic integration of what had been seen hitherto, at least across large sections of British public opinion, as a "common market" of still-sovereign states. A certain degree of so-called Euroskepticism (suspicion of the entire project of lowering barriers to trade, capital, and human movement between member countries) was already widespread. Only acquiring membership in 1972 in an organization founded in 1956, UK governments had shown little enthusiasm for joining until the early 1960s and then were opposed by President Charles de Gaulle of France because he saw the United Kingdom as a stalking horse for US geopolitical interests and still locked into an imperial mind-set that was at odds with his own as the putative leader of a France-based, Europe-wide bloc geopolitically independent of both the United States and the Soviet Union. Once de Gaulle was gone, the United Kingdom did join, but almost immediately got cold feet. In a 1975 UK referendum on continuing membership, a large majority (67 percent) voted in favor of staying after Prime Minister Harold Wilson wrested some concessions from the European Community (as it then was). The 1975 leave voting map bears little or no resemblance to the 2016 leave map we examine later. Scotland, for example, was then noticeably more Euroskeptic than the parts of England that had largest shares of leave votes in 2016. But continuing membership should not be construed as equivalent to wild enthusiasm on anyone's part. Grudging membership has long been reflected in a lack of acknowledgment of identity as Europeans, limited social network ties with the rest of the EU, and persisting economic connections across the Atlantic and to a wider world that gave the illusion that the United Kingdom could do as well or better economically without its EU membership (e.g., Dennison and Carl 2016).

On top of this long-standing reticence about the entire project of European integration, UK governments spent much energy after the country had joined carving out exceptions for themselves from major policies. Before the referendum, for example, and following in the footsteps of Harold Wilson in 1975, Prime Minister Cameron tried but failed to gain further carve-outs for the United Kingdom from the EU, hoping thereby to undermine whatever fire the campaign to leave might have. The most important of the exceptions already in place were the Schengen passport zone and the common currency, the euro. Ironically, then, the United Kingdom had long managed to have its cake and eat it too, in that it enjoyed the economies of scale in markets and regulations that came with EU membership but could avoid aspects of the enterprise that were not popular. Perhaps this could have gone on indefinitely?

In retrospect, observers have emphasized two events that proved crucial to the deepening of popular skepticism about the European Union and encouraged support for the idea of withdrawal, or what we know now as Brexit. The first was the expansion of EU in the early 2000s to include many relatively poorer countries in central and eastern Europe. Given that one of the pillars of the EU was the free movement of people, this meant that there was a net movement of Poles, Bulgarians, and Romanians, for example, westward to the richer countries such as the United Kingdom. These migrants found employment in sectors, such as commercial agriculture and personal services, for which there was increasing demand for labor but relatively few takers among the native British. The refugee crisis of 2015, with tens of thousands tramping from Greece through the Balkans and northward, and the association of immigration from Islamic countries with well-publicized terrorist incidents in the United States, France, and the United Kingdom, added fuel to the fire. That the United Kingdom had control over the immigration of non-EU people (estimated as four out of one hundred UK residents in 2015) did not seem clearly distinguished in the popular mind from the five in one hundred residents who had come from the rest of the EU. Terrorism, Islamism, and immigration were all fatefully interconnected. The EU was entirely incidental to this constellation.

The second event was the 2007–2008 economic crisis, which severely afflicted the British financial sector, a significant part of the overall UK economy. This in turn led to the bailout of banks and the imposition of austerity measures on government programs to finance the bailout. The complacency of the political class that had allowed the crisis to unfold in the first place and then the imposition of costs not on those who had brought it on but its victims (those with foreclosed mortgages, reduced expenditures on health services, and so on) gave rise to a widespread sense of betrayal and anger. Of course, this had nothing much at all to do with the EU as such. But the EU came to symbolize for many the slings and arrows of a globalization that had brought on the crisis and then made it difficult to resolve.

These trends, however, came together through an emerging watershed for the parties and institutions of government. Among other things, a number of signal events suggested a breakdown in politics-as-usual within the United Kingdom. For example, these included the ending of the historic pattern of single-party government in 2010 with the advent of a coalition government of the Conservatives and the Liberal Democrats, the rise of new parties such as UKIP and the nationalist parties in Scotland, Wales, and Northern Ireland, and the referendum on Scottish independence in 2014, notwithstanding the decision to remain in the United Kingdom, which spoke to the anomalous position of England within the UK without its own political institutions. UKIP was the linchpin of the referendum (Ford and Goodwin 2017). Its role as a spoiler for the Conservatives (and, in the 2015 national election, also for the Labour Party) combined with its clear commitments to leaving the EU and to restricting immigration, glued together by an emphasis on its Englishness, not least in the figure of its leader, Nigel Farage, to challenge the status quo. In tapping an increasingly antiestablishment vein of sentiments across a significant part of the English population, UKIP was able to pull the political ground out from under the other parties (Clarke et al. 2017, 101, 150; Flinders 2018). In other words, absent UKIP, no referendum.

In this chapter we begin by describing the result in terms of the geography of the leave vote. We then turn briefly to why there was a referendum in the first place—to placate a faction within the Conservative Party and quell worry about the electoral prospects of UKIP relative to the Conservatives—and identify the main parameters of the referendum campaign. This involves showing how much the issues of European immigration and globalization actually figured in the debate about Brexit. Though a good case can be made that for segments of the population these issues were fairly central, a wider skepticism about the EU and nostalgia for national sovereignty were also at work, particularly in parts of England. The rest of the chapter is taken up with examining the three facets of populism as described previously, specifically in relation to those who voted "leave." From this viewpoint, the vote to abandon the EU is interpreted as a populist move. The loosened ties to the main parties, all of which officially supported "remain," the role of Brexit leaders, such as Nigel Farage from UKIP and Boris Johnson from the Conservative Party, and the reliance on media campaigns make up the three elements of the story that we tell. Our main conclusions are that the referendum was never just about the EU or the "left behind," that votes varied from place to place in ways that suggest a disaffection with the established parties and their indeterminacy about the EU (and other questions), and that Brexit probably signals the beginning of a period in which, at least in much of England outside London, right-wing populism still has much mileage with regard to whether the United Kingdom is finally inside or outside the EU.

THE LEAVE VOTE

The leave vote left a particular geographical trace (Map 3.1). In many parts of England, particularly the South and Southwest, the two sides were not that far apart. But the country was not all the same. The people spoke, but with "forked tongue." Much commentary has focused on the relatively high leave vote in the English Midlands and urban North. This fits into the "left behind by recent economic events" narrative. Many of these places have also experienced long-term economic decline, so coping with it is not a new experience for their inhabitants. Even there, nostalgia more than current dire straits seemed the predominant motif. In Grimsby, for example, a historic fishing port with few if any fishermen left, the dominant leave vote paid no attention to the real cost Brexit would impose on the town's burgeoning

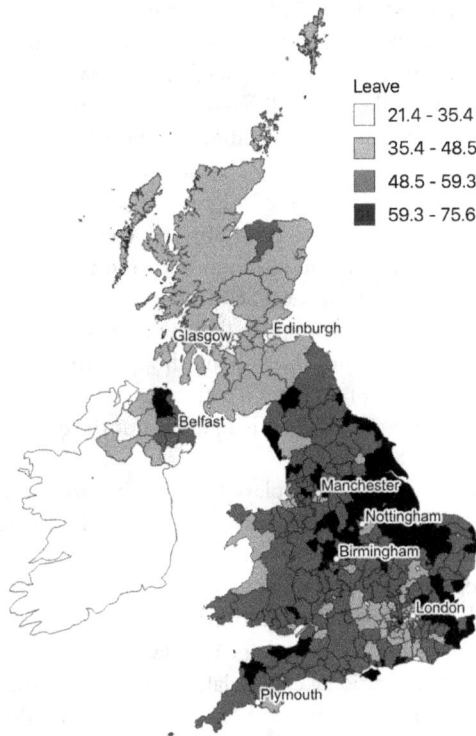

Map 3.1.   Geography of Brexit.
Source: https://www.electoralcommission.org.uk.

fish-processing industry with the loss of EU market access. Romance for a "seafaring nation" won out over actual job prospects (Segal 2018). But the emphasis on these areas misses the fact that large tracts of eastern and southeastern England, including the outer London suburbs, presumably more affluent areas, ceteris paribus, had the highest leave vote totals across the entire United Kingdom (Dorling 2016). Inner London, Scotland, and Northern Ireland generally went against the trend, although in each of the latter two areas there were exceptions to the rule. Loyalist/Unionist districts in Northern Ireland had higher leave totals, as did some areas of tradition-ally high support for the Scottish National Party in Scotland (Agnew 2018b). The cities and regions around Manchester and Liverpool (Merseyside) had the lowest leave votes in England save for Inner London. Parts of central Scotland shared this feature, as did Welsh-speaking Wales.

Most studies of the referendum results emphasize how much the age distributions and educational levels of local voting populations predict the relative frequency of the leave vote, with varying emphases on the resentful working class in "struggling areas" (e.g., Becker et al. 2016), the "squeezed" middle class (e.g., Antonucci et al. 2017), or cosmopolitan London (and Liverpool and Scotland?) versus the provincial hinterland (e.g., Johnston et al. 2018). None of these accounts says anything about the politics of Brexit, per se, particularly how the referendum campaign and the ac-tivities of the parties related to the age-education nexus, which just about everyone agrees settled the outcome at the national level. Northern Ireland and Scotland are also pushed off into a "well, they're different" category without asking what they might add to discussion about the referendum as a populist moment.

A straightforward tabulation from a UK-wide poll taken by YouGov in the af-termath of the referendum offers some insight into what happened nationally and thus, in terms of relative concentrations of different categories of voters in different places, how the map itself came about, even with the interesting anomalies (e.g., Liverpool on one side and northeastern Scotland on the other) that resist reduction to population characteristics and opinions flowing thereby from them alone (Figure 3.1). Some of the categories from the poll are dropped from this tabulation (SNP and other parties, for example), making it reflective in some respects of the vote in England more than in the wider United Kingdom. But the demographic and educa-tional variables are still UK-wide.

Prior voting decisions seem to have played a significant role in the vote, with 2015 UKIP and, to a lesser extent, Conservative voters providing much higher propor-tions of those voting leave. This is not that surprising, given the fact that it was the threat of UKIP and the division within the Conservative Party over membership in the EU that brought about the referendum in the first place. Beyond this, as noted previously, education qualifications and age correlate highly with the vote outcome. Older voters with fewer educational credentials are much the most likely leave voters, all other things being equal. It is worth bearing in mind that these two "variables" are highly related to one another. The expansion of higher education in the United Kingdom is fairly recent, and this means that most people with university degrees are

2015 Vote		
	Remain	Leave
Conservatives	39	61
Labour	65	35
Liberal Democrat	68	32
UKIP	5	95
Green	80	20

Age		
	Remain	Leave
18-24	71	29
25-49	54	46
50-64	40	60
65+	36	64

Education		
	Remain	Leave
GCSE or lower	30	70
A level	50	50
Higher below degree	48	52
Degree	68	32

Figure 3.1. How Britain voted.
Source: https://today.yougov.com.

younger rather than older. London and other cities are the places where these qualifications most pay off, given the structure of the UK economy. Higher education presumably also makes people worldlier or more cosmopolitan and hence more likely to favor a globalized world. When mapped or graphed, these two variables correlate highly with the leave vote: places with older voters with lower educational credentials had a much higher propensity to vote leave than did those with the opposite profile.

Also interesting is what does not really show up nationally when variables such as unemployment and share of immigrants in local populations are graphed against the leave vote. Nationally there is literally no correlation between unemployment rate and relative size of leave vote. On closer inspection, however, this is due almost entirely to the lack of such a relationship in London, Scotland, and Northern Ireland. In Wales and most of the English regions, there is only a mild positive correlation between the two variables, although there is a considerably higher one in eastern and northeastern England, two regions with above-average leave votes. So, in a couple of regions a case can be made for some degree of economic anxiety involved in a leave vote. When it comes to immigrant share of the local population (wherever those immigrants might be from) and leave vote, there is an inverse relationship nationally: leave votes are higher where immigrant shares are lower. This repeats at the regional scale, except that the inverse relationship is somewhat weaker in the East and in the East Midlands. All this suggests that if anti-immigrant attitudes played a role in the leave vote, it was mainly because of a generalized fear of immigration unmitigated by actual experience of immigrants themselves, except to a minor extent in the two named regions. It might be noted that, after London, the East has had the largest relative increase in immigrants of all British regions since the early 2000s, and many of these are from EU countries such as Poland, attracted by higher wages in agricultural labor. By and large, however, unfamiliarity can be said to breed contempt.

We will be emphasizing the overall mediating roles of relative turnout by age group and party affiliation in producing the map of leave voting. It is not that other social factors surveyed above do not count. It is more that their influence is filtered through the political lens that people bring to making decisions like deciding to vote and then voting to leave the EU. Of course, people do these things in the context of a public debate. It is to the broad contours of that debate and the conduct of the referendum campaigns that we now turn.

THE REFERENDUM: DEBATING BREXIT

In justifying his decision to hold the referendum on UK membership in the EU in 2016, David Cameron has said that holding the vote was necessary "because this issue had been poisoning British politics for years." Arguably, however, it had not. Except in a segment of the electorate affiliated with UKIP and among some of Cameron's own members of Parliament (MPs), public opinion across the country had not identified the EU as one of the most important issues facing the country until he called the referendum (*Economist* 2017a). The issue then dramatically rose in the ranks from mid-2015 onward, where it has remained after the referendum. Whereas for the previous decade the EU had always been identified as a serious issue by between 5 and 10 percent of the population, suddenly it rose to 40 and then 50 percent. This suggests that the referendum brought the EU into the wider frame of public opinion rather than being a response to a widely shared acute sense of malaise about the EU that needed exorcising. What it did more broadly was provide a focal point for the concerns and resentments that had been building up as a result of the growing distrust of mainstream parties and politicians and their increasing divorce from the anxieties and identities of large segments of the (English) population (e.g., Rose 2016; Flinders 2018).

The story of the referendum as an event as opposed to an aspiration on the part of UKIP and some backbench Conservative MPs reflects the confluence of two influences. One was a group of MPs who had met since the formation of the Conservative–Liberal Democratic coalition government in 2010 to challenge the government from the right. Without the coalition, perhaps they would never have organized themselves. The failure of David Cameron to follow through on a 2007 promise to hold a referendum on the Lisbon Treaty, which extended the powers of the EU, plus his governing with the EU-enthusiastic Lib Dems had emboldened the rebels. Ironically, the Lisbon Treaty included the very Article 50 that could now be used for a simple in/out decision on leaving the EU. A referendum on that treaty would have required framing in/out membership as a constitutional question rather than one decidable by popular plebiscite. Taking advantage of par-liamentary rules adopted in 2010, in October 2011 some of the rebels introduced a motion for referendum on EU membership. William Hague, responding for the government, said that it was not clear at all what going "out" of the EU would entail. What later became known as "soft" and "hard" Brexit after the referendum were thus raised in 2011 but never figured into how the United Kingdom would actually leave the EU, notwithstanding the desire of a majority of the voters to do so. That such nuts-and-bolts questions never came up suggests how emotional and nonfunctional the entire debate on the leave side would turn out to be. But eighty-one Conservative MPs voted for a referendum in defiance of the government. La-bour MPs, also threatened by UKIP or on the same ideological wavelength, joined in the fray. This was the beginning of a revolt about the EU from the benches of the UK House of Commons.

The second influence was a massive crisis concurrently faced by the EU itself, spe-cifically in relation to the eurozone and the bank bailouts, forced austerity, political turmoil, and so on. The electoral successes of UKIP in 2013 local elections and the 2014 European election then sealed the deal. "The level of political harassment [of Cameron] from UKIP and his own party intensified as Europe's fortunes declined" (Farrell and Goldsmith 2017, 239). On January 23, 2013, Cameron announced in a speech at Bloomberg's London office that that he would put a commitment to hold an in/out referendum into the Conservative Party's next election manifesto. Of course, before the referendum he went through the motions of trying to make EU membership more appealing by tripping around Europe to drum up support for changes in the workings of the EU. Needless to say, nothing came of this. So, the prime minister and the British people were painted into a corner by the in/out nature of the question and the fact that Cameron's effort to negotiate a "new deal" was never going to assuage the Euroskeptics.

Yet there was nothing inevitable about the outcome of the referendum. The campaign was crucial to the overall vote (Glencross 2016, 35–46). It was, as Andrew Glencross (2016, 35) reports, "a debate beyond the facts." It was about feelings and attitudes first and bringing in stories and data to illustrate those sensibilities second. The two camps that emerged to represent the two sides—Conservative-Labour (Vote Leave) and UKIP (Leave.EU) on the leave side and Britain Stronger in Europe on the remain side—focused on very different issues. The Vote Leave campaign advanced doubtful claims about exploding immigration, EU threats to national sovereignty, the need to redirect the United Kingdom's contributions to the EU budget into the National Health Service (NHS), and a future EU dominated by such current candidates for membership as Turkey, Serbia, and Albania. The UKIP Leave.EU campaign focused on immigration almost to the exclusion of anything else. This campaign proved particularly adept at exploiting fears aroused by the huge train of refugees that had entered Europe the previous summer. The remain side failed to ignite much passion, to say the least. It focused relentlessly on the risks to the national economy of leaving the EU, on the United Kingdom's image as an open society, and on the individual financial repercussions of Brexit.

Polls showed that as the campaign progressed in early 2016, voters who expressed views were highly polarized. In February a brief gap opened up in favor of remain. But this did not last as the campaign became increasingly about immigration. Strangely, then, those in the leave camp looking forward to a "Global Britain" with impeccable neoliberal credentials and replacing the EU with trading partners in the Anglosphere and the former British Empire had come to depend, in a Faustian compact, on the anti-immigration Euroskeptics of UKIP as the main agents for pushing them forward over the finish line. The leaders of the Vote Leave campaign, Michael Gove and Boris Johnson, started reproducing the core claims of Nigel Farage and the UKIP group. Even as foreign figures from within the EU and elsewhere, such as US President Barack Obama, counseled on behalf of remain, the tide turned in favor of leave. Nicknamed "Project Fear" by the leave camps, the remain campaign failed to offer anything other than the prospect of gloom in the aftermath of a leave vote rather than much by way of positives, such as the United Kingdom's actual contributions to the making of the EU and the fraudulence of many of the claims made by leave. Remain thus "lost control of the political narrative" (Glencross 2016, 45).

But the population was responding to much more than arguments about the distance from or democratic deficit of the EU. Many were thumbing their noses at the powers that be. In delegating power to "the people," the referendum revealed the dilemma at the heart of governing in a globalized world while claiming the repatriation of sovereignty: that plebiscitary mechanisms, by polarizing electorates, lead to the abandonment of the possibility of political accommodation. The leave campaign was organized around the claim that the people are no longer sovereign and used the lack of control over immigration as the main evidence for this by sticking the blame on the EU. As a result 62.5 percent of the electorate (counting both "remainers" and those who did not vote) did not vote to leave the EU, yet are somehow now part of the "will of the people" as expressed in one referendum (Freeden 2017, 7). This leads to the dissolution of a sense of the people rather than to its unification. This also calls into question the very capacity of representative institutions such as the UK House of Commons to manage a range of problems. So it is not just the political parties that suffer from a legitimation crisis. The outcome of the referendum is revealing about this dilemma. There was an utter lack of correlation between the geography of the outcome of the referendum in terms of leave/remain votes, on the one hand, and the expressed views of MPs representing different districts, on the other. About 75 percent of Conservative-held seats and 70 percent of Labour ones voted leave under majoritarian rules. Thus a total of 421 seats in England and Wales voted for Brexit. In contrast, only 147 MPs voted to leave the EU, compared to 454 who voted to remain (Glencross 2016, 67). This is particularly ironic given that one of the leave arguments was that in abandoning the EU, "UK parliamentary sovereignty" was going to be reestablished as "the people" took back control from Brussels. Such contradictions, unfortunately, only came to the fore in discussion after the referendum. During the campaign, passion was almost entirely on the side of leave. That is what proved decisive.

THE GEOGRAPHY OF ELECTORAL DEMOGRAPHY

Crucial to populist moments is disaffection with the status quo, including not only moves away from conventional party positions and votes but also the relative mobilization of groups of voters favorable to populist options. As argued previously, party affiliations had become increasingly labile in the United Kingdom since the 1980s as the "offers" of the two major parties became more alike and other parties such as UKIP, the Liberal Democrats, and the SNP provided alternatives to the two hitherto dominant ones. In the context of the Brexit referendum, given the internal divisions of those two parties about whether to go or to stay, it is plausible to say that what mattered was the mobilizing of potential electorates around the two options. The overall low salience of the EU relative to other concerns among the voting public before 2015 meant that the campaigns needed to bring out the segments of the population most favorable to one side or the other. Getting out "your" vote was the name of the game. Two aspects of this process are worth emphasizing, as discussed in Chapter 2: overall turnout and its geography, given that voter mobilization typically varies from place to place, and the generational character of the vote, assuming that different voters "come of age" in different political-economic circumstances and this colors their later voting behavior, including their attitudes toward the EU and the other issues raised by the campaigns (immigration, Englishness, etc.). Much research has shown that the values of different generational groups shape how they regard political issues (e.g., Ford and Goodwin 2014). Thus, who shows up to vote with which values is particularly important in the context of a referendum vote such as that about Brexit.

First of all, the nationwide turnout was high relative to recent national parliamentary elections. Indeed, at 72 percent of registered voters, it was the highest since 1992. Many people voted who had not done so recently or were doing so for the first time. About 2.8 million habitual nonvoters turned up to vote in the referendum, probably largely for leave (Eatwell and Goodwin 2018). One of the most important features of the referendum was how voting varied by age group (Figure 3.2). This is collinear with educational credentials (as noted previously), suggesting that the two went together. Overall turnout was lower among younger voters and those with more credentials. This seems critical to the overall outcome of the election. The various multivariate statistical studies agree on little else than this. Note that in Figure 3.2 the relationship graphed is between percentage turnout and percentage voting remain by age group. As age increases, the turnout goes up, and the percentage voting remain goes down. High turnouts by voters over age forty-five (particularly sixty-five and over) voting leave overwhelmed the higher propensity for younger voters to vote remain. All other things being equal, this was a vote by older people, with values acquired as they came of political age in the 1960s through 1980s, against those of people, voting in much smaller numbers and thus possibly complacent about the outcome, for whom the EU was a staple of daily life when they came of political age.

The geography of turnout reinforces this conclusion, even if in Scotland, Northern Ireland, and the three metropolitan areas of London, Liverpool, and Manchester, various mediating factors interrupted this strong relationship, such as popular parties that strongly supported remain (as with the SNP in Scotland and Sinn Fein in Northern Ireland) and long histories of relatively more tolerant attitudes to immigration than the English average in the metropolitan areas. Turnout was not at all even across the country (Map 3.2). It was low across Scotland and Northern

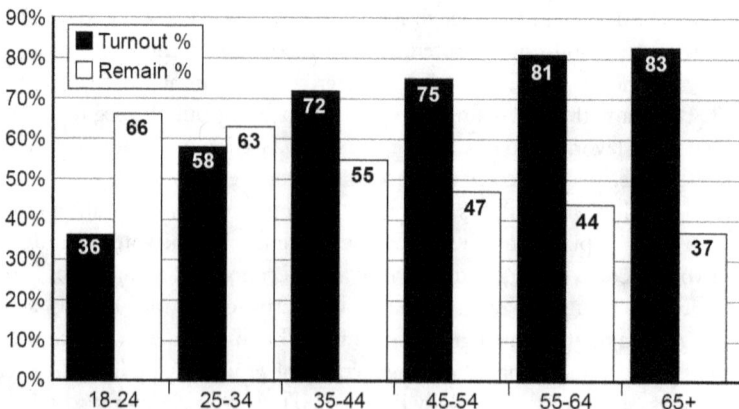

Figure 3.2. Voting by age group.
Source: https://www.bbc.com/news/uk-politics-45098550.

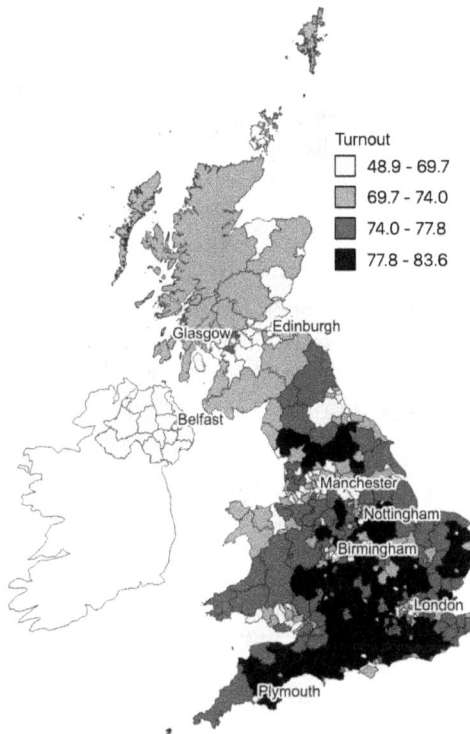

Map 3.2.   Brexit turnout.
Source: https://www.electoralcommission.org.uk.

Ireland, where the leave campaign did not ignite much fire. It was also much lower in most metropolitan areas than in the countryside of the Midlands and southern England. The remain campaign oriented itself to urban areas with their greater shares of younger, better-educated, and more affluent voters. It is clear that many of them simply did not show up. The main urban areas together recorded turnouts about six points below the UK average. Of course, no one can say for sure whether those who did not vote would have voted remain, but the previous association with age distribution and propensity to vote remain is somewhat suggestive. Turnout also tended to be higher where there had been above-average support for UKIP in the 2014 European election, particularly in Southeast England and in areas with concentrations of people aged sixty-five or older in Derbyshire, the Lake District, and East Dorset. Presumably many of the voters who turned out in these places voted leave. But some places where there is evidence of relatively high remain votes also had above-average turnouts. These are places with concentrations of people with more credentials working in tech and finance, such as Winchester, St. Albans, and South Cambridgeshire (Goodwin and Heath 2016).

The Brexit referendum, then, tended to bring out older rather than younger voters. These were the "radicals" largely drawn to the leave side of the political equation. Middle-aged and elderly voters were the ones most likely to turn out and vote. They overwhelmingly voted leave. They were the ones in revolt against the status quo, reflecting their long-term dismay with the elitism and cosmopolitanism of both the British political elite and their peers in Brussels. Such signs as prior UKIP votes alert us to this constellation of attitudes covering such issues as immigration, English identity, and economic insecurity, as well as hostility to the EU. Recollections of empire, of the "Dunkirk spirit," of two television channels, and of jobs available locally without the need for qualifications reinforced a sense of betrayal at the hands of perfidious party hacks. Many seemed to ignore the fact that the official leave campaign envisaged a UK economy even more subject to the whims of global competition, from which membership in the EU in a number of respects provided shelter. But younger voters, irrespective of their private predilections about the EU or immigration, have tended to be less politicized all around. Among countries with regular elections, the United Kingdom has long had one of the largest age gaps in electoral turnout between young and old (*Economist* 2017d). The voice of the young, therefore, one way or the other, was not heard in part because they have been systematically less likely to involve themselves with voting. This has plausible long-term consequences such as further future declines in turnout in regular elections, lack of support for packaged party platforms when they are used to customized consumption, cynicism about politics and politicians, and so on.

So, not only the leave vote itself should be seen as symbolic of a populist moment and the decay of the politics of accommodation. The relatively low turnouts in the Brexit referendum by younger, better-educated voters, vis-à-vis older, more poorly educated ones, also suggests the potential breakup of the link between this emerging generation and the exercise of electoral choice through parties and elections. The two largest parties are also internally divided over the EU and other issues and, as the Brexit referendum revealed, out of touch with their traditional electorates. Their task now presumably is to bring those back in while keeping an eye on the future generation. However, even if "the young across western Europe are more likely to hold a favorable opinion of the European Union, . . . it is their elders, who look upon it with greater skepticism, who hold sway with governments" (*Economist* 2017d, 5). If you do not show up for a referendum with a clear set of options, will you show up for an election when choice is more elaborate? If the answer is no, then what we saw in 2016 may well open up the future to alternatives to the liberal democracy that has prevailed in its predictably muddled way in the United Kingdom for so many years.

DEMAGOGUES OF LEAVE

A central feature of populist movements, notwithstanding their other differences, is the importance of their leaders and the leaders' personalities in attracting support.

They stand in for the institutional mechanisms that populism wishes to challenge and subvert. Without the leader there is little or nothing to glue such movements together. The campaign to leave the EU was no exception. In this case a number of personalities vied for top dog. Arguably, followers make leaders, so the key question is, What do they want that putative leaders can supply? Identifying and stimulating a sense of crisis seems critical, if one looks back at previous populist moments (Wills 2016). Disillusionment with existing and recent political leaders who had thrown in their lot with the EU but had also brought on the 2007–2008 financial crisis and led the country into the disastrous wars in Iraq and Afghanistan, in part through claims of superior knowledge and technocratic expertise, was also in the background. People were looking for "authentic" leaders who promised a fresh start in line with their own experiences and prejudices.

The great tension from start to finish in the Brexit referendum was not really between remainers and leavers but between UKIP leader Nigel Farage, on one side, and the two more establishment figures, Conservative Party ministers/newspaper pundits Boris Johnson and Michael Gove, on the other, in the campaign to recruit support for the leave position (Mount 2017). The latter worried that Farage would become too important and potentially alienate more moderate voters with an unrelenting focus on immigration and his pet aversions and reactionary opinions rather than a focus on the question of national sovereignty that exercised them. This is why the leave campaign was divided rather than unified under one umbrella. Of course, this is also a negative commentary on the remain campaign since it never really fought for any strong vision or found a leader to compete with the leave side. Jeremy Corbyn, the relatively new Labour Party leader from 2015, for example, was himself a long-standing Euroskeptic and can be said to have practiced at best a "constructive ambiguity" about Brexit even while officially in the remain camp (Diamond 2018).

The split-leadership scenario for leave turned out very well. The three main figures had a spatial division of labor. Farage went for mobilizing the UKIP vote and nonvoters, plus Labour voters attracted by the anti-immigration stance and opposition to Turkish admission to the EU, which he made the center of his campaign. Farage and UKIP spent much energy in places in northern England where their message had apparent resonance. Farage blanketed local media, organized rallies, and left much of the national television debates and so on to the Johnson/Gove group. UKIP's populism was all about British (English) blood and soil and how elites had betrayed them. Farage, irrespective of his French-sounding last name and German wife, embodied this. The Vote Leave leaders were figures from newsprint media more attracted to abstract arguments about sovereignty and statehood than to the details of policy (Davies 2018b). They targeted Conservative voters and others more attracted to repatriating sovereignty, "Global Britain," and spending at home what was claimed would be saved by withdrawing from the EU.

Farage comes across as a regular "chap." Rarely seen during his campaign without a pint of beer or smoking a cigarette, he was the antithesis of a "politically correct" politician. His manner of dress and speaking are also almost deliberately old-fashioned, from the flat caps and the tweed jackets to vocabulary from the 1950s (for example, saying "fizz" for "champagne") (Mount 2017, 29). Though obviously upper-class English in his speech and mannerisms, he directly appealed to a sense of Englishness that disarmed many who might have found him more than faintly ridiculous. His efforts at distancing UKIP from explicit racism became increasingly difficult as the campaign wound down. The murder of Labour MP Jo Cox by a neo-Nazi in the waning days of the campaign and Farage's authorization on the same day of a poster showing a line of young, male, dark-skinned Syrian refugees at the Slovenian border with the slogan "Breaking Point: The EU Has Failed Us All" seemed to be setbacks in the face of much criticism from various points of the political compass. In the end, whatever their reservations, many of the older voters who came out for leave seemed more bedazzled than dismayed.

Compared to Farage, Johnson and Gove were Johnny-come-latelies to the anti-EU cause. It was only in February 2016 that they entered into the campaign. This was the month when David Cameron returned empty-handed from his effort at trying to "reform" the EU. Johnson saw his opportunity. Hitherto not known for his hostility to the EU, he became the most important advocate of leaving it. Whether this reflected pure opportunism or a change of mind is hard to figure. Certainly he arrived on the scene as polls showed disappointment with what Cameron had wrought. Writing was beginning to appear on the wall. Leave could win. Johnson and Gove energized the Vote Leave campaign. The fact that Johnson was a former mayor of London and a television celebrity was vital to his role. From May 2016 until the day of the referendum, Gove jockeyed to be seen as the main protagonist, but his unpopularity with large segments of the population because of his ministerial record increasingly thrust Johnson into the dominant position alongside Farage, and those two became the twin faces of the overall leave campaign.

Polling suggests that once Johnson committed himself to the leave campaign, he quickly became the main figure in discrediting his counterpart on the pro-EU side, Prime Minister David Cameron (Figure 3.3). In terms of national coverage, Johnson made himself key by involving himself in many publicity stunts and appearances that rapidly became the centerpieces of the leave campaign. "In the battle for airtime, there was no greater asset than Johnson" (Farrell and Goldsmith 2017, 347). The most infamous perhaps was his appearance in Truro, Cornwall, on May 11, 2016, with the bus that had printed on its side the dubious claim "We send the EU £350 million a week, let's fund our NHS instead. Vote Leave. Let's take back control" (Wren-Lewis 2018). The slogan was already notorious, but it was Johnson's star status that brought it fully into the emotional limelight of the campaign.

SOUND BITE POLITICS

In the battle of communication during the referendum campaign, the leave camp had what turned out to be two major advantages over what, at first sight, would

Trustworthiness of politicians speaking about Brexit

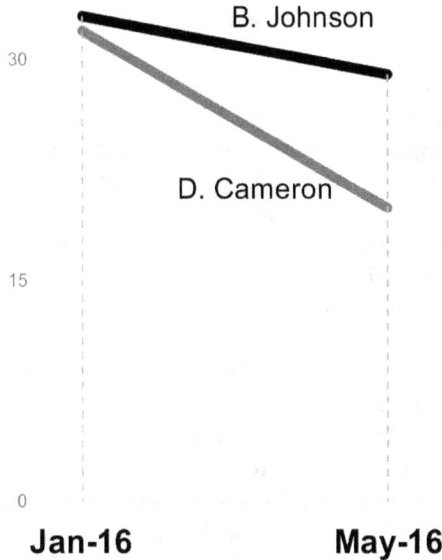

B. Johnson

D. Cameron

30

15

0

Jan-16   **May-16**

Figure 3.3. Trust in Cameron and Johnson.
Source: https://today.yougov.com.

be the natural advantage of the remain side supported by the sitting government and, at least in theory, the official opposition, the Labour Party, in addition to the smaller but well-organized Liberal Democrats. In Scotland and Northern Ireland the advantages were much weaker, given the support for remain by such well-entrenched parties as, respectively, the SNP and Sinn Fein. The two advantages were the fact that for many years and consistently during the campaign, a significant part of the so-called tabloid press (and its ancillary websites) was totally committed to leaving the EU and that social media, although seemingly much more a phenomenon of youth, turned out to be biased toward the elderly and the leave side (Jackson et al. 2016). It is worth reflecting on these two features of the campaign and how messages were conveyed for what they say about contemporary populism.

Apart from the *Independent*, *Guardian*, and *Mirror* newspapers, the national press in London had long been relentlessly hostile to the EU. The population had been softened up for leave long before the scheduling of the referendum. Not surprisingly then, such outlets as the *Daily Mail* invariably framed the EU in terms of conflict rather than collaboration with the United Kingdom. The owners of these papers, such as Rupert Murdoch, had long had nostalgia for the days of empire and the

Anglosphere. But their antiforeign coverage also sold papers. The decline of the regional and local press in England also meant that a rather relentless barrage of London-based messages descended on the country without much local mediation. The local BBC and commercial television stations provided little if any "balancing coverage." The either/or character of the referendum suited the tabloid model all too well (Seaton 2016).

The entire referendum was framed by much of the press in conflictual terms. "We give, they take" was the message. Likewise, immigration reporting across much of the press was extremely negative. Anecdotes about immigrants "sponging" off the welfare state and "bleeding" the NHS dry had long been the stock-in-trade of many tabloids. The immigration issue tout court was also tied to the EU, even though the UK government had considerable discretion about immigration from outside the EU. There was enormous simplification of the issues such that the complexities of, say, actually leaving the EU were never discussed. Most of the newspapers also reported the campaign from an explicitly leave perspective and presented it as a story about the Conservative Party and its personalities rather than about a major constitutional choice. Particularly marked was the nostalgia for an older England. A way of life had been undermined, and this was the last chance to bring it back. This was an appeal to hearts rather than minds (Berry 2016).

The relatively new social media also turned out to be advantageous to the leave campaign (e.g., Polonski 2016; Grčar et al. 2017; Davidson and Berezin 2018). The simplicity of the yes/no vote fit well with the logic of Twitter and Facebook. The anonymity and absence of editorial direction encouraged the use of violent language and sentiments and, once linked in to specific social networks, produced an echo-chamber effect among participants. UKIP had already had some experience with efforts at polarizing opinion via social media. Remain was locked into traditional ad campaigns and billboards. These were losing strategies (Garrahan 2016). A full 95 percent of Vote Leave's budget went to digital media advertising and interventions. Facebook's Instagram app was particularly important to the leave campaign (Polonski 2016). Most people on Facebook are "friends" with people in their vicinity. This sharing of posts drew in people who were not typically engaged politically and allowed for the open use of appeals to emotion and the proliferation of dubious facts. Even when opponents challenged their veracity, the questioning kept the facts in play.

Steve Buckledee (2018) has described at length "how Britain talked its way out of the European Union." He shows how the pro-EU camp failed to articulate in any of its press briefings and social media strategy anything other than negative arguments for remaining in the EU. At the same time, the leave side appealed openly and enthusiastically to emotional themes. Vitriolic and polarizing language paved the way. "The people" would have their way. But in the end the leave campaign also engaged with the particular fears and dangers that became increasingly clear-cut as referendum day approached. Combined with UKIP's "ground game" in northern England, the use of social media proved mobilizing of local social networks in places

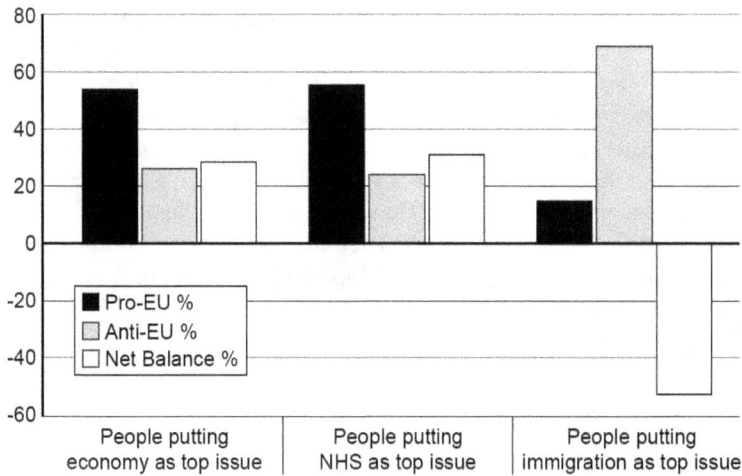

Figure 3.4. Key issues surrounding Brexit.
Source: https://today.yougov.com.

that mattered to the outcome. It was finally immigration (whatever that meant to any given voter) that trumped abstract construals of sovereignty or more funding for the NHS (Figure 3.4). This message found a very receptive audience.

CONCLUSION

The prior electoral success of UKIP, divisions within the Conservative Party over EU membership, and the failure to produce any sort of reworking of the United Kingdom's relationship with the EU conspired to produce the populist revolt that is Brexit. We have attempted to show that this was not an inevitable outcome encoded in the DNA of the British electorate, so to speak. Anything but, we would say. The campaign mattered, and, hands down, the leave side ran the stronger one, engaging with the passions of a substantial segment of the electorate by providing the sort of leadership and communication strategy that creating such passion requires. The campaign on the other side was a dud. The softening up of much of the English population with the media's conflictual framing of and disinformation about the EU for years on end is also an important part of the story. The blending of issues such as immigration sui generis into the campaign, particularly by Nigel Farage, proved crucial. A future free-trading Britain did not seem to excite quite so much. Many people literally had no real idea what they were voting about in policy terms. Overall, the referendum came down to a plebiscite about the resentments of "the people." Most of these relate to a sense of lost privilege in the world at large, to having to listen to people speaking foreign languages, to winning back what they have lost at the hands of "elites" on the other side, to rejecting collaboration with a wider world, and to striking back on behalf of English nativism (e.g., Sayer 2017; Goodhart 2017; O'Toole 2018; Dorling and Tomlinson 2019). After Brexit, how do you go back to the politics of accommodation? The party may well not yet be over for UKIP, but it might be a party that Nigel Farage would find much nastier than the one he left behind him after the referendum (*Economist* 2018b). The fiasco of negotiating Brexit since the referendum has left both the Conservative and the Labour parties and their leaders with much diminished support. They are massively divided internally. The electorate is increasingly "switched off" (Graphical Insight 2018). A new round of populism may find some willing recruits.

4

Reality Bites

The Unexpected Victory of Donald Trump

The victory of Donald Trump in the 2016 US presidential election was unexpected by most pundits. Indeed, there is speculation that Trump himself was as surprised by his win as anyone else. Beforehand, most electoral models showed that he had a very narrow path to victory, whereas his main opponent, Hillary Clinton, could win in a number of ways. Trump had to combine a solid victory in the US South and Appalachia with capture of Florida and several of the large midwestern states that had gone to Barack Obama in 2008 and 2012. The US electoral college system, with its indirect election of the president through the distribution of votes at the state level, produced the victory.

Despite Donald Trump's continuing exaggerated and patently incorrect claims about the scale of his 2016 US presidential election victory in terms of his share of the popular vote, the fact remains that he garnered just enough votes in a few key states—Michigan, Pennsylvania, and Wisconsin, specifically (just over eighty thousand votes all told)—to tip the balance of the electoral college in his favor. In fact, Hillary Clinton won a plurality of the national popular vote, 48.2 percent to Trump's 46.1 percent. She accumulated significant majorities in states such as New York and California that did not translate well in the electoral college. It is not the first time that a US president has been elected without winning the popular vote, the last time being in 2000, when George W. Bush was declared the winner. The 2016 outcome was, however, one of the most unexpected and unanticipated. Understanding this outcome provides insights into the motivations of voters, the rise of Trump, and the populism he represents in the United States.

The result of the 2016 presidential election serves as a stark reminder that it is the electoral college, and not the popular vote, that determines the winner of presidential elections in the United States. Briefly, each of the fifty states is allocated electoral college votes based on the number of members in its congressional delegation.

Electoral college votes from each state are given, winner-takes-all, to the presidential candidate who obtains the most popular support in the state, except in Nebraska and Maine, which can split electoral college votes between candidates by congressional district. With a grand total of 538 electoral college votes available, a minimum of 270 is necessary to win a US presidential election. In 2016, Trump received 306 to Hillary Clinton's 232. At the outset it is worth emphasizing the role of turnout in producing this outcome: 46.9 percent of those potentially eligible to vote (adult US citizens) did not vote in 2016. In only eight states and Washington, DC, did more people vote for one or the other of the two main candidates than did not vote: Iowa and Wisconsin for Trump and Colorado, Minnesota, Maine, Massachusetts, New Hampshire, Maryland, and Washington, DC, for Clinton. Across the country, then, of those eligible, 25.6 percent voted for Clinton, 25.5 percent for Trump, and 1.7 percent for Libertarian candidate Gary Johnson. As we shall see, however, it was the combination of the distinctive pools of potential voters available in different places and their relative mobilization in the context of the electoral college that gave rise to Trump's victory.

This chapter emphasizes, however, that Trump's win did not simply come out of nowhere. The candidate himself may have played an important role in his electoral success by exploiting his reality television persona and his notoriety as a celebrity, but the sentiments and attitudes that he tapped into had been both explicit and latent in US politics for some time. One of these was the increased attitudinal polarization between the political parties and those who identified with them, if less so within the population as a whole, on a range of cultural and economic issues. In the Republican presidential primaries after he declared his candidacy, Trump openly identified himself with a popular "base" that the Republican Party had cultivated largely on cultural issues (race, sex, gender, ethnicity, etc.) rather than making any effort at appealing to moderate or centrist voters. Largely southern, Appalachian, and white, this "base" was presumed to be inadequate quantitatively in conventional electoral analysis to deliver a positive national outcome. But 2016 was not a typical presidential election by any stretch of the imagination. Polls before and during the campaign showed that Trump and Clinton were both regarded as flawed and unpopular candidates across the wider electorate. The relative inadequacies of the candidates have thus become one of the most important features of postelection analysis.

Beyond this, however, the two sides had to address the new world of political communication that conditioned electoral competition. Trump came to rely almost to the point of parody on Twitter to convey his messages, often seemingly tweeting deep in the middle of the night. At the same time, he used one of the oldest techniques around, the rally, in which he repeated ad infinitum to gatherings of his fans his favorite themes, such as stemming the immigrant invasion, restoring black football players' respect for the flag, discrediting the "fake news" media, and so on. Rather than relying on free media attention like Trump, Clinton conducted a more traditional campaign, relying on her superior knowledge of government, grasp of empirical detail, and likelihood of becoming the first female president to push her cause. The televised presidential debates were her forte.

We begin the chapter with a brief overview of the context for the rise of Donald Trump as a presidential candidate, including how he emerged into contention in the Republican primaries. Attention then turns to the backdrop of his conquest of the Republican Party with respect to recent trends in the sociogeographical polarization of the US electorate and how these emerged. A third section describes the results of the 2016 presidential election in terms of the swing from the 2012 Barack Obama–Mitt Romney contest at the level of congressional districts and with respect to the electoral college. We then turn to the three overarching themes we have identified as crucial to the current populist "moment." The first is the role of turnout in 2016 relative to 2012, particularly with respect to racial/ethnic groups and in what ended up being the key states of Michigan, Pennsylvania, and Wisconsin. Trump's significance as a polarizing candidate able to mobilize his potential voters in crucial places more successfully than Hillary Clinton is then discussed. The emergence of Trump and "Trumpism" is framed within our understanding of populism, with particular focus on his position as the exclusive, singular, and indispensable voice of contemporary American populism. Finally, the role of new social media and television are emphasized particularly in relation to Trump's claims about the bias of traditional media against him and his claims. We show how Trump's messaging and use of digital technologies, from his invidious use of social media to his open and dog-whistle appeals to white nationalists, serve to reinforce support from his base, infuriate and immobilize his opponents, and paradoxically both strengthen and jeopardize his own position and legacy.

NOT JUST A NOWHERE MAN

Trump would like everyone to believe that his 2016 electoral success was all about him. New York TV "personality"/property tycoon Donald Trump's surge to the top of the list of candidates for the Republican nomination for the 2016 US presidential election in national polls, as well as in early primaries and caucuses, has been interpreted in a variety of ways. From one viewpoint, he appealed to the interests and prejudices of all those, particularly older, poorly educated white men, who felt that they had lost out to women and minorities in an increasingly "politically correct" America. Or, he was a blunt talker whose views on immigration, globalization, and guns were free of the caveats that mar the politicians and party hacks he freely insulted on the campaign trail. Alternatively, he was seen as a "strong leader" precisely because he lacked nuance, and his personal history as a property tycoon and reality TV star offered welcome relief from the professional politicians who pivoted hither and thither on this issue and that. He was thus "authentic." He was the most effective communicator with an audience that viewed "nuance" as betraying a lack of faith in basic premises about the commonsense nature of reality as they see it. Trump's peculiar career as a developer of towering apartment and office buildings and sprawling golf courses offers a clue to his success as a political communicator. There's nothing very distinguished aesthetically about any of them. But they indicate enormous skill at selling an image: Trump himself. His name must appear on anything he owns, even if the mortgage is totally overleveraged. According to one architectural critic, "His biggest building is Chicago's 98 story Trump Tower. Designed by the same architects as the world's tallest tower, Dubai's Burj Khalifa, it has a resemblance in the sculptural massing, the setbacks and streamlined corners. It is Mr. Trump's best building but still marred by its massive sign: The Donald is always present, even when he is out" (Heathcote 2016).

Snake-oil salesmen, pastors selling the prosperity gospel, and branding that masks disappointing content are nothing new in American life. But never before has American national politics seen such a political performance that lacks any grounding in prior political office or even previous party affiliation. He has switched back and forth between party registrations without much evidence of any conviction, beyond a history of seeing himself in world-historical terms and as a long-standing critic of trade agreements and "open borders," except for his own foreign investments. Trump's supporters seem obsessed with the "leadership" he could provide. But this is not about a history of active involvement in politics. They like it when he says that President Obama is "weak" or his opponents are "losers." The very casualness of his campaign, the statements made and then withdrawn or denied, the journalists disdained and regular campaign activities such as massive TV advertising avoided all speak to the uniqueness of Trump's approach to campaigning (Wallace-Wells 2015). It is exactly his outsider status and rhetorical excess that provide his appeal, even while he obviously hails from within the national business elite that one might suppose they would find suspicious. Despite the fact that he inherited considerable wealth from his father, his ability to portray his business "success" in self-made terms is possibly crucial here. It fits into a national narrative of individual achievement and presents him as the opposite of those, such as Hillary Clinton, who can be portrayed as having become rich as a result of their political connections. Of course, success in New York real estate and national television is not without its own reliance on political connections to receive favorable land rezonings in exchange for campaign contributions and on media allies to push your cause. Trump had a long history of both. In the end, his name recognition and pugilism toward shared enemies, such as Bill and Hillary Clinton and Barack Obama, apparently trumped any doubts about his own bona fides.

From the outset, his campaign themes and the concerns of what became his popular "base" were conjoined. Trump clearly identified issues vital to a segment of the US population that regular politicians, so to speak, tended to avoid: illegal immigration, hostility to the Black Lives Matter critique of police shootings of African Americans, the bias of government in favor of minorities and women, and the threat of terrorism from outside the United States. These were either nonissues or ones on which political opponents held exactly opposite views (Scott 2018). Trump came to polarize rather than to mollify or reassure. To his primary supporters, the biggest challenges facing the country were "terrorism and immigration" (they were against both, period). They wanted not only to "Make America Great Again," Trump's slogan, but to make it "bigger, better, stronger." Above all, as pollsters reported from their pro-Trump informants, "He tells it like it is," "can bring change," and is "from outside the establishment." The term "establishment" refers entirely to practicing politicians. Billionaires—well, at least this one—are exempted. Yet, interestingly, and reflecting the aging demographic at the core of his support, Social Security ranked after terrorism as the top issue for many of his strongest supporters (those who selected Trump as their top pick in their state's primary or caucus) (Chan 2016). This is a nationalist bloc disillusioned with globalization and the broken promises of the Reagan years, during which they had been led to believe that the rising tide of money in private hands from lowering taxes on the wealthy would redound to their advantage in terms of jobs and growing incomes. When Trump says, "We're being ripped off," he means by foreigners because our elite is weak and corrupt and allowed this to happen (Sargent 2016). His audience seems to hear not only this but also that because he sounds like them, he is an outsider, an antipolitician. At the same time, and crucially, his supporters no longer seem to believe that the political system is self-correcting. The middle ground offers no solace (Salam 2012).

Only a strongman from outside the typical universe of politicians can put things right. He is their cowboy on horseback, an authoritarian like them. He'll straighten out Washington and the world, they say, just like we would like to do. His supporters say that you can tell he is one of them from how he speaks, at a fourth-grade level, without affectation or the circumlocutions of the politicians but with the aura of celebrity. And because he says he is financing his own campaign, he can't be bought. All the slogans of his campaign—"Drain the swamp" (referring to Washington politicians and lobbyists), "Lock her up" (referring to longtime Washington politician Hillary Clinton), and "Build the wall" (the key slogan meaning deter and keep out immigrants)—follow from the "them versus us" emphasis of his campaign. No other candidate—none of the contenders on the Republican side on which Trump decided to run because he judged the party more vulnerable to his appeal and not Bernie Sanders, only a registered Democrat from 2015—could offer this political recipe. All the others were tainted to one degree or another by their insider status.

The collapse of the Republican Party as a coherent center-right vehicle for articulating and aggregating relatively conservative interests is certainly a large part of this story. Trump just exploited it. This collapse is a surprise because as recently as 2004, the possibilities for a new conservative-based Republican Party seemed all but assured (Dochuk 2006). The fiasco of the 2003 invasion of Iraq and the financial crisis of 2007–2008, intimately associated with the Republican presidency of G. W. Bush, are certainly partly to blame. But the imminent collapse of the Republican Party as anything recognizable to its founders, such as Abraham Lincoln, or more recent representatives, such as Nelson Rockefeller and John Lindsay or even Ronald

Reagan, goes back to Richard Nixon's strategy of welcoming into the ranks of the party's voters those southern whites disaffected from the Democratic Party by the civil rights legislation of the 1960s. Even as recently as 1982, when Reagan endorsed a stronger version of voting rights enforcement (in the Civil Rights Act of that year), the Republican Party still stood for a more inclusive vision of the United States than that historically characteristic of the Democratic Party (Lichtman 2018). Nixon's "southern strategy" led to the geographic flipping of the South from the Democrats to the Republicans but with fateful consequences for the Republican Party's coherence as a general-purpose as opposed to ideological party. But it certainly did not happen overnight. Trump was a long time in the making. He was the modern "doughface," the term used to describe northerners during the US Civil War who supported southern (white) "principles," who would finally turn the Republican Party into a fully fledged populist one (Sinha 2018).

The Republican Party thus finally took over where segregationist former governor of Alabama George Wallace left off in his presidential campaigns of 1968 and 1972. Of course, that unraveling of the South from the embrace of the Democratic Party had deeper roots in the Dixiecrat movement of the late 1940s and in the long history of slavery (Feldman 2013; Acharya et al. 2018). As a result, though, since the 1970s the Republican "base" has been increasingly southernized both electorally and culturally. The ascendancy of Newt Gingrich to the Speakership of the US House of Representatives in 1994, with a policy of no compromise with the Democrats and a largely southern-infused cultural agenda—get tough on crime, shrink the federal government, impose a set of religious litmus tests on judges, and so on—as the main attraction to potential voters reinforced the regional bias in national politics (Kornacki 2018). Until the 1980s, for example, many Republicans tended to support the Supreme Court's 1972 *Roe v. Wade* decision legalizing abortion across the United States. Indeed, the Republicans had historically been more attuned to the notion of such "rights" (and to environmentalism) than had the Democrats (Halpern 2018b). But since the 1990s, the white South with its much more socially conservative views, to say the least, has come to completely dominate the Republican caucus in the US House of Representatives. The southern front-loading of the Republican presidential primaries in late February and early March also gives the South disproportionate influence in deciding the party's candidate (Dionne 2016).

The central issues of the 2016 Republican presidential primaries—from the continuing false charge of Obama's foreign birth and disdain for anything he had done, to the centrality of opposition to any sort of gun control and hostility to recent legal shifts on same-sex marriage—are also symptomatic of bias toward those regions of the country where these issues rule the Republican primaries. Karl Rove's strategy of recruiting for G. W. Bush in Protestant stadium churches among the pious but previously politically unaffiliated, rather than pivoting to the center to capture so-called independent voters, reinforced this trend. The Tea Party movement infiltrating the party after the election of Barack Obama and the bailout of the financial sector following the 2007–2008 financial collapse provided an identity politics of the Right representing "a visceral anger at the cultural and, to some extent, political eclipse of an America in which people who looked and thought like them were dominant" (Fraser and Freeman 2010, 81). But the Tea Party was never primarily about the state of the economy (Lepore 2010, 2011; Skocpol and Williamson 2016). Very quickly, with Barack Obama in the White House—the president whose very US citizenship was questioned most vehemently by none other than Donald J. Trump—this became white Christian nationalism in all but name, with Sarah Palin, 2008 Republican vice presidential candidate, as its most public face.

What Trump added was his feel for the theatrical. Elections are always about drama. But they are not usually entirely theatrical. "Political candidates are judged as much by the performances they give as by the policies they propose" (Chou et al. 2016). As Charles Guggenheim, who worked for Robert Kennedy, once said, "People expect drama, pathos, intrigue, conflict, and they expect it to hang together as a dramatic package" (quoted in Davies 1986, 98). With his background in so-called reality television on NBC's *The Apprentice*, where he got to say, "You're fired!" to dozens of putative protégés, Donald Trump was cast perfectly for the role of a lifetime. But the Trump phenomenon is more than the typical electoral dramaturgy. As a TV protagonist, Trump is "the boss." He forces the viewer to line up on one side or the other in judging him. He will not allow you to be neutral. Show ratings depend on his being as outrageous as possible. Nobody tunes in to watch a "reasonable" presentation. Trump's checkered history as a businessman with numerous bankruptcies and failed ventures was eclipsed by his television persona (Keefe 2019).

As in professional wrestling, where it's the fights that get the audience, however fake everyone knows them to be, so in Trump's campaign: "he is a savior or a disaster; a bigot or a patriot; a truth-teller or a buffoon; a commanding front-runner or a bubble on the verge of bursting" (Poniewozik 2015). Trump took the logic of reality TV and transferred it to a campaign for the US presidency. Certainly, it was not only this; the populist anger he tapped into was real enough. But the Trump campaign was theatrical in an unprecedented way for US presidential politics. Among other things, the candidate called for banning all Muslims from the United States, promised to build a wall to keep out Mexicans, hinted at conspiracies about 9/11 and much else, and mocked a disabled reporter. He reinvigorated ethnocentrism on the part of white Americans. In the primaries he reversed the usual polarity of campaigning: "Where traditional candidates have gaffes, he has publicity opportunities. Even his ugliest remarks—saying, after a rough debate on Fox News, that the moderator Megyn Kelly had 'blood coming out of her wherever'—seemed, among his followers, to burnish his reputation as a straight shooter. It's 'The Real World' approach to politics: Let me show you, America, what happens when candidates stop being polite and start getting real!"(Poniewozik 2015)

PLACE AND POLARIZATION

A commonplace of US politics today is that the country has become increasingly divided between "red" (Republican) and "blue" (Democratic) states. Whereas the former are clustered in the South, Midwest, and prairies, the latter are concentrated in the Northeast and on the West Coast. In fact, most of the population inhabits local areas that are purple rather than either red or blue (Hopkins 2017). National surveys show that the population is not that much more polarized ideologically on a range of issues today than it was in 1970. The parties, however, have become increasingly polarized since the 1980s, with the Republican Party in particular drifting to the right. With party activists more polarized, candidates have become so too. This trend can be seen in the polarization of registered party voters across a range of key issues (Figure 4.1). This has happened even as those who register to vote as independents and those who fail to vote have eclipsed numerically those registered for the Democratic and Republican parties. This means that party primaries for both congressional and presidential elections increasingly produce more extreme candidates for general elections (Sanders 2017). As a result, voters are faced with less moderate candidates. Consequently the minorities of voters who can be mobilized by the more extreme candidates increasingly determine the outcomes of elections. Many voters, actual and potential, are thereby sidelined in the new menu of electoral choices. Absent this process, Trump could never have emerged as a plausible candidate (Campbell 2016; Grossman and Hopkins 2016).

The world over, as argued in Chapter 2, electorally based "catch-all" political parties are having trouble attracting popular support. Whatever their ideological roots or political goals, they increasingly fail to mobilize or actually put off potential voters. In a globalizing world, national governments find it increasingly difficult to reach the goals they set for themselves. Borders are too leaky. If you say you'll tax it, capital moves. Shocks from elsewhere no longer stay over there. As populations judge the failure of promise to match outcome, election turnouts are trending downward everywhere that elections are held (Mair 2013). The dwindling of support for a major party, therefore, is not something entirely particular to the United States. Besides the disintegration of a party, the rise of Trump could also indicate the beginning of some sort of realignment between parties or a new party system. The United States has been through "party systems"—conjunctions between party ideologies and bases of support—before (Lepore 2016). Arguably, the sixth one began with Ronald Reagan's victory over the incumbent Jimmy Carter in 1980. The electoral coalition Reagan put together is now coming apart. Bill Clinton's centrist Democratic Party is also now on the rocks, facing a revival from the left. Populist moments often herald the collapse of the old and the slow emergence of the new. Plausibly, the liberal economics and liberal interventionism that have defined the US place in the world since World War II—favoring an open global economy, exporting liberal democracy, and disdaining dictators who operate too independently—are now open to widespread popular doubt from both right (Trump) and left (Sanders). The "establishment candidates" could now be left in the dust (Simpson 2016).

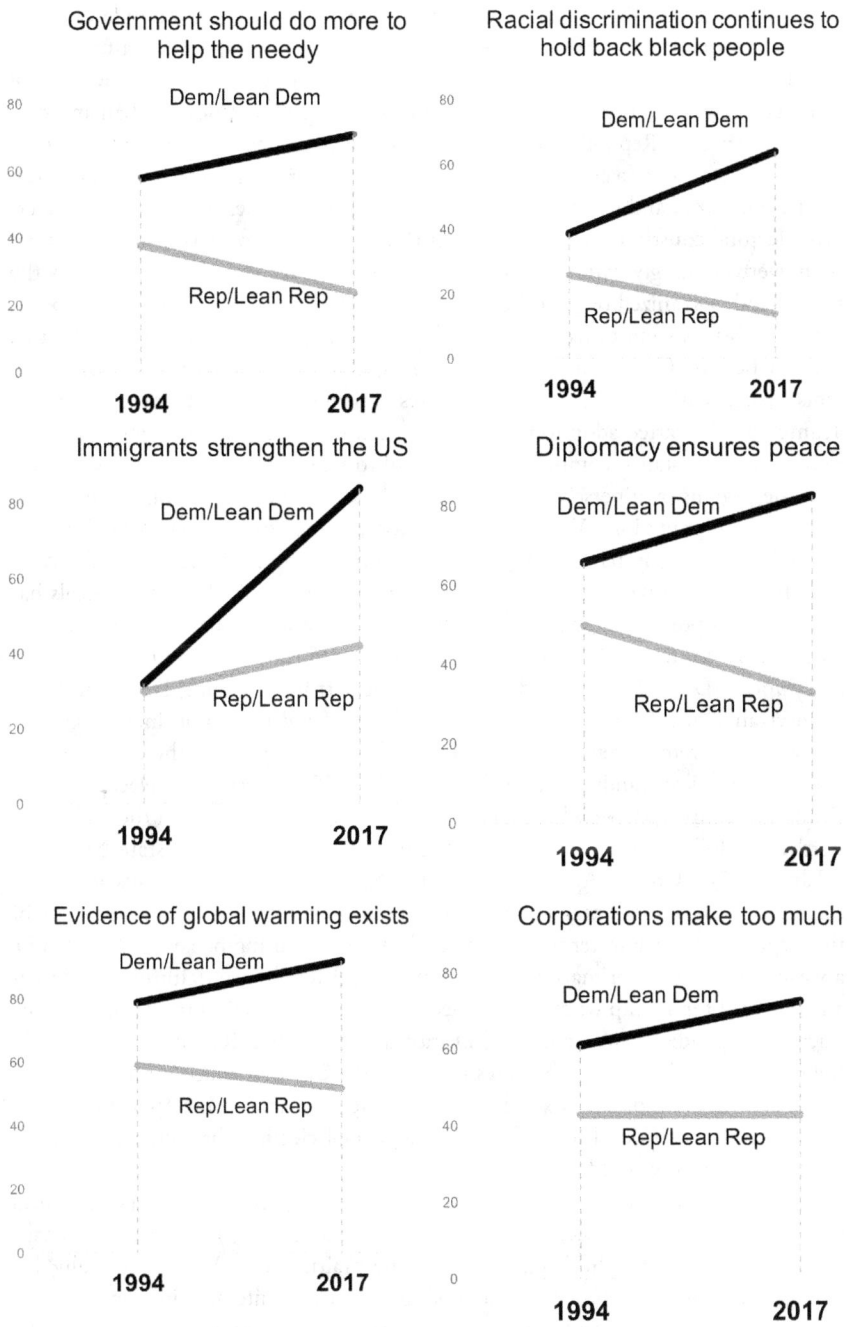

Figure 4.1.   Dimensions of polarization in the United States, 1994–2017.
Source: Adapted from http://www.people-press.org/2017/10/05/the-partisan-divide-on-political-values-grows-even-wider.

In 2016 the Republican Party, with Trump as its presidential candidate, ended up with at least three distinctive and increasingly nonoverlapping constituencies: a populist base drawn disproportionately from white working-class voters, evangelical Protestants (who are themselves increasingly diverse), and traditional urban and suburban upper-class Republicans. The Republican Party's hostile takeover by Donald Trump is the result of a confluence of the mood of a large segment of the population, on the one hand, and the party's prior failure to glue together its increasingly divergent electoral constituencies, on the other (Luce 2016). Donald Trump's success has been overwhelmingly with the first of the core groups, leavened, surprisingly, by the second and, galvanized by promised tax cuts, the third. In the primaries many born-again Christians seem to have preferred Trump to Republican contender Ted Cruz, possibly because Cruz, who geared his campaign to all so-called evangelicals, represents a particularly theocratic brand of Protestantism (Schaul and Uhrmacher 2016). Trump's wholehearted adoption of positions on abortion and other crucial issues for right-wing Protestants, combined with his call to nationalism, gave him an unlikely edge, despite his own personal history as anything other than a devout Christian of whatever denomination. Although biblical comparison to the pagan king Cyrus as a people's savior may have helped Trump in some evangelical circles, his ability to fuse the American nativism and theological Manichaeism of many evangelicals has been more important (Stewart 2018; Heim 2019). In a national poll taken by the *New York Times* in late December 2015, among eleven thousand Republican-leaning likely voters, Donald Trump had his greatest support in the South, New York State, Pennsylvania, and Michigan. More specifically, he fared best of all in a geographical swath very reminiscent of the only parts of the country where there was a swing toward Republican candidate John McCain in the 2008 presidential election, when the national turn was overwhelmingly in the opposite direction: from the Gulf coast northward, following the Appalachian Mountains all the way to upstate New York (Cohn 2015). "Greater Appalachia" is what Steve Inskeep (2016) calls it. Across this region and beyond, many of Trump's supporters seem to be on the periphery of the Republican Party in terms of personal histories of voting behavior. This can be a weakness in closed primaries where only the registered party faithful rule. But it augured well for Trump when he survived to the general election in that he then attracted independents and disaffected Democrats, as much as Republicans, in exactly the places where he needed the votes to win in the electoral college. That's the rub. It was the cleaving of the Republican Party that gave Trump his opportunity. He could put together a coalition of voters in a general election that other Republican candidates arguably could not.

Trump's success could signal the beginning of a new pattern of sociogeographical polarization. As we shall see, his largest margins tended to be with rural and small-town voters in the South, Appalachia, and the prairie states. More specifically, his strongest constituency consists of non-college-educated white men in places that are either in economic decline or facing cultural changes emanating from outside their daily experience that they find unacceptable. The more prosperous metropolitan areas that benefited from globalization and are associated with more avant-garde cultural positions all tended to back Hillary Clinton in 2016. But the trends follow a more localized and regionalized pattern of responses to what are essentially national-level issues rather than a state-by-state coloration. It is not so much, then, that different places have their own "issues" (although such issues as legalization of marijuana, climate change, and incarceration take on markedly different casts in different places) as that social and economic differences across the country (and demographic differences such as the relative densities of different ethnic groups and such subgroups as college-educated white women and non-college-educated white men) increasingly condition the likelihood both of voting and of voting for a candidate like Trump or Clinton. This is the current process of place and polarization, not the blue state/red state opposition. As a result, unless places in relative decline experience a massive reversal of fortune, the auguries cannot be that good for future populist candidates like Trump unless they can suppress votes for their opponents through gerrymandering and voter ID laws.

HATING THE PLAYERS AND DESPISING THE GAME?

Never in the history of US presidential elections have two candidates been more disliked than Hillary Clinton and Donald Trump. In some polls offering the choice of Hillary Clinton, Donald Trump, or neither, the "neither" choice won (Murray 2016). In the months and weeks leading up to the election, some opinion polls indicated that many Americans planned to vote against one of the candidates rather than for the other (Pew Research Center 2016). Such negative views held by voters in 2016 were unprecedented in the history of modern political polling. With both candidates similarly disliked and scoring record lows on favorability, the 2016 presidential campaign was among the most negative in history (Enten 2016). Indeed, long after the election, many of those who voted for Trump tended to invoke their disdain for his opponent rather than anything positive about him in explaining their choice (*Economist* 2018d).

That said, elections are always about making choices on the basis of imperfect options. In this case two factors beyond the favorability of the candidates were crucial to the outcome. One was that Trump proved better at putting together a geographical coalition of voters to win in the electoral college. This surprised most commentators, who generally placed enormous faith in national polls based on demographic categories that tended in practice to take on different meanings and affect voting differentially in different places. In fact, the Clinton campaign relied heavily on presuming that women voters everywhere, for example, would end up siding more with their candidate than with someone with Trump's reputed long history of sexual abuse of women. The focus on voting as an entirely rational act in pursuit of material interests likewise tended to miss the fact that Trump appealed first and foremost to emotional attachment to a certain idea of American identity rather than to the "bread-and-butter issues" that Clinton emphasized. Much evidence suggests that Trump won handily among voters who decided at the last minute, particularly in the crucial swing states, and among those who saw the candidates as equally good or bad and went with the one they thought represented "change" (Jacobson 2017, 25). The second factor was Clinton's failure to adequately mobilize the coalition that had produced successive victories for Barack Obama. Although Clinton did run slightly better among white women than had Obama in 2012, she lost significant ground with white men, particularly non-college-educated ones, and among African Americans and Latinos of both sexes. Although she did better among younger age cohorts than Trump, their numbers paled to insignificance nationwide given their overall lower turnouts compared to older voters. Clinton voters in the age range of eighteen to twenty-nine reported much less enthusiasm for her than did Trump voters of the same vintage. With greater enthusiasm from this cohort perhaps, her vote would have been higher in crucial states (Galston and Hendrickson 2016). In the final analysis, Clinton "failed to connect with enough of the remaining electorate to offset her huge deficit among white men, especially those without a college education, and particularly in the Rust Belt regions of the Midwest" (Jacobson 2017, 26.)

Two maps give a clear idea of what came to pass once the votes were tabulated for the 2016 US presidential election. The first shows, by congressional district, where in 2012 Trump outpaced Romney and Clinton did better than Obama (Map 4.1). By looking at percentage shifts by district, this map avoids showing local trends merely as deviations from a fictive national trend derived by use of the mean and standard deviation. Rather, it shows them as the real trends on the ground, so to speak, in the places where the election was won and lost. Two results speak volumes about the outcome. The first one is that Clinton built up impressive swings in metropolitan areas and some areas where Democrats do not typically do well, like Utah (in this case because of hostility to Trump from Mormon voters). Unfortunately, as in California, this meant that she had substantial wins in the popular vote that did not translate into sufficient electoral college votes. Her votes were too concentrated in states like California, New York, and New Jersey, when a better spread would have led to greater reward. The second is how well relative to Romney Trump did in what earlier we termed "Greater Appalachia" (West Virginia, Tennessee, etc.) and in the Midwest. Much of this has been ascribed to a rural/small-town effect nationwide. In fact it is an effect that is particularly strong in these regions as opposed, say, to New England or even parts of the South. It is also not really a story of places in economic eclipse. It is more a story about a sense of cultural alienation in a changing country in which the main cultural industries are located in New York and California. On top of his holding onto votes in the Deep South and adding them in Florida, Trump's success compared to Romney in Ohio, Michigan, Wisconsin, and Pennsylvania in the end gave him the edge in the electoral college. Indeed, some of his success came in counties that had voted for Obama in 2012. Whether this signifies that Obama voters had shifted to Trump or that different people were mobilized for Trump and Obama voters stayed home is hard to say. There has been much discussion of this

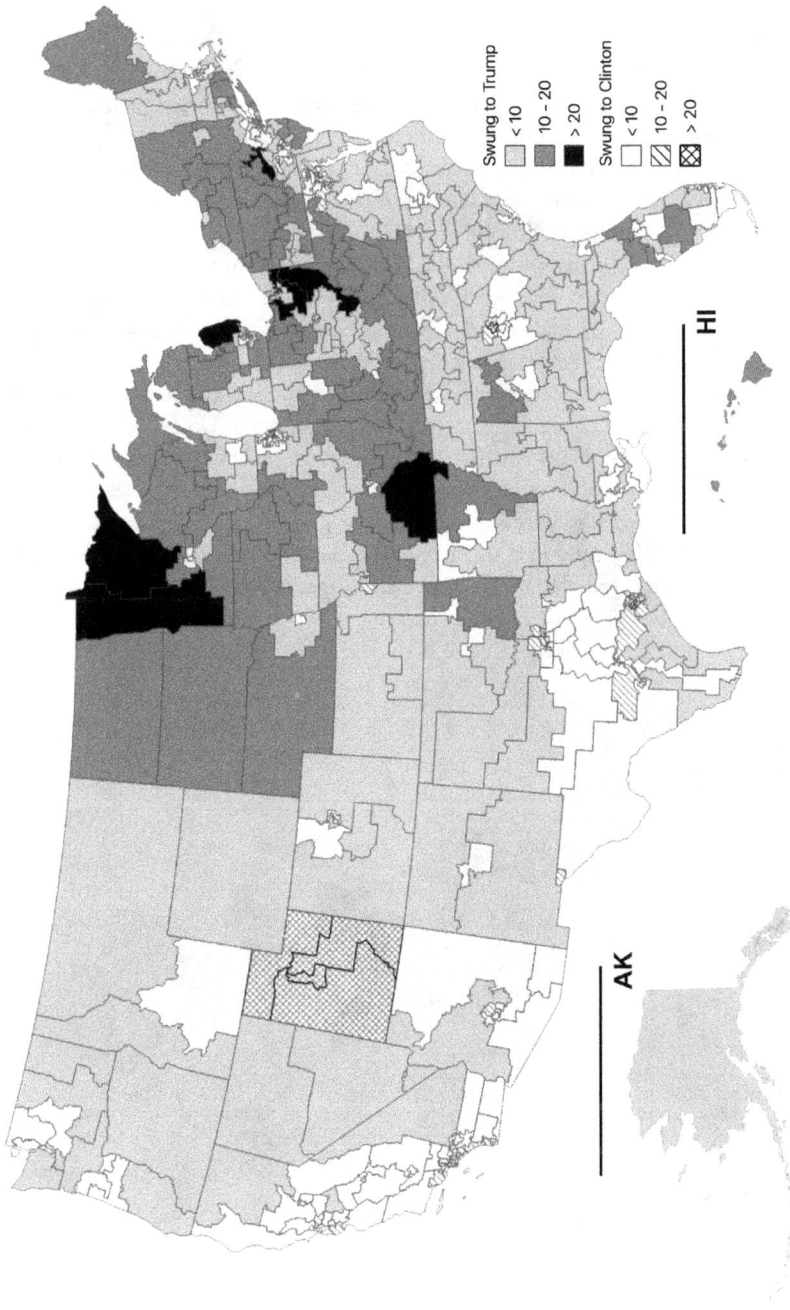

Map 4.1. 2016 presidential election margin versus 2012 presidential election margin, by US congressional district.
Source: https://www.dailykos.com.

without any ready resolution. On one side, some writers stress the "left behind" voters of Ohio and Michigan who had lost faith in the economic policies of the Democrats and turned to Trump. On the other, some, more convincingly in our view, argue on the basis of survey evidence that racial anxieties had increased during Obama's second term, turning some voters, particularly working-class males, toward the raw antiminority and anti-immigrant rhetoric of Trump (Sides et al. 2018; Beauchamp 2018). Differential turnout across different groups in different places, as we shall see, however, was critical to the outcome, notwithstanding the seeming paradox of Obama counties shifting to Trump.

The second map is the determining one. This is the map of votes in the electoral college (Map 4.2). It shows how much a "winner-takes-all" model at the state level (save for the anomalies of Maine and Nebraska) reproduces the federal system by privileging the states as units for aggregating votes but at the expense of a democratic commitment to one person, one vote. The resulting map gives rise to the blue state/ red state opposition as the singular feature of the geography of US presidential politics. Clinton won in the Northeast (with the exception of one Maine district) and on the West Coast, with outliers in Illinois, Minnesota, Colorado, and New Mexico. Trump won everywhere else. Not surprisingly, and particularly in light of the 2000 and 2016 elections that produced winners in the electoral college who had lost the popular vote, the electoral college has been scrutinized, criticized, and defended.

When it was determined that Trump had not won the popular vote and had in fact lost by a whopping margin of over 2.8 million votes, commentaries on and calls

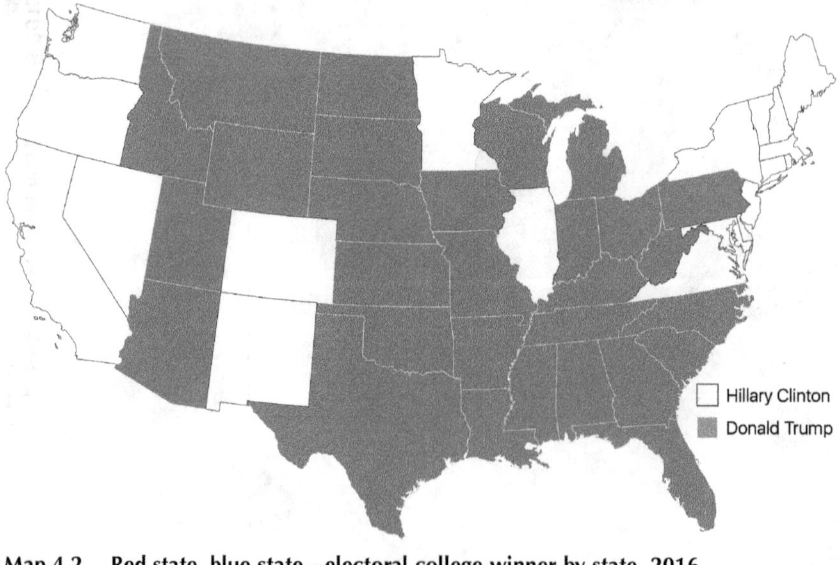

Map 4.2.   Red state, blue state—electoral college winner by state, 2016.
Source: https://www.dailykos.com.

to abolish the electoral college quickly appeared. Proponents of the electoral college and those who have emerged victorious claim that it remains relevant and effective today because "every state counts." In other words, since each and every state contributes to the final total, candidates must engage in national campaigns and cannot focus entirely just on the most populous cities and states. Though smaller states are given a disproportionate amount of influence in the selection of a president, this can be considered an advantage of the electoral college because candidates must respect this fact in a constitutionally federal republic. Though a total of 538 electoral college votes are available, votes from several states are virtually guaranteed to one party's candidate or the other. For instance, in this highly polarized era of American politics, the Democratic presidential candidate can count on the fifty-five electoral votes from California, just as the Republican candidate can depend on the thirty-four electoral college votes from Texas. The strategies and tactics of presidential campaigns clearly reflect this electoral geography of the United States, as they direct their attention and resources to those states where support for both parties is believed to be close and fluid. These are the "battleground," "contested," or "swing" states where modern-day data-driven campaigns target undecided voters and algorithms are fed voter lists and big data to get out the vote. In 2016 the Trump campaign, whether by design or accident, seems to have done a better job of calibrating its strategy.

TUNING OUT INSTEAD OF TURNING OUT?

With neither candidate inspiring much of what can be called positive enthusiasm in 2016, turnout was an absolutely central issue. Who could most successfully mobilize his or her "side" while also attracting more of the increasingly important bloc of independent or swing voters, particularly in swing states? Only 53.1 percent of US adult citizens voted in 2016. This compares to 62.3 percent in 2008 and 57.5 percent in 2012. About 74 percent of voters were white, down from around 85 percent in 1992. The geography of turnout reveals an incredibly wide range of rates of participation in 2016 (Map 4.3). At 43 percent, Hawaii had the lowest statewide turnout (probably because it has long been a one-party Democratic state in presidential elections, and by the time voting closed there, the election winner had been declared), followed by West Virginia (50 percent). Minnesota had the highest statewide turnout (74 percent), followed by Colorado (73 percent) and New Hampshire (72 percent). But turnout was particularly low in a swath of counties curving from New Mexico through Texas, Oklahoma, Tennessee, and West Virginia to central Pennsylvania and upstate New York. This belt, with a few exceptions, provided Donald Trump with some of his highest percentages. His victory was built in part on low turnouts in places that supported him. Perhaps potential voters for the other side simply stayed home.

But low voting in 2016 spanned a much more differentiated spectrum of places. On the map, rural and small-town areas dominate. But far more potential votes were

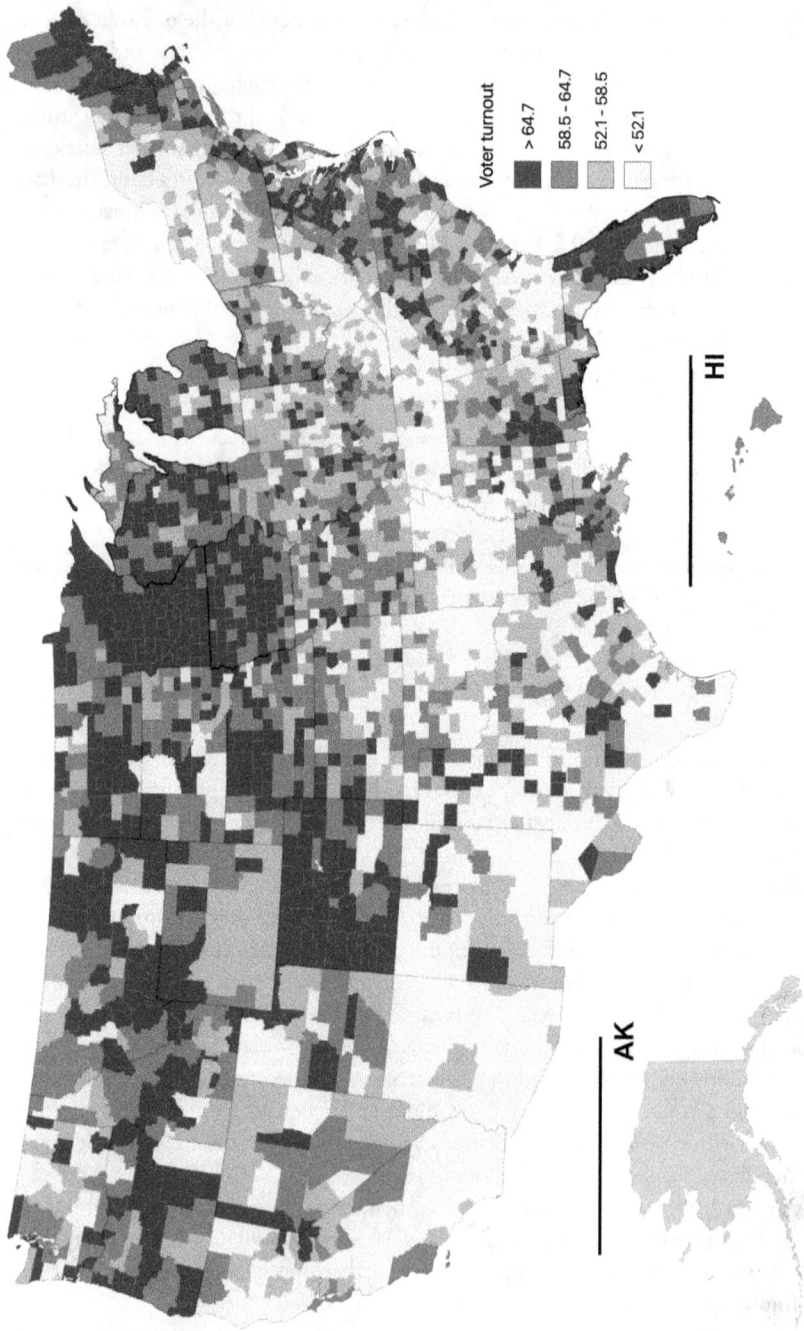

Map 4.3. Estimated voter turnout by county, 2016.

Source: https://www.census.gov/programs-surveys/decennial-census/about/voting-rights/cvap.html.

Voter turnout

- > 64.7
- 58.5 – 64.7
- 52.1 – 58.5
- < 52.1

AK

HI

lost in metropolitan counties because of differences in population density (Mellnik et al. 2018). For example, four of New York's five boroughs, as well as all or parts of Houston, Dallas, Memphis, St. Louis, Baltimore, and Oklahoma City, had among the lowest turnouts nationwide, ranging from 48 percent in the Bronx (New York) to 55 percent in St. Louis. Four hundred of the one thousand lowest-turnout counties are more than 80 percent white in population. But another two hundred or so are majority African American or Latino. Many of these are urban counties. There has been a persistent "turnout gap" in US presidential (and other) elections between whites and nonwhites even when, as in 2008 and 2012, an African American was one of the main candidates (Fraga 2018). Overall, however, traits other than race/ethnicity seem to set low-turnout places apart. In over seven hundred of the low-turnout counties, majorities had high school or less in terms of education. High-voting counties, to the contrary, tend to have higher percentages of people with more education. Some of the statewide differences come down to ease of voting and voter-suppression efforts (usually in Republican-controlled states) (Lynch 2018). County differences reflect both prior histories of voting, get-out-the-vote efforts by parties, and the relative attractiveness of parties and candidates.

The final consideration certainly played a part in the states of Michigan and Wisconsin in 2016, which, along with Pennsylvania, determined the outcome of the election in the electoral college. Even if in these states as well as others, such as Ohio and Iowa, some Obama voters in 2012 switched to Trump in 2016, more important were very large declines in turnout in predominantly urban and African American counties that potentially deprived Hillary Clinton of crucial votes (Figure 4.2). The point here is not to blame African American voters for the election of Trump. Far from it. It is simply that a group mobilized in 2008 and 2012 by a candidate who genuinely excited them simply could not be taken for granted by a very different candidate, Hillary Clinton, in 2016 (see Sides et al. 2018, Chapter 8). Alternatively, she could have tried to attract a different constituency as a possible solution to her dilemma of finding sufficient votes in swing states. Of course, hindsight allows us to see what was not obvious at the time. Pundits of all political persuasions had shared the assumption that African Americans had no choice in the face of a candidate on the other side like Trump.

TRUMP AND TRUMPISM

What the Clinton campaign lacked in inspiration, the vulgarity and brashness of Donald Trump and his campaign more than made up for. From his insulting nicknames for opponents—like "Low-Energy Jeb" Bush, "Lyin' Ted" Cruz, "Little Marco" Rubio, and "Crooked Hillary"—throughout the Republican primaries and presidential campaign to the revelation of his lewd remarks about how he treated women, Trump embraced and epitomized the adage "There's no such thing as bad publicity." For many, the final outcome of the 2016 US presidential election con-

Change in voter turnout by race, 2012 - 2016

■ Black □ White

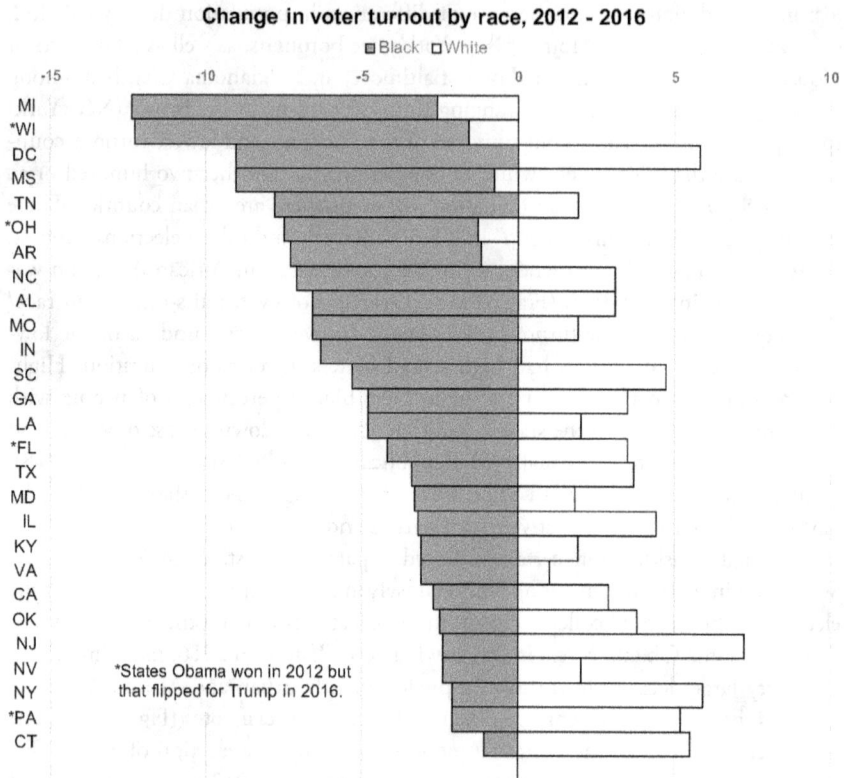

Figure 4.2. Change in voter turnout by race in selected states, 2012–2016.
Source: Adapted from https://www.washingtonpost.com/news/monkey-cage/wp/2017/05/08/why-did-trump-win-more-whites-and-fewer-blacks-than-normal-actually-voted.

firmed this statement. By dint of rhetorical excess and domination of the news cycle, Trump had conquered the country and the Republican Party, in that order. Trump has what conservative columnist Bret Stephens (2018) calls a "feral" political intelligence. He may be a bigoted con artist, and his followers may all be dumb. But used, due to his background in reality television, to communicating with a mass audience of "the less educated" (a phrase he himself used to describe many of his supporters), he was able to keep all eyes on him: "There's more than one type of intelligence. Trump's is feral. It strikes fast. It knows where to sink the fang into the vein."

From this perspective, Trump is the quintessential postmodern populist. It is not his policies, whatever they are on a given day, that excite his supporters. It is his attitude, his vehemence in venting their frustrations at the state of the world and advocating how simple solutions could actually be if not for these laws and norms that interfere with doing "the right thing." When he makes things up, that is fine because that is what they want to hear. "Trump reflects back to his supporters a general feeling for what *ought to be*, a general truthiness in their guts" (Hurst 2018). They desire confirmation that a celebrity shares their prejudices and voices them in public. For his part, he sees himself, not this or that policy, as the solution to their problems. It is an emotional attachment, not a rational agenda, that connects him and them. He also embodies an oppositional stance to all things that they find worrisome: undocumented immigrants who do not speak English, the disappearance of jobs in manufacturing, foreigners cheating "us" at trade and investment, expenditures on foreign aid, and government policies that favor "minorities" at their expense, particularly health-care and welfare expenditures. Trump managed to articulate, in his own inarticulate way, exactly how many of his fans see the world around them. This was his political genius. His campaign rallies (continuing into his presidency) and the use of Twitter lent themselves to the overstatement of threats (those dangerous women and children refugees at the US southern border) and outright misrepresentations of reality that became the leitmotif of his campaign. During the course of his presidential bid, Trump told thousands of documentable lies. Simplicity is so simple.

Trumpism, therefore, is not a coherent ideological formation based on programmatic goals that favor the material interests of his voting bloc, such as income redistribution or health care for all. Far from it. At the time of the election, it was clearly a communication strategy behind which many of the policies favored by the Republican Party for many years—from appointing hyperconservative judges and shrinking the regulatory reach of the federal government to instituting massively regressive tax cuts—could be put into place. At the same time it has also involved a recognition of the changing party base, whose outlook over the previous ten to twenty years has grown consistently more nationalist and less in favor of free trade and open borders than was traditionally the case with the leadership of the Republican Party. This is no longer Ronald Reagan's Republican Party, although it has its roots within the changing base of that party since the 1960s.

The essence of Trumpism, therefore, is cultural backlash (e.g., Green 2017). It may marginally address the question of job loss and other economic concerns of the less educated who supported Trump, but it is mainly a politics of resentment (Oliver and Rahn 2016; Norris and Inglehart 2019). It is a reaction against multiculturalism and a multiracial America. It is antiestablishment because the Hollywood and Washington elites have gone over to that side. It is also openly nationalist or focused on "popular sovereignty" in the sense that it rejects cosmopolitanism and the virtues of knowing and understanding the world at large. We are fine as we are, is the refrain; leave us be. Finally, it is obsessed with others, foreigners and minorities, "taking advantage of us." It is time for us to show them a thing or two. It is about the "clash of civilizations." His largely white evangelical Protestant supporters are more American nationalist than Christian, as that latter term is typically understood (Kuruvilla 2018). The sad side of this ideological complex is apparent if you examine the interesting highly positive correlation between enrollment in the US government health-care program Medicaid and votes for Donald Trump across counties in the state of Kentucky. As the *Economist* (2018c) reports in the context of Republican attempts in 2018 to reform the program by adding work requirements to eligibility, "Of the ten rural counties in the country with the highest share of adults enrolled in Medicaid, six are in Kentucky. These areas are also the Trumpiest. . . . During the 1990s, racial animus, especially the notion that lazy blacks were crowding the welfare rolls, was shown to be especially powerful in shaping attitudes to the safety net. Yet the people most likely to suffer from the new efforts at [reforming Medicaid] are the poor whites who helped send Donald Trump to the White House." Under this peculiar variety of populism we are calling Trumpism, the more you or your neighbors depend on government, the more you seem to despise it (see, e.g., Porter 2018).

Whether this is sustainable over time is doubtful. The incoherence of Trump's political offering then sets limits on the future of Trumpism. Without him what could it be? Thus, he's right: during the election and since, it has been largely about him. But the American leader stirring up fear and loathing is not entirely new. Trump may be the candidate par excellence whose lack of filters signals authenticity. However, he is also channeling long-held anxieties and fears on the part of large segments of the population who think that a retreat from global interdependence "back" to a future in which they can once again think that they are in charge (however fictive that past might be) will also make them safe. As Benjamin Barber (2004, 36) once noted when writing about the threat of terrorism and how it is not really about an anarchic world "out there" but intimately related to the US hegemonic position in the world at large, Americans have long supported the idea that "fear can only be defeated by fearsomeness. While the world trembles, Americans release their cold fear in shivers of applause for a militant Americanism punctuated by 'USA! USA!'"

FROM TELEVISION TO TWEETS AND TRUTHINESS

Following the 2012 election in which Barack Obama secured his second term as president, Donald Trump used the social media platform Twitter to declare—rather "Tweet"—that the electoral college was a "disaster" for American democracy. Shortly after his 2016 victory, Trump tweeted that the electoral college is "actually genius in that it brings all states, including the smaller ones, into play" and followed up by stating, "If the election were based on total popular vote I would have campaigned in NY, Florida and California and won even bigger and more easily." Calling this reversal in thinking about the electoral college ironic is an understatement in the age of Trump. It is, however, emblematic of political communication that allows Trump to speak directly to his base(s), the role of technology, and how what he says/tweets does not matter. It's all a distraction. In fact, the real business of government apparently gets in the way of Trump's distractions. Expertise and administrative competence count for very little in Trump's world (Lewis 2018). It's the rhetoric, stupid.

Communication, therefore, was key to Trump's ascendancy (Hall Jamieson and Taussig 2017). The role of the media in shaping, defining, and reinforcing this populist moment across America and elsewhere can neither be overlooked nor overstated. Moreover, the traditional mass media are today simultaneously enhanced and diminished by a range of digital technologies and social media platforms like Facebook and Twitter. Once heralded as innovative tools to promote democracy and citizen engagement, these same digital technologies can now be used to disrupt and undermine democratic institutions and practices. Our particular interest is how this new social media landscape facilitated the emergence of Donald Trump and subsequently strengthened his role as the singular and exclusive leader of this populist moment in America. Yet, in the final analysis, was this really how he overcame the odds against his victory?

The Trump campaign's communication strategy rested on three legs: support from Fox News and right-wing talk radio, particularly pundits Sean Hannity and Rush Limbaugh; the use of Twitter and Facebook to disseminate stories favorable to Trump but without the mediation of the so-called mainstream media (the quality newspapers such as the *New York Times* and the main television networks); and the use of targeted communication with likely voters employing explosive rhetoric (particularly at rallies packed with rabid supporters) reported on widely by the mainstream media in place of advertising. In contrast, the Clinton campaign relied very much on television advertising and the "science of politics": targeting voters and determining the most effective ways of persuading them to vote for Clinton through "big data" analysis and mailings and focus groups. Trump struggled to build a professional campaign. Considerable evidence suggests that in many respects Clinton's campaign actually worked better than Trump's in terms of having a positive impact on the vote totals (Sides et al. 2018, Chapter 8).

In brief compass, we would emphasize several aspects of Trump's approach that set his campaign apart from Clinton's and previous ones. The first was the open use of the Fox News network, which made little or no effort at appearing evenhanded in its coverage of candidates. Trump both favored the network in granting interviews and used its media personalities to push his stories-of-the-day, including farfetched claims about, for example, the crimes of immigrants and insults directed at his adversaries. Trump particularly favored recycling phrases and ideas that he had picked up from Far Right websites. These were then taken as gospel on Fox News and repeated ad nauseam to the Fox faithful. Far Right conspiracy theorists like Alex Jones and Rush Limbaugh thus found their previously marginalized ramblings had become central to the Trump campaign, at least for one news cycle, before Trump moved on, in reality TV fashion, to something else. This created what Yochai Benkler et al. (2018, 75) call a "propaganda feedback loop." It was particularly effective in cementing the base that Trump had identified and built up in the primaries going into the general election.

A second aspect of Trump's communication would be the way that a number of actors favoring Trump, including the government of Russia, intervened in the election surreptitiously through the planting of pro-Trump and anti-Clinton stories on Facebook and other social media. Whether this involved collusion between Trump and these other actors remains an open question as of 2019. The intervention on his behalf is not. Facebook in particular was crucial to Trump (Halpern 2018a). His campaign recycled all manner of misrepresentations about Clinton and her positions, relying on accusations of malfeasance on her or her husband's part and even charging that she was terminally ill. At the same time, anonymous sources, some of which turned out to be sponsored by the Russian government, were trolling news websites and planting false stories on Facebook to gin up Trump's supporters and demoralize Clinton's and to recruit potential voters, such as African Americans, in crucial electoral college states. Trump's and many Trump supporters' attraction to Russian president Vladimir Putin's positions on issues from homophobia to undermining the European Union was perhaps reciprocated in Putin's desire to see Trump rather than Clinton elected to the US presidency (Harding 2017; Hall Jamieson 2018; Romm 2018). Be that as it may, Instagram and Facebook provided mechanisms for the dissemination of information that reinforced the polarization of the US electorate even as it generally favored Trump over Clinton. The older white voters targeted by the Trump campaign were much more likely to share fake stories on Facebook than were any other demographic groups (Guess et al. 2019). Even if the motivation to support Trump was already strong, the sharing of stories that put him in a positive light and his opponent in a negative one could well have reinforced mobilization on Trump's behalf and pushed some voters into his column.

In the third place, Trump's neglect of traditional campaign strategies employed by the Clinton campaign turned out to be his strength. His use of rallies and constant attacks on the media for publishing "fake news" (news unfavorable to him), as well as the media's reporting of his attacks, conspired to produce an echo effect among both consistent and potential supporters. As the Clinton campaign and liberal mass media and pundits alike pinned their hopes and expectations on data and analytics to get out the vote, Trump and his comparatively slim campaign made little of this approach, save for what turned out to be the not very helpful "psychographics" offered by the British firm Cambridge Analytica, whose main contribution turned out to be leaked Facebook data that allowed for better targeting of misinformation. Trump instead believed that his rallies and his physical presence at them were key to generating support and firing up his base. In retrospect, this proved a very effective strategy. Given his bombastic persona compared to, first, his Republican primary opponents and, then, Hillary Clinton, as well as the fact that his rallies were often raucous, brazen, and sometimes violent affairs, Trump benefitted tremendously from free media coverage. In fact, it has been estimated that the Trump campaign had received the equivalent of $2 billion worth of media coverage at no cost by the end of February 2016, well before he secured the Republican nomination or won the presidential election (Confessore and Yourish 2016). With Hillary Clinton betting on voter turnout models and the microtargeting of millennials, women, and minorities with big data tactics, Trump captured the hearts and minds of those in the largely white places that ultimately mattered in the election (Sides et al. 2018). His loose connection to empirical truth, what has been called "truthiness"—if I believe it's true, it becomes so—connected him to the like-minded, who then showed up and voted for him.

This final point seems crucial. In the end it was not social media or Fox News that determined the outcome of the election. Many of the people who voted for Trump already inhabited social worlds in particular places where alternative political perspectives were simply absent. By watching Sean Hannity and through their preexisting "friendships" on Facebook, they already espoused the worldview that Trump arrived to amplify and exploit. As the writing of those such as Arlie Russell Hochschild (2016) and Katherine Cramer (2016) reminds us, Trump could simply play into an existing political consciousness that was not built on watching Fox News or participating in social media. It was already there for the taking. As Hochschild (2016, 14) puts it, "Our home enclaves often reflect special cultures of governance tying politics to geography. . . . Rural areas in the Midwest, South, and Alaska lean right while large cities, New England and the two coasts lean left." The different lives these reflect condition what people come to feel is true and worthwhile. Trump simply tapped into the resentments and home truths of predominantly older and male white Americans whom previous politicians either did not recognize so fully or could not bring themselves to exploit.

CONCLUSION

Trump's victory in 2016 closely fits the bill for much of what goes for contemporary populism. The leader appeals to a discrete demographic that he masquerades as "the people" and excites these people at rallies and through his command over news sources extolling himself as their savior from the failings of politics-as-usual. The policy content of the popular appeal is minimal. In Trump's case it was encapsulated by slogans about building a wall with Mexico, hostility to Washington politicians and bureaucrats, and calls to abandon traditional US foreign policy for a maverick approach based on personal connections and a rejection of multilateralism.

Yet this did not come out of nowhere. It had been cultivated for years within a Republican Party that finally succumbed to almost a parody of where it had been pointing since at least the 1990s. The Obama presidency, coinciding with the aftermath of the 2007–2008 financial crisis and representing the ascendancy of the United States' first African American president, undoubtedly also ginned up a large segment of the US population to look past Trump's own checkered history as a person, businessman, and celebrity to see him as an agent of their own rescue from the cultural and economic contradictions of contemporary America.

Trump's lack of interest in expertise and effective governance as opposed to constant political campaigning suggests the limits of this mutation of populism. Trump's popular base of older white Americans who identify predominantly as Republicans is a rapidly declining slice of the total electorate that just happens to turn out more predictably to vote than do many others (Rubin 2019). But its relative shrinkage suggests real limits to the Trump style of populism. Eventually, when crises arise that demand some degree of consensus building across the population or compromises with adversaries at home and abroad, the strategy of division and rancor upon which Trump has built his entire approach will also lead either back to more democracy or into some sort of authoritarianism. Then we shall see how resilient US political institutions prove to be, as well perhaps as the emergence of a less sectional and ideological Republican Party that can attract support from a broader swath of the population.

5

Two Steps Forward, One Step Back?

Marine Le Pen and the National Front in France

France provides a case of a recent European populist moment involving a movement that has been in existence since the early 1970s. This is distinctive from the other three cases, the US and UK ones in particular, in that the French National Front (NF) (renamed as the National Rally after the 2017 elections) has evolved out of a long tradition of far-right movements in France rather than being simply the direct result of recent economic and social events. If contemporary populism in Italy goes back to the 1990s when there was a clear break in the political system, the NF represents the remarkable recent strengthening on an "antisystem" party. Even though in 2017 it did not overcome the political and electoral barriers in France that stand in the way of a movement like the NF achieving national political office, its presidential candidate did make it to the second-round runoff election—in large part because the NF of 2017 had moved with the times.

French presidential elections under the rules of the Fifth Republic, in place since 1962, have two rounds of voting, with only the highest two vote gatherers moving on to the second round two weeks later (April 23 and May 7 in 2017). The winner serves in office for five years. Since 2002, parliamentary elections take place following the presidential election and work on the same general principle; in theory candidates can be elected in the first round, but very few are. In both contests the electoral system favors centrist candidates in the second round who can accumulate votes from those who had voted for others in the first round. But this also encourages dramatic falloffs in turnout, as well as the casting of blank and spoiled ballots to protest the choices on offer. If, once in office, the president of France becomes something of a monarch, getting there favors those who occupy the political middle ground. The NF may well be considered a populist "threat" to the centrist bias of the French electoral system, but its very periodic potency is a sign of a polity in which "normal channels of negotiation and debate are closed off" (Mount 2018, 5).

THE NATIONAL FRONT
AS "SCARECROW" OF THE FIFTH REPUBLIC

The NF has long been, as Perry Anderson (2017, 17) says, "the ideal scarecrow of a neoliberal republic." Since the 1980s it has provided the outsider electoral threat that guarantees an alternation between center-left and center-right parties by making the second rounds of presidential elections plebiscites for one or the other. Only in 2002 and 2017 did the NF make it through, whereupon the other parties ganged up against its candidates to make sure the status quo remained undisturbed. In 2002 Jean-Marie Le Pen, the historic leader of the NF, beat Lionel Jospin of the Socialist Party for second place in the first round, but he was then roundly beaten by Jacques Chirac of the Center-Right in the second round. In 2017 his daughter, Marine Le Pen, led in the polls during the first round, made it into the second round against Emmanuel Macron, and, following the same pattern, lost heavily in the second round. This time around, it was not the old parties but an entirely new centrist one, recently invented by Macron, that was the victor.

The French Fourth Republic that prevailed from 1946 until 1958 was a parliamentary one in which parties ruled. It was widely derided as a "parliament without windows" or a world unto itself (Williams 1964). The regime that replaced it under the command of President Charles de Gaulle, in response largely to a crisis over the decolonization of Algeria and the repatriation of French settlers back to France, was powerfully centered on the office of the president. Until 2002 presidents were elected for seven-year terms. In that year, legislative and presidential elections were timed to happen concurrently every five years after a period in which a president from the Center-Right had to cohabit with a parliament dominated by the Center-Left. The change was introduced to produce concurrence between legislative and executive branches but as a result also created even greater concentration of power in the hands of the executive branch of government. The coattails of the winner of the presidency would guarantee a compliant legislature. Both in design and even more as a result of its 2002 mutation, the electoral system institutionalized a technocratic authoritarianism in which presidential legitimacy was never so much a result of interparty competition as the direct mandate of the people who showed up to vote in the second round. This "Bonapartism," going back to the days of Napoleon I, means that a party such as the NF is not alone in its populist appeals to "the people." In a sense all French politics is populist in orientation. It is the ethnonational element in the positions of the NF that sets it apart from the others, even when most of the parties claim the mantle of Frenchness for themselves. The NF's relative emphasis on exclusion is crucial.

The centrist preference built into the presidential electoral system is worth a few words at the outset. The fact that in the first round, none more so than in 2017, many candidates could gain significant shares of the overall vote and that there was typically a large decline in turnout between rounds shows how much the system closed out voters who felt underrepresented politically as much as culturally and economically out of sorts with the establishment parties and politicians. That these parties and politicians had proven increasingly incapable, particularly after 2008, of responding to the cultural fears and economic problems of many voters was icing on what had for long been a political cake into which their identities and interests were never baked (Berger 2017). The carriers of this disillusionment and hostility for discretely different groups of voters were for many years the NF along with the Communist Party. Only latterly they had begun to overlap as the NF narrative about the costs imposed on France by immigrants and the EU had picked up support among some working-class voters hitherto more likely to vote Communist. The story of the NF in the 2017 presidential election is mainly about how this greater consensus was achieved notwithstanding its inability to overcome the mobilization of bias built into the two-round electoral system.

Following on the heels of the vote for Brexit and the election of Donald Trump, much was made in the media in France and elsewhere in 2016 and 2017 of the "threat" posed to French politics by the NF (e.g., Cohen 2017; *Economist* 2017b). In the face of the very unpopular outgoing president François Hollande of the Socialist Party and the collapse of the campaign of the center-right candidate François Fillon as a result of corruption allegations, the planets seemed to align finally for the NF. Appealing, as do other populist movements, to "the people," the NF was able to mobilize around 20 percent of the electorate nationwide in the first round of presidential voting, a similar percentage to the candidates of three other parties, but it lost overwhelmingly in the second round as a result of vote switching to the more likely victor and overall decline in turnout.

In this chapter we start with an overview of the National Front and its history in French politics, including the historic currents of opinion it has tended to tap into. We emphasize how much its ideological metamorphosis since 2011 under a new leader, Marine Le Pen, albeit the daughter of the former one, has contributed to its recent success. Dynastic inheritance it may have been, but the fact that the new leader was a woman in a populist pantheon across Europe and the United States, where this is exceedingly rare, bears some emphasis. Attention then turns to the NF and the geography of its support in 2017. The main themes here are the nature of the geography underpinning the vote as explained by many commentators (e.g., center versus periphery, urban-rural, etc.) and the ways in which the NF has brought under one political umbrella several constituencies in contrast to its past support.

Finally we take up the three overarching themes of turnout, leadership, and political communication to explore the details of how the NF finally failed to break out of the political ghetto in which it has historically been confined. We raise the question of whether in fact the composition of its electorate is not now too diverse for ideological coherence, even though that is paradoxically what it needs to reach the second round of presidential elections. In particular, positions taken to attract a more working-class (and formerly Communist-voting) population that is also in demographic decline are difficult to square with the nationalistic identity politics of many of its previous adherents. Only its frankly xenophobic anti-immigrant and increasingly subdued anti-EU rhetoric continues to glue the parts together. This makes finding common ground with more leftist populists an unlikely proposition.

THE NATIONAL FRONT AND ITS HISTORY

France has a long history of populist-nationalist groups arising in conditions of acute social crisis. In the twentieth century such groups have all tended to combine elements of populist critique of the republican "establishment" and, with respect to French political traditions, a counterrevolutionary elitist view of France with a "closed, exclusive conception of a nation under siege" (Winock 1993, 152). From the Action Française and the Croix de Feu of the 1920s and 1930s, through the Poujadistes (followers of Pierre Poujade and the Union for the Defense of Tradesmen and Artisans [UDCA]) of the 1950s, to the NF, such groups have thrust themselves into national politics (Camus 1997). In electoral terms the NF has turned out to be by far the most significant. Much of the enduring appeal of such groups, whose efflorescence has tended to coincide with widespread consciousness of political exclusion and neglect of interests, has been to the large component of French society that is self-employed and vulnerable to abrupt shifts in consumer demand and changes in government fiscal (tax) policy. With widespread deindustrialization and the collapse of the Communist Party since the 1990s following the disintegration of the Soviet Union, the NF has expanded its base of support into working-class communities. The siege mentality has acquired a new constituency (Perrineau 2017).

Gabriel Goodliffe (2012) refers to this segment of the population as having "class-cultural roots" in a distinctive French political economy that has long been under threat from the inroads of big business, the erosion of trade barriers, the end of empire, and the emergence of European integration. He also notes how much the cultural differences revealed by the Dreyfus Affair, when in 1894 a Jewish officer was wrongly accused of treason, economic tensions of the interwar period, when small business took a major hit, and the experience of the collaborationist Vichy regime during World War II, when the traditionalist values promulgated by the regime found favor with *les petits indépendants* (small business owners, traders, and craftsmen), laid the groundwork for the anxiety about and hostility to the Fourth Republic in the 1950s that produced Poujadism and then, in the 1970s, the NF. Jean-Marie Le Pen, the founder of the NF, was a notorious agitator in Poujade's UDCA.

The NF was founded by Le Pen in December 1972 out of a unification of far-right groups, including an openly fascist one, Ordre Nouveau, to challenge de Gaulle's Union of Democrats for the Republic (UDR) (Charlot 1986). Running in the 1974 presidential election, Le Pen received only 0.76 percent of the first-round vote. In 1981 he failed to collect the five hundred votes needed to get on the presidential ballot for that year. The performance in legislative elections was similarly miserable. Things turned for the better in 1983, when the party achieved some success in municipal elections, and in 1984, when it garnered 11 percent of the vote in the European elections. With a national government in which the Center-Left dominated both the presidency and parliament after 1981, Le Pen could present himself as the true voice of the Right. President François Mitterrand encouraged this identification so as to outflank the Center-Right by encouraging the registration of immigrants to vote and switching legislative elections to proportional representation in order to split the Center-Right in the National Assembly (Reynié 2016). Arguably, much of the NF's electoral improvement was due to the increased saliency of immigration as a political issue in the context of the still raw wounds of postcolonial experience and the deepening of European integration and globalization. Above all, however, it was the question of the racial differences between the new immigrants and the native French (including immigrants of European provenance) that became the centerpiece of Le Pen's appeal.

If grounded in the siege mentality of old, it was nevertheless a substantive addition to the prior complaints. Along with limiting the state to its main regulatory functions (police, defense, judiciary, diplomacy), otherwise reducing bureaucracy, and reinstating the death penalty and laws against homosexuality, Le Pen openly preached anticommunism and the menace to national identity from nonwhite immigration. He would deny accusations of racism, adding that "he condemned all racisms including anti-French racism" (Charlot 1986, 37). This has now become a leitmotif of right-wing populists everywhere, from Trump in the United States to Matteo Salvini in Italy. Attacks on the media and the expression of conspiracy theories about globalists and Communists were combined with a hyperbolic presentation to produce a "neoliberal populism" (Ivaldi 2015). After the Maastricht Agreement in 1992, the party, like others on the Far Right across Europe, became increasingly Euroskeptical. If the NF remained enamored with the defense of "Europe" and its values, radical gestures were avoided in favor of a more ambiguous attitude and the use of the EU as a "political resource" in terms of the European Parliament as an arena for connecting with populist movements of similar character in other European countries, even as the leader could criticize the workings of the institution and its possible expansion to include "unacceptable" countries such as Turkey (e.g., Reungoat 2015). Among the political leaders Le Pen claimed to most admire were Francisco Franco (the former Spanish dictator) and Augusto Pinochet (then dictator of Chile). While preaching for a "strong" state, therefore, he was also in favor of a globalized capitalist economy.

Even though Le Pen made it through to the second round of the 2002 election, something he had never achieved previously (he had scored 14.4 percent in 1988 and 15 percent in 1995), his 16.9 percent in the first round (against Jospin's 16.2 percent) led only to 17.8 percent in the second round against Jacques Chirac's winning 82.2 percent. That same year the NF failed to win a single seat in parliament. Something of a fade-out seemed in the cards. In 2007 Le Pen received only 10.4 percent of the first-round vote. He seemed increasingly out of touch with the NF electorate, let alone the broader population. His old brand of straightforward racism and xenophobic contempt was out of step with what Dominique Reynié (2016) calls "heritage populism" in which populists portray themselves as defenders of European and Western "freedom" and "secularism" against immigrants, Islam, and globalization. Others in the higher echelons of the NF had noticed this disjuncture between party program and social changes as early as 1998. A slow drain of leaders out of the party continued in the following years. This reduced the role of various archreactionary currents, such as ultra-Catholics and admirers of the Vichy regime (Betz 2013).

The tensions finally came to a head in 2011. By maneuvering within the party organization, Marine Le Pen was then able to acquire the presidency of the NF. On appointment in 2012, she immediately set about cleansing the party of anti-Semites and the remaining old-line reactionaries in an effort at what she called "de-demonization." The role models of leadership were no longer the old-school French counterrevolutionaries such as Maurice Barrès and Charles Maurras but modern populists "unencumbered by the disreputable legacy of the past, such as Oscar Freysinger, the flamboyant poster boy of the Swiss People's Party, who had gained notoriety as one of the main organizers and promoters of Switzerland's successful anti-minaret referendum, and to some extent, Geert Wilders, the no less flamboyant Dutch anti-Islam agitator" (Betz 2013, 2).

So, very quickly the content of the NF program changed significantly by "pushing to the backburner those within the NF as well as those within the party elite who [held] more racist and xenophobic views" (Williams 2011, 693). After establishing herself as leader, and even more so after expelling her own father from the NF in 2015, Marine Le Pen was able to impose her own vision on an otherwise factionalized movement. Arguably this was a turn from the extreme Right toward a recognizably postmodern populism as we have described it previously. Specifically, democracy is now defended, rather than decried, and posed against "the elites"; "national capitalism" and "national preference" are posed against "transnational hyper-capitalism" (although here the danger is of recycling old anti-Semitic myths about the Rothschilds and so on); protecting France's cultural identity (particularly in the form of a hyperbolic "replacement" of the Christian French by adherents of Islam) is distinguished from biological racism; and antiliberalism now substitutes for anticommunism (e.g., Betz 2013; Kauffmann 2016). Even though now framed in terms of imminent threats associated with the present day, in fact all of these "new" positions resonate with historic examples of rightist populism in French history (Kauffmann 2016).

Particularly salient beyond the reframing of immigration as a threat to national identity rather than in explicitly racist terms has been the increased emphasis on republican secularism (hostility to the veiling of Muslim women, retreat from homophobia, and so on) and the overt shift in economic policy from neoliberalism to social populism (Crépon 2015; Ivaldi 2015). Notwithstanding these changes, the party remains far from "normalized." It still feeds off discontent that does not as yet translate into much actual political representation, local or national (Shields 2014; Anderson 2017). Ironically, it has met with the most success in elections to the European Parliament, somewhat like the United Kingdom Independence Party.

But this is due to low turnouts and single-round proportional representation more than absolute popularity.

THE GEOGRAPHY OF THE 2017 NATIONAL FRONT VOTE

The 2017 presidential election campaign began with both of the main parties discredited. The Socialist Party under President François Hollande had reached the nadir of its support, and the Center-Right, though with higher support in opinion polls, was vulnerable because it was still associated with the presidency of Nicolas Sarkozy when the financial crisis hit in 2008. Still, it looked as if the Center-Right could pull it off. This was strengthened when François Fillon emerged as the candidate of Les Républicains. A former prime minister under Sarkozy, in December 2016 he looked like a shoo-in with a 7 percent lead over NF candidate Marine Le Pen in polls of first-round voting intentions. The other candidates did not look likely to make the cut. Inevitably, Le Pen would be voted down in the second round.

This was not to be. A scandal over Fillon's using public funds to pay his wife and children for no-show jobs erupted in late January 2017, and Fillon never recovered from this blow. For their part, the Socialists were demoralized and divided after the disastrous Hollande years. Their candidate, Benoît Hamon, could not even garner support from the main figures in the party following a primary election in the same month that scandal enveloped Fillon. This opened the door to Emmanuel Macron, who had declared his candidacy in October 2016 after creating his own party, En Marche, the previous April. Macron had perceived the weakness of Hollande's reelection potential and struck out on his own. The new party explicitly declared the redundancy of the Left-Right opposition, arguing for a renewal of the Center as economically liberal and socially progressive. Recruiting the centrist Catholic politician François Bayrou to his cause, Macron was well placed to make it to the second round, where he would predictably beat Marine Le Pen.

The only wrinkle in this plot was the possibility that, rather than from the NF, the real challenge to Macron would come from the left. There, Jean-Luc Mélenchon, a refugee from the Socialist Party of the Mitterrand years, under the label La France Insoumise (LFI, Unsubdued France), provided a left-populist option by campaigning for "the people" against the elites in control of a bankrupt political system. Its main demands were a call for a Sixth Republic based on a parliamentary republic with the rights of recall and referendum. Beyond this its platform looked amazingly like that of the NF, except for the anti-immigrant invective of the latter, including being militantly antiglobalist and in favor of welfare protection and state intervention (Perrineau 2017). On the EU, the NF was more "classically" Euroskeptic, given its ethnonationalism and hostility to immigration whatever the progeny of the immigrants, but warmed to it as the election approached, being ambiguous about its position on the euro. Like other leftist populists, such as Podemos in Spain, the LFI's problems with the EU were not so much with the idea of European integration as with its current form. This reflects the broader difference between the two versions of populism across Europe (e.g., van Elsas et al. 2016). Interestingly, rather than openly addressing the "immigration question," the manifesto of LFI said nothing at all about immigration, a significant silence (Anderson 2017, 20). Late in the campaign Mélenchon rapidly increased his support, not least because he was widely thought to have been the victor in the presidential television debates.

On election eve Mélenchon closed in on Fillon in the polls and produced the possibility of a narrow separation between four candidates going into the election (Map 5.1). The real problem with the polls for this and the second round would turn out to be the difficulty of sorting those who would not vote from those whose preference was weak or based on opposing a candidate (such as Marine Le Pen) rather than favoring another (such as Emmanuel Macron) (Enten 2017). Turnout was to be crucial to the outcome.

Indeed, the first-round vote saw four closely bunched candidates, although Macron had a clear lead at 24.01 percent. The other three were separated by scarcely one percentage point: Le Pen at 21.3 percent, Fillon at 20.01 percent, and Mélenchon at 19.58 percent. Mélenchon undoubtedly stole considerable thunder from Le Pen by winning youthful and unemployed workers who might otherwise have voted for her. He came in first in Marseille, Toulouse, Montpellier, and Lille and did very well in

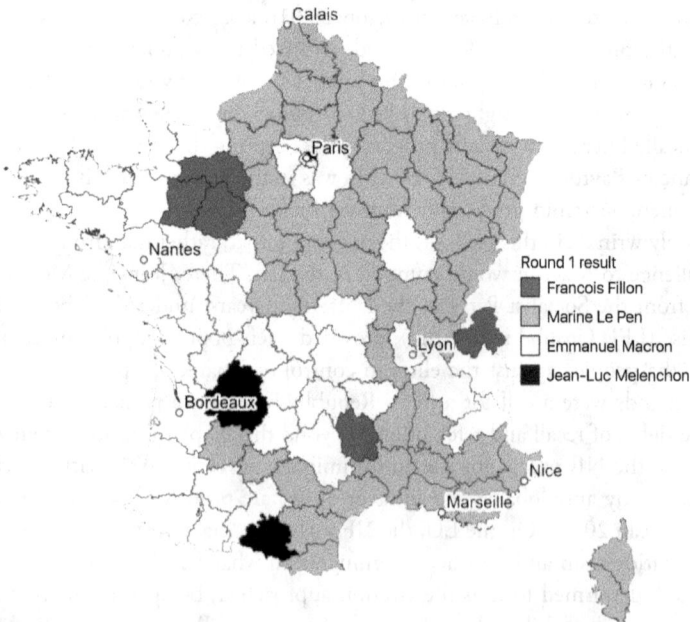

Map 5.1. The geography of Round 1 results.
Source: L'Institut National de la Statistique et des Études Économiques.

the immigrant suburbs of Paris and Lyon. But his movement had not replaced the NF, which still had a big lead among the petit bourgeois and working-class groups that had been its base in the 2014 European and 2015 departmental elections. Together, though, the populists showed how much dismay there was with the standard parties. Combined, they won 40 percent of the first-round vote. But 24 percent of voters did not vote. Adding them in, two out of five voters, therefore, did not support a "conventional" candidate such as Macron, Fillon, or Hamon. This counted for naught in the runoff, of course. With nonvoting at its highest level in fifty years, Macron won by a huge margin. In an electorate of 47.5 million, Macron won 20.7 million votes; 10.6 million voted for Le Pen, and 16.2 million did not vote or submitted blank ballots. Excluding the nonvoters, then, Macron won 66 percent of the vote and Le Pen 34 percent. The majority of first-round voters for Fillon, Mélenchon, and Hamon switched to Macron in the second round, although about one-third of both the first two's voters did not vote in the runoff (Burn-Murdoch et al. 2017).

At the departmental level in the first round, there was a clear regional concentration of votes for Marine Le Pen (Map 5.2[a]). This was not new but was more intense in the sense that the areas in question were now more inclined toward the NF than previously. If half the electorate was working-class and from the North and Northeast, the rest was concentrated in the far South and consisted of the traditional NF constituency of *pieds noirs* (returned settlers from Algeria and their offspring)

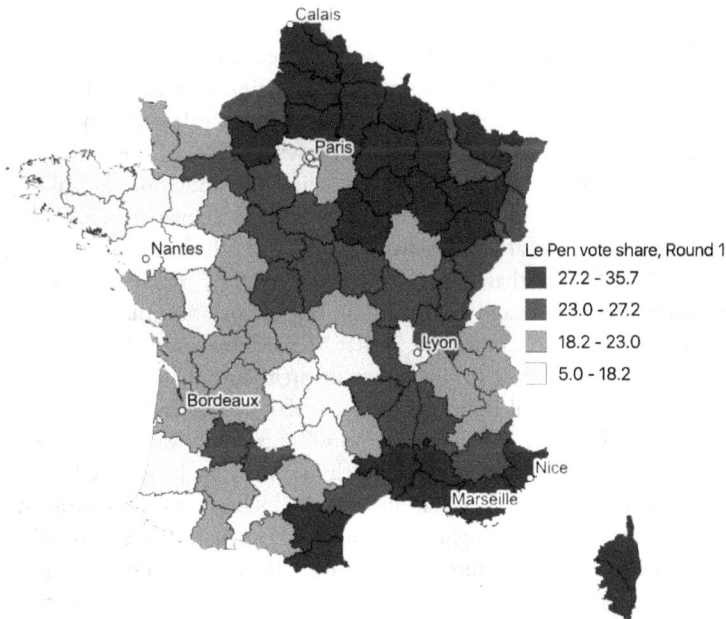

Map 5.2(a). Le Pen vote share, Round 1.
Source: L'Institut National de la Statistique et des Études Économiques.

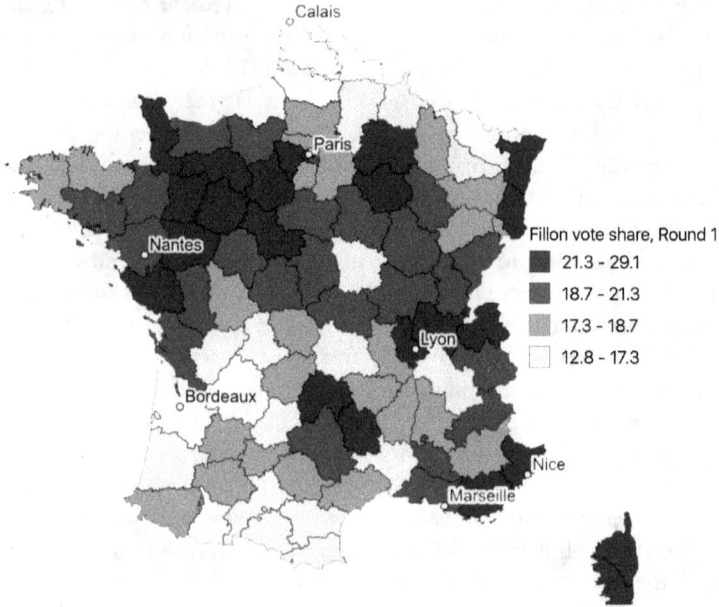

Map 5.2(b). Fillon vote share, Round 1.
Source: L'Institut National de la Statistique et des Études Économiques.

and petit bourgeois Catholic conservatives. In the second round, hard-core NF voters were supplemented with others from the more mainstream Right and a few from the Far Left (Burn-Murdoch et al. 2017). These were recruited largely in the same places rather than spread around or from places where Fillon, for example, did well in the first round (Map 5.2[b]). This suggests just how much the NF has become rooted in certain places and almost completely rejected elsewhere (e.g., Huc 2017; Ivaldi 2012, 2018). Its local social networks produce both rewarding patronage ties and a sense of familiarity that mitigate the predominantly negative image it might have elsewhere (e.g., Marchand-Lagier 2017). But the prospect that the NF had indeed become the Right, celebrated by Robert Ménard, mayor of the NF stronghold of Béziers in southern France, turned out to be premature (Chassany 2017).

In terms of overall social indicators that correlate ecologically with the second-round votes at the municipal level, the most important was average education level (Burn-Murdoch et al. 2017). Very much like with the leave vote in the Brexit referendum, in which age and education were the highest correlates, areas with the lowest educational levels had higher votes for Le Pen. As in the United Kingdom, younger people tend to have more educational credentials than do older age groups (Le Bras 2015, 128). Even so, Macron still won more votes than Le Pen in the "least-educated" municipalities. Income is highly collinear with education, so not surprisingly it also correlated with lower votes for Le Pen. Given the new significance of the "left behind" in Marine Le Pen's narrative, one might expect areas with higher percentages of people in working-class occupations and higher unemployment to put larger numbers in her column. In fact, however, once age and education are controlled for, there is not much to either of these predictors. This seems to be the case almost entirely because in the main metropolitan areas more working-class and unemployed voters either voted for Macron or did not vote. In the first round they were much more likely to be Mélenchon voters (Burn-Murdoch et al. 2017; Gilli et al. 2017).

There also seems to be absolutely no correlation between the presence of immigrants and voting for the NF. Again, as we saw with leave voters in the Brexit referendum, surveys suggest that NF voters are severely exercised about the impacts of immigration and vote for the NF largely for this reason. This is the case even when there are not many immigrants in their vicinity. More speculatively, some research using survey data suggests that more "pessimistic" voters (responding to the question "Relative to your generation, the situation of the next generation will be: Better, The Same, Worse") voted for Le Pen, and Le Pen did much better than Macron in areas with lower life expectancy for women (Burn-Murdoch et al. 2017).

This all adds up to an interesting geography of the Le Pen vote in 2017. In the first place, there now seems to be an extraordinary spatial morphology to the NF vote as reported by Hervé Le Bras (2015, 14–15) for prior years. Across elections the same places produce a mobilization of votes for the party that is almost completely absent elsewhere. Le Bras (2015) speculates interestingly that this correlates with areas where earlier populist movements enjoyed some success, previous deposits of immigration, higher crime rates, and nucleated settlement. Unfortunately this logic does not always work, as Le Bras himself points out. For example, Poujadiste voters were concentrated in central-western France, exactly the opposite of the pattern for the NF. Nevertheless, there is something to the idea that these places, clustered regionally in terms of aspects of their local and regional histories as well as current population characteristics, seem to provide a set of milieus in which the NF has tended to thrive and that cannot be accounted for by singular social indicators. People in certain places are making, in Le Bras's terminology, a "desperate bet," one with a low probability of success but nevertheless logical from their perspective and picking up support among new generations because of increased blockage in social mobility, overall economic stalling, and cultural embattlement. The "heritage populism" of Marine Le Pen is their bet.

In the second place, some commentators have tended to view the France of the NF as entirely provincial or peripheral in comparison to France's dynamic urban centers where the mainstream parties garner their support. An urban France is posited in opposition to a rural France, with the NF associated almost entirely with the latter (e.g., Guilluy 2014). The argument is that the new jobs and prospects for the future are in the dynamic metropoles, and those left behind, who are resentful and angry at their lot in life, are concentrated in the rural areas. The NF vote is the "revenge of the villages." This approach has been common in trying to explain the vote for Trump in the United States and the leave vote in the Brexit referendum in the United Kingdom. It is not that there isn't something to it. Popular books about the bitterness of the people in postindustrial northern France make this point quite eloquently (e.g., Eribon 2013; Louis 2017). But it is overstated, to say the least.

There is no such clear opposition, particularly if you look at the first-round votes, which are a better guide to actual voting behavior than the forced choice in the second round. In 2017 only 21 percent of the votes for Le Pen in the first round were in small towns and rural areas. Other candidates performed equally well in such places (Gilli et al. 2017). Le Pen was not the candidate of the periphery or rural areas. Using percentages at the scale of spatial units such as municipalities and departments misses the fact that, in absolute terms, cities are much more important than rural areas to the votes of all the parties, populist or otherwise. The typical use of maps (such as ours) can mask this complexity. This "cartographic trap" (Gilli et al. 2017) misses the extent to which electoral outcomes are based on the fact, for example, that most poor people live in the biggest cities, not in the rural provinces. Jacques Lévy (2017, 80–91), for example, shows how much the vote for Le Pen (and Macron) is determined between the regional scale, on the one hand, and the major Northeast and Southeast versus West and Center dimensions and urban-rural gradients, on the other, with the suburban and outer-urban areas being crucial to outcomes, rather than in terms of a simplistic nationwide urban-rural opposition. The overgeneralization into this rural-urban polarity has continued with interpretations of the so-called Yellow Vest protests about fuel taxes and other Macron policies across France in late 2018, even when the geographic pattern again is much subtler (e.g., Nossiter 2018; McAuley 2019b).

TURNOUT AND NOT VOTING

As Jacques Lévy (2017, 86) says, nonvoting and expressing dissent by casting blank or null ballots make for the "biggest party" in France. In 2017 about 47 percent of those eligible in the first round did not vote for the any of the candidates on the ballot. There is some tendency for people in lower socioprofessional categories to vote less than people in higher ones, but the difference (ranging between 21 and 31 percent from the highest to lowest socioprofessional categories) does not seem to be the decisive factor in overall turnout. Of course, there are all sorts of reasons for not voting, ranging from a sense of exclusion from the concerns of parties and politicians, to indifference to politics, to deliberate rejection of the electoral choices available. Not voting is greatest in smaller towns, particularly industrial ones, and in the suburbs of the largest cities. In certain cases, however, city centers are also affected. This is the case, for example, in Brest, Havre, Mulhouse, and even some cities with smaller working-class populations, such as Toulouse, Marseille, and Grenoble. In 2017 the turnout question was particularly central because, if hardly new, two candidates, Le Pen and Mélenchon, were now appealing in the name of "the people" precisely to many of those not affiliated with the main parties and inclined to give elections a pass because they saw themselves as outsiders in a "crooked system."

Turnout in France in 2017 had three aspects. The first is the 12 percent of potential voters in 2017 who were not registered to vote. These were largely French people abroad or immigrants. The second and most important aspect entails people who just do not vote. In the first round in 2017 this was 22.3 percent of those registered to vote. At 10.6 million eligible individuals, this outnumbered the 8.7 million votes received by Emmanuel Macron. The third case is possibly the most interesting. These are people who vote but spoil their ballots or do not express a preference; 11.5 percent of the ballots cast in the second round in 2017 (around 4 million votes) were of this type. This is "true" abstentionism in the sense that the voters are politically engaged but actively refusing to cast a ballot for any of the options available. This went up in the second round because of the reduced menu of choices and the fact that some first-round candidates, like Mélenchon, encouraged their voters to do so. Overall, on May 7, 2017, the 31.4 million voters who cast a ballot for either Macron or Le Pen comprised only about 60 percent of those in theory able to participate in the election.

Mapping turnout in the first round at the departmental level (Map 5.3[a]) shows an interesting regional pattern. Lowest turnouts are in very much the same places where Le Pen's votes were concentrated: the Northeast and Southeast of France. Likewise the higher turnouts are where Macron's votes tended to be highest and the election overall more competitive: the center and West of France. Given that turnout shrank without much geographical variation for the second round (Map 5.3[b]), Le Pen was not able to make up any ground by mobilizing previous nonvoters. From this viewpoint, Le Pen's mobilization was less successful than Macron's. Fear of Le Pen was his strongpoint. Looking back to the first-round votes (Map 5.2[a]), it does not seem that Marine Le Pen was able off the bat to successfully recruit sufficient numbers of the disaffected to the cause of the NF. Some of the places where she had her highest support in the first round experienced some of the largest drop-offs in turnout between rounds (Map 5.3[c]). Places with higher percentages of younger people, presumably less affiliated with existing political groupings and open to populist alternatives such as those offered by the NF and LFI, showed a particularly lower propensity to vote in the second round than did those with lower percentages, although this also included places where Mélenchon had done relatively well too (Map 5.4). Null voting was less important than differential turnouts to the outcome. But it again shows that Le Pen was not able to pick up those who presumably voted in the first round for someone else and then voted with a blank ballot the second time around (Map 5.3[d]).

Though centrist, Macron represented a new political formation without the tainted labels of the older parties. He has been described, partly tongue-in-cheek but also because of his antiestablishment rhetoric, as an "antipopulist populist" (Bordignan 2017). But neither he nor Le Pen managed to stimulate much enthusiasm for their causes beyond those already motivated as much to keep one of the two out of

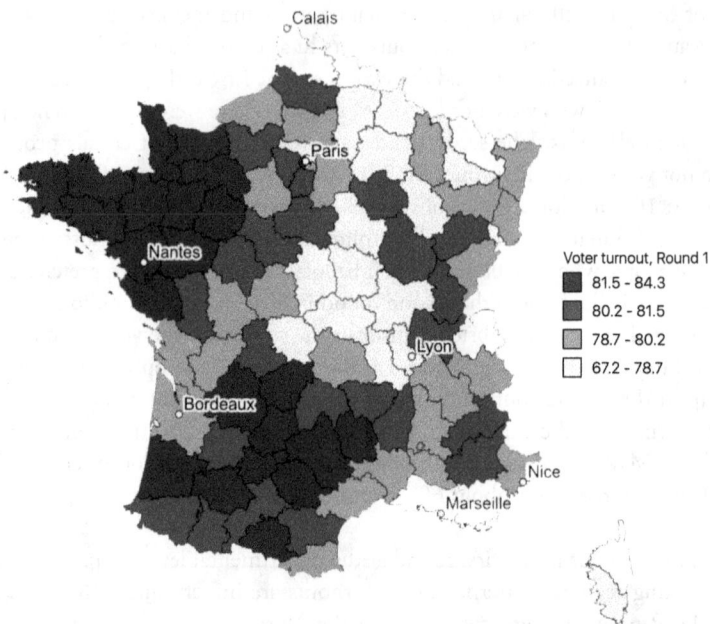

Map 5.3(a).   Voter turnout, Round 1.
Source: L'Institut National de la Statistique et des Études Économiques.

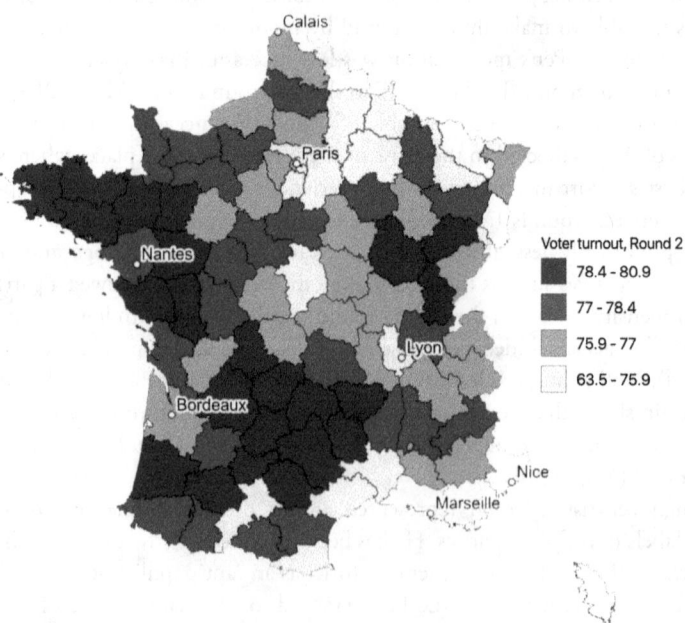

Map 5.3(b).   Voter turnout, Round 2.
Source: L'Institut National de la Statistique et des Études Économiques.

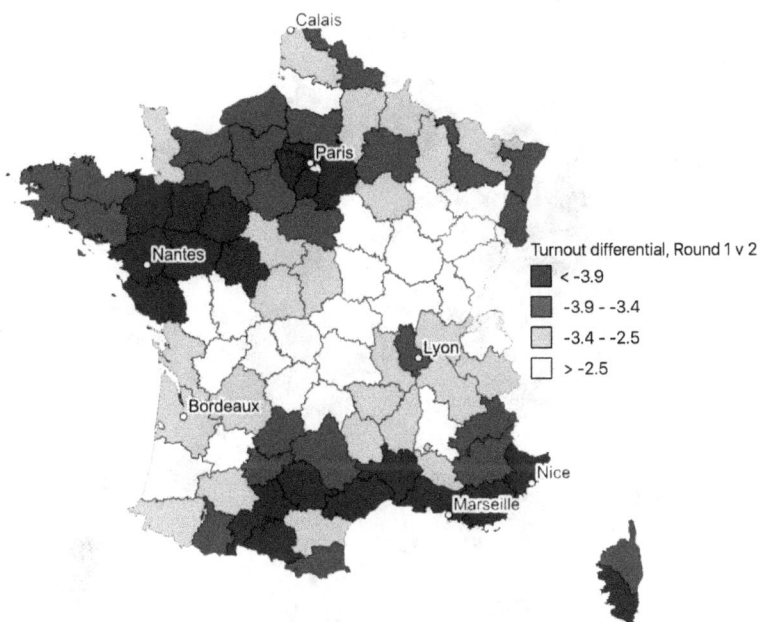

Map 5.3(c). Voter turnout differential, Round 1 versus Round 2.
Source: L'Institut National de la Statistique et des Études Économiques.

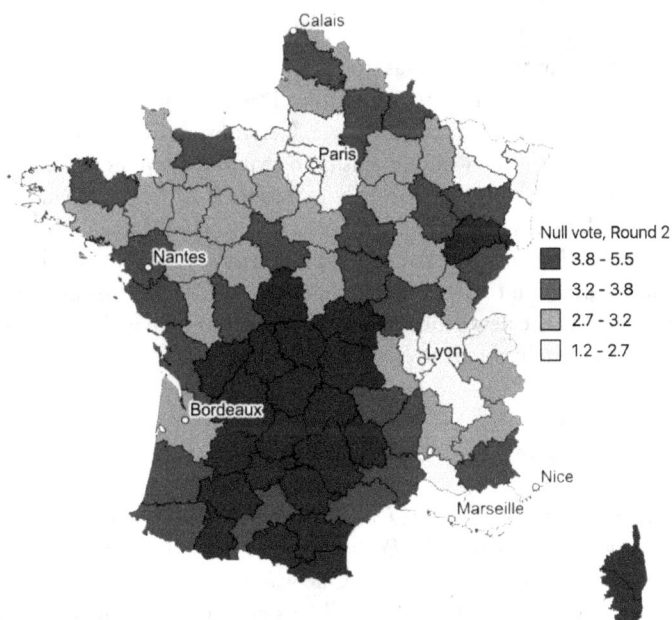

Map 5.3(d). Null vote, Round 2.
Source: L'Institut National de la Statistique et des Études Économiques.

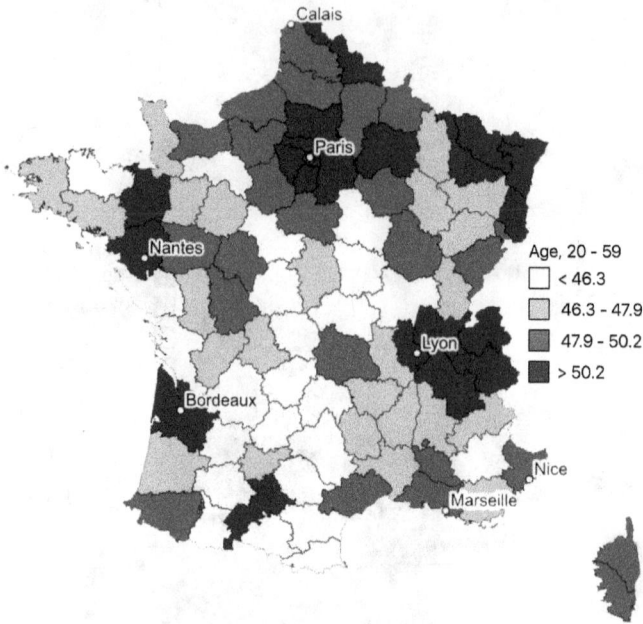

Map 5.4. Geographic age distribution in France, 20–59.
Source: L'Institut National de la Statistique et des Études Économiques.

office as to vote a favorite in. This was similar to the Hillary Clinton–Donald Trump choice in the United States in 2016, except that Trump managed to squeeze through because of the artifact of the electoral college. Certainly, those mobilized by Mélenchon seemed to show little or no propensity to switch their votes to Le Pen. Leftist and rightist populisms remained mutually exclusive. If Mélenchon had made it to the second round, perhaps he would have been able to give Macron a better run for his money in bringing younger and other disaffected groups into the fold. Having adjusted the NF program to better match the times, Marine Le Pen could not stir up enough votes among the new generation to turn an election in which the old parties, as such, were completely absent to her electoral advantage.

LE PENISM

To what extent was the NF of 2017 a different political animal than in previous elections, and what was Marine Le Pen's role in the so-called new NF? As early as 2011 there were signs of a change afoot. One was a clear shift in attempting to appeal to former Communist Party voters well beyond what her father had done. This was as much about adjusting the party's program as it was about using language that might appeal to former Communist voters. This was forthcoming even though it went somewhat against the trend of contemporary right-wing populism in countries such as the Netherlands and Italy to combine cultural conservatism with free market rhetoric. The point was to expand the electoral base of the party beyond an aging/declining Catholic and traditionalist population (Williams 2011). This was why after 2012 the NF shifted toward a more statist and popular-welfare focus in its policy statements. The 2017 FN manifesto is full of references to "the have-nots," "the unemployed," and "the downtrodden," all of them put down to capitalism and *libéralisme* (pro-market economic theory), which sounded more like the Communist Party of old than it did her father's NF. In candidates' debates these were also among Marine Le Pen's favorite words (Liogier 2017). We should bear in mind, however, that the trend for an increased NF vote from workers of various stripes was well under way before the advent of Marine Le Pen as the party's leader and presidential candidate (Gougou 2015), although her arrival (as expressed in the 2012 presidential election) did encourage a much higher number of female working-class votes than had hitherto been the case. The dilemma, of course, is that the working-class segment of the population is not large enough to produce a majority of votes in a second-round election and is also in demographic decline.

But the approach to the electorate as a whole also changed strategically in ways that suggested a new style of leadership, even as the party was cleansed of holdovers and looked toward expanding its base of support. Three strategic elements characterized the rise of Marine Le Pen as the leader of the NF. We can perhaps think of these three, added to the continuing orientation to working-class voters in declining industrial areas, as the essence of "Le Penism." The first was to move away from speaking so much about "France" and "the nation" toward referencing "the people" and "the national interest." The effort was to shift from being situated on the right toward being a catchall party that could attract voters from across the spectrum but particularly among those suffering from the effects of deindustrialization (Perrineau 2017).

To Marine Le Pen, rejecting "untamed globalization" was an important part of this logic, and "the people revolting against a system that is no longer serving them" was another (*Foreign Affairs* 2016). Of course, this could also potentially attract voters previously on the left but increasingly disenchanted with globalization and the EU. In fact, it has not been so easy putting the past at bay. As she rejects "the power of money," "denounces consumerism," and mocks "antiracism" as "fundamentally racist," Marine Le Pen is obviously moving away from the incredibly toxic racism that was her father's stock-in-trade. But the hints of de-ideologization being replaced by sound bite themes hide what is still a largely conspiratorial worldview. Immigration remains overwhelmingly the most important topic for the NF and its voters. "Its discourse always presents France as enslaved, invaded, threatened by various aggressors" (Eltchaninoff 2018, 109). The novelty has been to avoid the senior Le Pen's provocations while still signaling to the old-timers that a crucial part of the script is much the same.

The second strategic element was the focus on how other parties and politicians were adopting NF positions and using this as a strategy to "normalize" the NF when it was often seen in the dominant media, particularly television, as a "far-right" phenomenon. This had begun when Sarkozy was president, but Marine Le Pen made it a vital part of her repertoire. Along with distancing the party from neofascists, Nazis, and so on, by adopting a language about immigrants and racial/religious differences that reframed the issues in terms of "national preference" and "national security" rather than cultural identity (already started in the 1990s), the effort was to show how much, for example, a concern about terrorists from Islamic-immigrant backgrounds had long been a calling card of the NF. This "law and order" orientation was guaranteed to appeal across the Right and into the wider French political spectrum (Kauffmann 2016). It obviously had powerful resonance in the years leading up to the 2017 election because of the numerous terrorist attacks within France and the recruitment of French-born militants into Islamist campaigns abroad.

The third element was leadership style and strategy. Even though she shares much of the rhetorical style of her father, Marine Le Pen has avoided his penchant for gaffes and relentlessly disciplined the messages of the party to avoid the insults and jibes that once tended to characterize its public persona. She is charismatic in person and, as a woman, is praised in "manly" terms (for strength, vigor, and so on) even as her female side also makes her less threatening (e.g., Matonti 2013). This has benefited her relative to her father, given the associations of the Far Right with naked racism and collective violence. She also has reworked the NF version of French history. Vichy and other questionable periods are gone. Now the Third Republic provides the base for nostalgia (Eltchaninoff 2018, 90–93). Of course, this period ended in 1940, so that has its problems too. Le Pen performs particularly well in rallies when preaching to true believers. When she is faced with critical interviewers on television or participates in televised debates with opponents, her recourse to NF "talking points" often comes off as stilted and rehearsed to the point of parody.

In 2017, even as she reworked the material, the substance of the messages she conveyed was remarkably similar. They concerned fears of crime and violence, including so-called zones of lawlessness, usually ascribed to immigrants or their offspring; "globalist enemies" who sound suspiciously like the Rothschilds of yore (Macron's former job as a banker with the Rothschilds and his apologies for globalization proclaimed, "Bingo!"); and an Islam in the process of rolling over what little is left of European civilization. The language was similarly extreme. Everything was "dramatic," "catastrophic," and "devastating." Her positions were "indisputable" and required "urgent" solutions. Crisis was the leitmotif, hyperbole the main style of delivery (Alduy 2015). The newfound anticapitalism wasn't much of an antidote to all of this, but Paris could well be worth this version of a mass (to paraphrase the former French king Henry V) if it expanded the base. But then you would really get something other than anticapitalism. Many voters did figure that out. The base did not expand very much at all.

THE MEDIUM FINALLY MATCHES THE MESSAGE

The NF never got very good press under the leadership of Jean-Marie Le Pen. The mainstream newspapers and television regarded him as an extreme, fringe political personality even as they covered him and indirectly gave him the recognition as an outsider that was crucial to his success. Of course, that success came at the price of restricting his political reach. Under Marine Le Pen the overt effort to de-demonize the party within the main mass media has been fairly successful, at the same time that the new social media have allowed the party to deepen its connections within the subculture surrounding the NF. These two features of political communication have allowed the NF to both expand its message into traditional enemy territory and also to deepen its commitments among activists.

Perhaps the most important contribution to the expansion of the NF vote between 2012 and 2017 has been the growing acceptance in the mass media, particularly the newspapers and on the part of the main pollsters, of a "new" NF that fits the image told in the stories promoted by the NF itself. The main storyline is the de-demonization of the party under the leadership of Marine Le Pen. Some of this concerns the humanization of Marine Le Pen as an "ordinary" person. As she is the main figurehead of the party, this has been a critical part of the overall change in press/media coverage. But much of it is an increasingly broad acceptance, from *Le Figaro* and *Les Échos* to *Paris Match* and the main polling agencies, that the new NF is profoundly different from the old. In fact, as Alexandre Dézé (2015) shows at length, much of the coverage has reflected a tendency to become overcommitted to the idea of the normalization of the party that has then taken on a life of its own. By way of example, pollsters ask and interpret questions in ways that suggest normalization is under way, and newspapers write stories with headlines that likewise presume that Marine Le Pen represents a new NF without much regard for what that entails empirically. As alleged in the previous section, there is much about the new NF that is very redolent of the old.

The backdrop to this process was the disappointing Hollande presidency, with the media on the lookout for new political celebrities to enliven debate about the elective French monarchy. The media were also under attack for their establishment ties and ownership by big business. Heavily state-subsidized, they also have been faced with declining subscriptions that have encouraged a more celebrity-oriented and combative approach to politics. During the 2017 election the ways in which the press attacked François Fillon went beyond what might once have been expected. His employment of family members may have been scandalous, but it was by no means that unusual among politicians of varied political stripes. Even though she had benefited from their "normalization" narrative, Marine Le Pen took a leaf out of Donald Trump's book and repeatedly accused the media of favoring Macron because he was part of the same "establishment" (Agnew 2017).

At the same time that the NF had become less ghettoized in relation to the mainstream media, the party and its activists were also investing in a very different strategy of their own to deepen connections with the party base and also open up lines with more youthful voters familiar with social media (Facebook, Twitter, and so on) as potential recruits. Here, of course, the messaging was totally different. At the same time that the use of social media allowed for pursuing the normalization strategy, it also, and crucially, allowed the party to create an "echo chamber" in which activists and supporters could get their "news" unfiltered by the mainstream sources hitherto dominant, such as local newspapers and television stations. More generally, the internet allowed activists to troll the websites of the main newspapers by placing critical comments after articles that might cast the NF or its putative allies (such as Vladimir Putin) in a dim light.

The NF was the first French party to set up its own website in 1996 and the first to establish a presence on Facebook in 2006. This reflected in part its being closed out of traditional mass media compared to the regular parties but also its early commitment to the internet as an instrument of political mobilization (Boyadjian 2015). By 2015 Facebook was particularly important to the NF for both disseminating its messages and establishing virtual links among its supporters. As of May 5, 2015, the NF had the largest number of "fans" of any French political party on Facebook, at 224,079 twice as many as the second-place Union for a Popular Movement (UMP) (then the main center-right party) at 121,217 (Boyadjian 2015, 151). By 2017 Marine Le Pen had over 1 million Facebook fans and 1.3 million Twitter followers, far more in both categories than Emmanuel Macron. Only Jean-Luc Mélenchon came close (Stothard 2017).

Given the greater importance of Facebook in France in terms of popular reach compared to Twitter, the Facebook presence and impact was of some significance. Populist parties generally have had a greater presence on the web than traditional ones. So the NF is not alone. As studies show, the internet lends itself to both anti-establishment messaging and casting doubt on the stories emanating from conventional sources of information (Hendrickson and Galston 2017; Dittrich 2017). It is also ideal for character assassination.

Decreased trust in traditional media and the increased use of unfiltered news through sites like Facebook have been a godsend to populist parties like the NF (Stockemer and Barisone 2016). In the end, though, perhaps most surprising, given the dominance of the NF and the LFI on the internet, is that neither was able to turn the corner in recruiting new voters in numbers that finally made much difference. This suggests that social media are indeed more of an echo chamber than a device for recruiting simply because the media are reflections of the real-world social networks that remain grounded and subject to all sorts of other influences in place (e.g., Dunbar et al. 2015).

CONCLUSION

The bias built into the French presidential electoral system favors centrist over extreme candidates. It was designed to do this. Given this fact, the prospects in

2017 for Marine Le Pen and the NF were limited. Notwithstanding the apparent improved standing of the party and its leader in the main media outlets and the powerful presence on social media, they were not able to expand beyond around a third of the total vote in the second round after achieving about a fifth in the first. This is a substantial improvement beyond what the senior Le Pen was able to achieve in his day but not what the hysteria about an immanent victory for the NF suggested in the days leading up to the election.

Two main conclusions seem apt. One is that the party remains largely ghettoized in its support among declining parts of the electorate and is not able to mobilize younger, better-educated voters to its cause even though it has a major presence on the social media that they use on a regular basis. Its desire to capture the so-called Yellow Vest protesters may prove difficult given the anarchist character of that movement and its indifference to the main themes of far-right populism. The second is that in the current electoral system, the prospect of a centrist victor puts off voters who might prefer some other option. Though some of them show up in the first round, many of them fall off subsequently. In 2017 Le Pen and Mélenchon between them captured an amazing 40 percent or so of the vote in the first round. This could be called a "populist vote." But the two sides differ so strongly on central issues, particularly immigration and attitudes to the wider world beyond France, that there is no prospect of them throwing in their lot with one another. Until and when France turns its back on the system of elective monarchy that is the Fifth Republic, the NF for one will continue to serve solely as a convenient "other" for the center rather than a real possibility as a governing party.

6

When in Rome . . . Populism and the Five Star Movement in Italy

Italy has long been fertile ground for political movements seeking an alternative approach to conventional political parties locked in electoral competition for parliamentary seats. Strangely, perhaps because of its very pervasiveness, Italian scholars have been loath to identify populism as a central concept for understanding Italian electoral politics (Bobba and Legnante 2016). As rulers in the European context of a late-unifying "nation-state," Italian governments have been faced with the task of creating a national mythos through which the people will identify with the national *patria* rather than their local or regional *paese* (Agnew 2017). This reached a crescendo under Italian Fascism in the period 1922 to 1943. Frequently alleged to have a political culture with "no sense of the state," compared to, say, France and Britain, with their elites drawn from the same schools, universities, and social strata, Italy has also had a mismatch between a Jacobin state-juridical apparatus (which presumes that a political class directs society) dating back to unification and a strongly fragmented society (Pombeni 1993, 93, 96).

The ready reversal after Fascism to a set of regional strongholds of different political parties from 1945 until 1992—the Christian Democrats dominant in the Catholic Northeast and the Communists in the socialist/anticlerical center, most notably—suggests how shallow Fascism's success in creating much in the way of a national political culture had been (Almagisti 2016). The South remained beholden to a patronage politics from which it has never completely escaped (e.g., Putnam 1993; Agnew 2002; Caciagli 2010; Sannino 2018). Though there was undoubtedly a degree of nationalization of party politics from the early 1960s until 1979 in terms of the geographical diffusion of support for the two largest parties, this was also a period in which extraparliamentary and antiparty politics blossomed, particularly on the far left and far right (Agnew 2002). But rather than on "competition for power [between parties]," this model was based on "a competition among powers and then on a competition among the fragments of power that various forces control. This dynamic is given nobility by the concept of political pluralism and vulgarized when associated with the term *lottizzazione* (sharing out of the spoils)" (Pombeni 1993, 63). By the 1980s, then, national elections were not so much competitions among parties as auctions among factions and interest groups of their shares of the national economic pie. Italian political parties appeared to have a high degree of unity but in fact were riven by many ideological, geographical, and social divisions.

We briefly trace populism's storied history in Italy, which has recently culminated with the popularity of the Five Star Movement (Movimento 5 Stelle, M5S) established by comedian/blogger Beppe Grillo and the late Gianroberto Casaleggio. We map the popularity and success across Italy of the M5S, as well as of its populist competitor, the League, most recently in the 2018 national election, again to demonstrate and illustrate the unevenness of one of the most successful populist movements worldwide. The Five Star Movement in Italy also serves as an important reminder to consider not only rising levels of political disengagement, the rejection of conventional politics, and the real and perceived role of a leader but also the broader political implications for the success of populist movements based, as in this case, on the outright rhetorical rejection of institutional and geographical mediation (e.g., Bickerton and Accetti 2018).

POPULISM IN ITALY BEFORE IT WAS POPULAR ELSEWHERE

In the immediate aftermath of World War II, there had already been strong signs of popular aversion in Italy to mainstream parties and politicians. This hostility to "normal" politics was manifested most clearly in the Fronte dell'Uomo Qualunque, founded by Guglielmo Giannini, a satirical journalist and comedian. The Fronte's newspaper garnered a sizable readership in 1945 and for a short time thereafter through its skepticism about the new political alternatives emerging out of the ruins of Fascist Italy and the return behind the new labels of many of the old "political class" whose errors were seen as bringing about the catastrophe of Fascism in the first place (Tarchi 2015, 176). Interestingly, Giannini preferred the word *folla* (multitude or throng) to that of *popolo*, because he saw the latter as a word used to trick or swindle common folk, as had been the case under Fascism. In this construction of "the people," "the multitude is the good and the chiefs are the bad, always and everywhere, also if, together, they both form the broader community. The first is the receptacle of each virtue the second embody the worst vices and are committed without end to a wicked conspiracy to make themselves an instrument of domination" (Tarchi 2015, 178).

So, it is not so surprising that when the party system that had prevailed since World War II disintegrated dramatically between 1989 and 1992, populist sentiment was not just in the air but already under mobilization. The main initial beneficiary of the ignominious collapse of the Christian Democratic and Socialist parties in the wake of the Tangentopoli scandals over corrupt party funding practices and the end of the Cold War was a party created in 1989 from a number of regionalist "leagues" in northern Italy, particularly the Veneto and Lombardy: the Northern League (Moioli 1990). Born from local activists, it incarnated an ideal-typical populism in almost all respects. Its leader until 2012 was Umberto Bossi, a showman/man of the people, who steered the League between attacks on the national government ("Roma ladrona," or "Rome the thief"), proposals for northern secession, and in 1994 entry into a governing coalition led by Silvio Berlusconi. An on-again-off-again alliance characterized this relationship (alongside the neofascist Alleanza Nazionale, with which Berlusconi merged Forza Italia from 2006 to 2013) down until 2011, with the League veering from secession to federalism and building up its hostility to immigrants (particularly Islamic ones) and to the European Union and its entire works (Bonomi 2008). The 2006 national referendum combining League policies on regional devolution with Berlusconi's desire for a more presidential executive in Rome failed to achieve a national majority. In retrospect this was the death knell for both strains of populism. The leader since 2013, Matteo Salvini, has turned the League into a nationally oriented anti-immigrant party, flirting with fascist groups such as Casa Pound that Bossi would have seen as redolent of the very Italian nationalism the Northern League was in part formed to counter. The xenophobia, though, while not new, is no longer directed at southern Italians on an equal basis with foreigners. This allowed it to spread its influence and support beyond the North and in so doing to drop its regionalist for a nationalist populism (Albertazzi et al. 2018; Brunazzo and Gilbert 2017; D'Alimonte 2018).

The alliance with Berlusconi was crucial to the long makeover of the League (Pajetta 1994). He entered national politics with his own new party, Forza Italia (the chant of supporters of the national soccer team) in 1994 just in time for the national elections of that year. Then and subsequently he presented himself as an "outsider" coming to sweep away the "political caste" that had held sway for so long over Italian politics at all levels of government. Known for his background in construction and control over the main private television channels, Berlusconi was in fact the quintessential political insider. Indeed, the grant of his television channels was made possible through his patronage of Bettino Craxi, the Socialist prime minister in the early 1980s and one of the main perpetrators of the corruption revealed in the scandals of 1989 to 1992. So Berlusconi and his party can be seen as constituting a phony populism compared to both Uomo Qualunque and the Northern League. Nevertheless, Berlusconi took advantage of the political vacuum that opened up in 1993 and 1994 to pursue a political career that rested firmly on his personal appeal as a "man of providence" who could challenge "the Communists" who still dominated the Left (if under new names), present himself as an antipolitician, and, above all, frame himself as representative of an ethic of the common man, laboring for his family under difficult circumstances (Orsina 2013). These are all strong hints of Giannini's *qualunquismo*, therefore, even when, as Diamanti (2003) suggests, Berlusconi's understanding of "the people" has tended to come down to two different if related constructions: the electorate and public opinion, with the latter seen as the key to the former. Needless to say, these are somewhat more instrumental conceptions of the people than what Jean-Jacques Rousseau had in mind for the general will.

Also intriguing about Italy beyond the range of movement populisms and their mutations is that the mass or catchall parties that have appeared since the 1990s, particularly the center-left Democratic Party (Partito Democratico, PD), have also taken on a populist cast. So, Matteo Renzi, prime minister from 2014 to 2016 and, as of that year, never elected at the ballot box by the electorate, makes no apology for communicating directly with the people rather than engaging so much through traditional party channels (e.g., Revelli 2015). They are all populists now. This is the result of the increased importance of the party leaders following on from Berlusconi, who appeals directly to the country as a result of the increased marginalization of the parliament. Recent electoral systems (from that of 1993, through that of 2005, to that of 2015) give party leaders previously unprecedented power over the selection and allocation of seats.

Finally, the past ten years have seen the rise of an altogether novel, manifestly populist political movement that as of March 2018 had become more popular electorally than the regular parties: the Five Star Movement (e.g., Loucaides 2019). This movement recapitulates many traditional populist themes such as hostility to professional politicians, experts, and standard centrist economic policies. It has also been hierarchically organized around a leadership given to ex cathedra decisions and expulsion of nonconforming members. The death of one leader, Gianroberto Casaleggio, in 2016 and the retreat of the public face of the movement, Beppe Grillo, shortly thereafter introduced both a more fluid and a less predictable organization into the movement. In the 2013 national election for the Chamber of Deputies, it had scored the highest number of votes nationwide of any individual political entity. It could have entered into national government at that point if its leaders so chose. It did not. Major success in municipal elections in major cities, particularly Rome and Turin, in June 2016 gave the movement a major boost in terms of potential administrative experience as well as popular support. Consequently, an avowedly antiestablishment movement perhaps stood on the verge of becoming the establishment.

POPULISM BEFORE THE M5S:
BERLUSCONI, BOSSI, AND THE ROLE OF THE LEADER

Populist movements, in dismissing the mediating role of parties, institutional management, and geographical distinctions in interests and identities, always seem to rely as a result on a leader whose persona provides a focal point for the movement that would otherwise be absent. What, then, makes for a leader who is seen at the time and subsequently as the very personification of the movement? For one thing, most of the best-known leaders arrive on the political scene at times of crisis in world or domestic politics. Silvio Berlusconi arrived suddenly on the Italian political scene at precisely that moment at which, while the old party system had died, a new one had not yet been created. Such moments are rare yet provide the opportunity for ambitious and resourceful leaders to emerge outside the usual tracks of political recruitment to high office. The "charisma" of the outsider is the main resource. Berlusconi can be rightly regarded as the "prophet" of the populist League and M5S movements, which in March 2018 together took over 50 percent of the vote in the national election (e.g., Verbeek and Zaslove 2016).

From the populist viewpoint, politics is no longer a profession but a mission. The leader is a savior who requires absolute authority in return for a promise of absolute love for the country (Zagrebelsky 2010). Believability is crucial. The narcissist's belief in self against all odds and all others is absolutely central here. Any inkling of self-doubt condemns the leader in the eyes of potential followers. Such leaders are believable because of their absolute confidence in the performance of the self, what they have already achieved, and what they can do in the future. As then journalist Boris Johnson (Johnson and Farrell 2003, 13), with his quintessential bravado, said of Berlusconi at the height of his rule, "There is something heroic about his style, something hilariously imperial"; he then went on to sycophantically list how the populist had moved mountains to make a palace for himself in Sardinia.

Of course, Berlusconi's ability to blanket the television airwaves with his life story as a self-made billionaire who, as demonstrated by the use of crass and vulgar language, was still very much "one of the people" and to spin the political crisis as he preferred also gave him a tremendous and long-standing advantage over possible competitors. But this was never enough in itself. The timing was vital. Berlusconi came to political prominence in an era in which his career as a media entrepreneur and impresario gave him unique insight into the character of contemporary charisma: its close connection to celebrity (Gundle 2010). We live in a time when many people are famous for being famous rather than for any sort of talent or accomplishment. Berlusconi knew this very well from his experience as a purveyor of precisely the sort of television that trades in celebrity: *Survivor, The Bachelor,* and so on (Stille 2006). In this regard, the heroic political leader is not just a man of destiny but also an everyman: a "cool" guy you would like to have a beer with. At the same time, however, he is also the personification of the populist movement with his active, virile, and repeatedly doctored physical body as a stand-in for the country itself (Belpolito 2009).

After 1992 three political formations came to dominate Italian national politics until 2013: a center-right grouping under the leadership of the media tycoon Berlusconi, a center-left grouping that has become the Democratic Party, and a regionalist/populist party, the Northern League. The electoral systems of 1993 and 2005 undoubtedly contributed to this through their encouragement of pre-election coalitions (Pasquino 2014). Berlusconi made himself the indispensable figure in putting together for substantial periods cross-regional and -locality coalitions between his own party, initially and more recently again called Forza Italia; the Alleanza Nazionale (a party that developed from the neofascist Italian Social Movement (MSI), with most of its core support in Rome and scattered places in the South; and the Northern League (Diamanti 2003; Shin and Agnew 2008). Over the long haul, Berlusconi's grouping was particularly successful in the North, especially in and around the largest cities such as Milan, and in the South around Naples and in Sicily. The Center-Left, meanwhile, retained a strong hold in central Italy and gained a hold in Basilicata in the South. The Northern League, for its part, tended to its greatest success in the more rural parts of Lombardy and the Veneto in the North but with some expansion into similar settings in the Piedmont region (in the Northwest) and in Emilia-Romagna (a "traditional" stronghold of the Left) between 2006 and 2008 (Shin and Agnew 2008).

The Northern League too was populist but had a different genesis and appealed to a very different constituency from the populism of Berlusconi. It started out as a set of protest movements in the small cities of Lombardy and the Veneto against the bias of Roman bureaucracy toward the South. Few commentators expected it to last as a significant presence in national politics. Obviously, the movement found a niche for itself within the center-right constellation that Berlusconi put together in the early 1990s. Initially uncomfortable in the role of junior partner, after 1999 the League's leaders turned the party into a party of government, at local, regional, and national levels (Diamanti 2011; Mancosu 2014). After that the party's historic leader, Umberto Bossi, drifted away from the secessionist logic and neopagan rhetoric about northern cultural roots that had characterized the party in the late 1990s and continued to inspire a certain element among the party's active supporters (e.g., Passarelli and Tuorto 2014). By early 2012 Bossi's diminished health, reliance on dysfunctional family, and lack of ideological coherence had taken a toll. In the 2013 national election, the League faded across the North, particularly in Piedmont and the Veneto, although this decline was at least partly a result of reentering into alliance with Berlusconi.

The dependence of the Northern League on Bossi's rhetorical excess or what the journalist Marco Belpolito (2012) calls his "oratory of gestures" had kept the party in the news at a time when the culture of celebrity was in ascendancy in Italy as elsewhere. But in the end this diminished the party. The failure of the party to deliver much to its electorate by way of federalism or a shift in Italy's public economy in favor of the North during its long period in office alongside Berlusconi was perhaps most important (Ricolfi 2012). But beyond this, the centrality of Bossi's family and circle of friends to the enterprise and the lack of internal democracy within the party left it open to the scandals it had always alleged were those solely of the "old parties."

In national terms over the 1994–2013 period, then, two coalitions organized along a basic Left-Right continuum increasingly accounted for most votes everywhere in Italy. This was so even if the Left was increasingly neoliberal and decreasingly social democratic and the Center-Right increasingly clerical and statist and decreasingly liberal in ideological orientation. The polarizing capacity of Berlusconi was undoubtedly important in this regard as he recruited other right-wing factions into his camp and institutionalized his alliance with the Northern League after 2001. If rhetorically competitive, Berlusconi and Bossi were nonetheless organizationally cooperative. Yet there was a definite geography to the overall national bipolarity (Almagisti 2016). If in the North Berlusconi had to share votes and seats with the Northern League, elsewhere he was faced with serious competition in the South but a dearth of opportunities in the center, where the center-left party still exercised a considerable draw. Down the years, Berlusconi's personality and activities, both business and personal, became increasingly central to his political appeal and to the arguments of his adversaries. No Italian political leader since Benito Mussolini had attracted the attention and criticism that Berlusconi did inside and outside the country (Agnew 2011).

This attention was largely because Berlusconi's rise to political prominence had much to do with protecting his business interests. To paraphrase the famous Prussian military strategist Carl von Clausewitz on war as a continuation of politics by other means, politics to Berlusconi is a continuation of business by other means. In turn, his wealth as one of Italy's richest people allowed him to behave according to norms that were exceptional by the public standards for other Italian politicians. He was self-funded and thus seen by many Italians as beyond the systematic bribery that had undermined the previous party system. His brand as a successful rentier capitalist, ironically using the very connections with politicians to obtain special treatment for his property and media interests that his populist assault on those very politicians decried, was crucial to his popular appeal. Given that his financial interests and leverage to acquire new assets were almost entirely of Italian origin, the posturing as a defender of the people's interests neatly intersected with his own. As a political leader he was particularly attractive to those who held instrumental views of government, feared increased state regulation of their activities, and were drawn to the model of wild consumer capitalism with which Berlusconi was strongly associated through the programming and advertising on his private television channels (Stille 2006).

Such people are to be found all over Italy but have certain geographic concentrations. Italy has the largest number of self-employed people of any major industrialized country, a reflection of the small average size of most businesses. But as maps of tax evasion (overwhelmingly in the South) and intensive television watching (in urban peripheries everywhere and the rural South) show, there are also geographic pools of such people in places with histories of off-the-books employment, narrow profit margins in small businesses, and credit-based consumption. Berlusconi's promises to reduce tax pressures, condone illegal building, and limit entry into professions all speak to this side of his appeal. Liberty from laws rather than equality under the law was the tacit understanding between the leader and this segment of his people (Viroli 2012). At the same time, and ironically in light of charges about his personal behavior, he allied himself with the church on questions relating to euthanasia, gay rights, and women's rights. Such positions made him attractive to the most conservative Catholic constituencies concentrated in parts of the Northeast and the South. Toward the end of his tenure in office, he also became openly hostile to the European Union, thus tapping into what has been a major refrain of right-wing populism across Europe as a whole.

It was the unraveling of the Italian public economy because of increased spreads in yields between Italian and German bonds in late 2011 that put paid to Berlusconi's last government. Berlusconi had been prime minister for all but five of the seventeen years from 1994 to 2011. He could not finally evade some responsibility for the weakness of Italy within the eurozone, of which Italy had been a member since 1999 (e.g., Pianta 2012). Even though his credentials as a successful businessman had helped bring him repeatedly to office, his ultimate failure to seriously address or arrest the declining state of the Italian economy must be the only suitable epitaph on his role as a political leader. Perhaps the very secret of his political success, appealing to entrenched conservative business interests and religious identities, also created the barrier to moving Italy as a whole in a new direction.

Berlusconi's leadership style has continued beyond the tenure of the man himself in the tendency of Matteo Renzi, prime minister from 2014 to 2016, to put himself above his party and to question the role of mediating institutions such as the parliament and the judiciary. Some elements of *Berlusconismo* live on beyond Berlusconi (Flores d'Arcais 2016). Replacing the then prime minister Enrico Letta in an intraparty coup in 2014, Renzi had portrayed himself as a *rottamatore* (breaker) who wished to change Italy by reforming the structure of the parliament, liberalizing the national economy, and using referenda to garner popular support beyond the confines of the parliament. The defeat of the October 2016 referendum on changing the electoral system (but keeping its "top up" of seats for the largest party grouping) and reducing the powers of the Senate showed that this brand of populism did not have much shelf life.

Though Berlusconi made a remarkable comeback in the February 2013 national election after his resignation in disgrace in 2011, partly by making promises about repealing and restituting previous payments for the property tax introduced by the technocratic Mario Monti government in 2012, he was not able to reconstitute the coalition of political forces located in different regions that had been the secret of his previous national electoral success (Pasquino 2014). This success had relied on putting together a strange cross-regional alliance of political groupings rather than really being able "to go to the people" as a national collectivity, even given his obvious power to send political messages over the television airwaves (Shin and Agnew 2008).

THE COMING OF INTERNET POPULISM AND THE GEOGRAPHY OF THE 2018 ITALIAN ELECTION

The year 2013 was the coup de grâce for Berlusconi's version of populism because of the dramatic rise of the Five Star Movement in that year's national election. This movement is a synthesis of the long career of the comedian Beppe Grillo as a political provocateur and, after 2005, a successful blogger and Grillo's now legendary alliance the previous year with the internet entrepreneur Gianroberto Casaleggio. From 2005 until 2007 a series of "meetups" were held around Italy to gather together followers of Grillo's blog. Grillo described himself as an "amplifier" of the demands of those disgusted with the lack of political response to local problems. On June 14, 2007, he announced "V-day" for September 8 of that year. This then took place in over two hundred piazzas around Italy and abroad. The *V* in V-day signified three things: Churchill's victory sign made with two fingers, *V* for "vendetta" in the story of that name, and *V* for *vaffanculo* (Go f--- yourself"), which is directed at loud voice toward Italian politicians. Grillo himself appeared in Bologna, where he announced three popular initiatives for changes in laws governing parliamentary representation: no parliamentary candidates with criminal records, a maximum of two legislatures for any representative, and a new electoral system based on direct preferences of the electorate. The attack on the "political caste" was to be the foundation of the movement.

Starting with support for "civic lists" of candidates in local elections, Grillo was quick to move forward in creating what he considered the "virus of deliberative democracy" (Corbetta and Gualmini 2013, 49). This involved making sure that selected candidates were not affiliated with current parties and that they accepted a set of stringent rules about their performance. Although scattered lists did appear on ballots across Italy in the 2008 national election, Grillo maintained his critique of how the electoral system was "against the Constitution" (Corbetta and Gualmini 2013, 49). On March 8, 2009, with his Carta di Firenze, he enumerated the main objectives of the program for a civic list now dubbed "a 5 stelle." The five stars referred to the core themes of what was becoming a national movement beyond simply criticizing the current regime: safeguarding water and the environment, the growth of public transportation and internet connectivity, and sustainable development (Fabbri and Diani 2015).

On August 2, 2009, Grillo announced the birth of what he called the Five Star Movement. This saw good results in regional elections in Piedmont in 2010 and Molise in 2011, and in May 2012 over 150 *grillini* were elected as mayors and councilors in local elections, including in the city of Parma. In October 2012, M5S became the largest party in the Sicilian regional assembly, with 15 percent of the vote. In the 2013 national elections it polled the largest number of votes of any single "party" for the Chamber of Deputies, although it was outnumbered overall by the two main electoral alliances. Its success led to its having the balance of power in the Senate. The movement was organized almost entirely on the web, which Grillo has used to effect mainly through his comedic mediation, rather than geographically through offices on the ground, so to speak.

Unlike the Northern League and Forza Italia before it, M5S initially did not colonize an older party's voters or even split off a specific slice of voters from another party (Riera and Russo 2016). Both the League and Forza Italia took votes from the former Christian Democrats as well as attracting some new voters, particularly the latter for the Northern League. Rather, M5S cast its net widely among previous non-voters as much as among those previously affiliated with other parties. Its voters were typically younger, better educated, and less prone to look at politics in terms of the Left-Right continuum (Passarelli and Tuorto 2018). The appeal is to an "antipolitics" that casts all traditional political parties in a dim light as instruments of corruption and destitution. Beyond this, the movement has emphasized its role as a voice for "the people," understood as "ordinary citizens," its antielitism, and, crucially, its view of politicians as delegates of the people rather than representatives in their own right (Franzosi et al. 2015). It found ideological resonance with those mostly younger generations tuned in to the new technologies (although Grillo himself is in his sixties) and facing a terrible job market in an Italian economy that has seen better days. Unfortunately, the Italian youth vote is of shrinking numerical significance. Across Italy there are now more people over sixty than under thirty (*La Repubblica* 2018). So a political movement cannot simply appeal to younger adults and expect to achieve electoral success. But support for the M5S also reflected the increasing disassociation between politics, in terms of popular demands and issues, on the one hand, and the realities of representative democracy, with politicians increasingly out of touch with ordinary people, on the other (Diamanti 2012b). Its own parliamentary members after 2013 were overwhelmingly neophytes to the role and to politics. In a survey, 40.4 percent reported that they had not voted though eligible to do so in 2008, the year of the previous national election (Farinelli and Massetti 2015).

But it is not simply an antipolitics movement. The "Grillo" phenomenon signifies a new way of articulating interests and identities but as yet without the capacity to aggregate these satisfactorily into a legislative agenda in the presence of existing parties with which the movement must negotiate. One dilemma it faces is that many of its first supporters and voters hailed generally from the center-left. Its early support in Emilia-Romagna, a traditionally "red" region, reinforces this conclusion. But increasingly, as it has attracted more voters from the right side of the political spectrum (particularly from the League) and also among those who are mainly protest voters, particularly in the South, it has also become a less obviously radical or progressive movement in its substantive commitments to civic democracy (Paparo and Cataldi 2013; Nasi 2015; Biorcio and Natale 2013; Diamanti 2016). For example, its official position on the future of the euro and Italian membership in the European Union has been somewhat labile to say the least. Yet it has affiliated in the European Parliament with such groups as the United Kingdom Independence Party. Grillo often has more typically right-wing views, for example, on undocumented immigrants and Roma camps, than did most early M5S activists and voters (Biorcio and Natale 2013, 143). It seems not to have transcended the Left-Right divide so much as to mirror both sides internally, notwithstanding its own rhetoric about being outside the bounds of the traditional polarity (Russo et al. 2017).

Another dilemma is that devotion to the instant popular participation promised by the internet goes against the logic of representation implicit in running in elections. Elections are determined on a geographical basis, with territorial constituencies and lists of candidates that differ from place to place. In reaching distinctive geographical constituencies with different views about the role of national government and policies that meet their identities and needs better than others, parties must accept that choices are not simply those of individuals, on the one hand, and the accumulation of national averages on issues, on the other. Yet M5S remains committed to the idea of transcending geography in both electoral and substantive terms by eventually instituting a direct democracy that would bypass traditional institutions, such as the parliament, and conventional elections themselves (e.g., Molinari 2018, Chapter 8). As yet, however, the internet/web is more an instrument of protest and revolt than of anything else.

Be this as it may, as M5S has spread across Italy in local and national politics, in order to bolster its support it has had to adapt its appeal (Almagisti 2016, 251–57). Even as its electoral base has shifted, however, M5S has not become a thoroughly right-wing populism. It has retained its antielitist and antiausterity messages. It remains hostile to all types of political intermediation exercised by interest groups (unions, media, intellectuals, and so) and to forming alliances with other parties or movements, even though in the aftermath of the 2018 election it entered into coalition with the League. Its emphasis on problem solving as the modus operandi of politics, however, leads to the symbolic devaluation of political decisions as "objectivized administrative praxis, delegitimizing partisan politics and politics itself" (Caruso 2015, 336). Its lack of much intraparty discipline, largely because of the devoted amateurism of its activists and their disdain for professional politicians, means that M5S is vulnerable to sidelining by better-organized populist parties like the League.

Faced with rooted competition from the League in the North and with at least residual support for the center-left Democratic Party in the center, in expanding its support southward and outside major metropolitan areas, in particular, the M5S had to appeal both to a constituency living without as much internet access as its core supporters and to those looking to Rome for economic support. This electoral calculus conflicted with the goals of renewing governance and addressing environmental issues, the original purposes of the Five Star Movement as reflected in its name (e.g., Canestrari and Biondo 2018). Its rightward drift, therefore, has had an electoral as much as an ideological logic. Its alliance in national government with the League after the election showed that, apart from the "citizens' income" directed in a vote-collecting manner toward its poorer and older voters, it shared much of the agenda of Euroskepticism and hostility toward established institutions of its more obviously far-right partner. In office, however, it has had to make accommodations to both the EU and economic realities, particularly an incredibly high government debt, which it criticized previous governments and parties for doing (e.g., Legorano 2019).

The geography of the 2018 election offers clues to what has happened to the party of internet populism relative to its competitors. First of all, in 2018 there was a clear regionalization of the concentrations of votes of the various parties. In an electoral system in which people vote for the Chamber of Deputies and the Senate and for single members and party lists in multimember districts, we focus just on the Chamber of Deputies. Nationwide in the Chamber of Deputies, in the proportional contests M5S received 32.68 percent of the popular vote, the League 17.35 percent, Forza Italia 14.00 percent, and PD 18.76. In the single-member contests, the Center-Right received 37 percent, M5S 32.68 percent, and the Center-Left 22.85

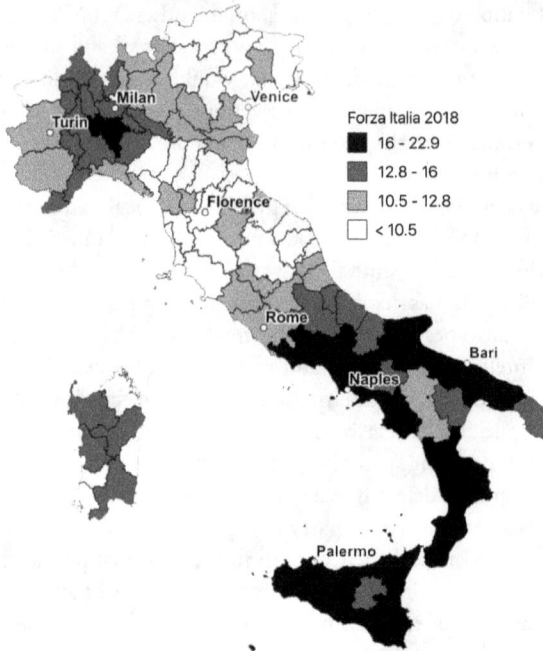

Map 6.1(a).   Geography of Forza Italia, 2018.
Source: Italian National Election Studies (ITANES).

percent. The League, competing in the center-right coalition with Forza Italia and Fratelli d'Italia, not surprisingly did best in the North but also with a significant set of clusters further south, particularly in central Italy. The M5S for its part emerged as a metropolitan hinterland and southern party (Map 6.1). The core of the center-left coalition, the PD, was left with a rump of areas in central Italy, where it did somewhat better than elsewhere. Overall, it was the main loser in 2018 at the expense of the Center-Right and the M5S. Within the Center-Right, the League enjoyed the most surprising success, eclipsing Forza Italia in northern Italy for the first time. After the election this outcome was to make the League the force toward which the M5S had to turn to realize a government with a parliamentary majority. Even though the League had been his putative ally in the election, Berlusconi was finally no longer able to present himself as the kingmaker of Italian governments.

Various factors seem to have contributed to the 2018 result. The electoral system introduced by the PD-dominated government for the 2018 election had the opposite of the intended effect. It was supposed to dissipate the M5S vote. In continuing with the use of single-member districts (37 percent of seats) alongside

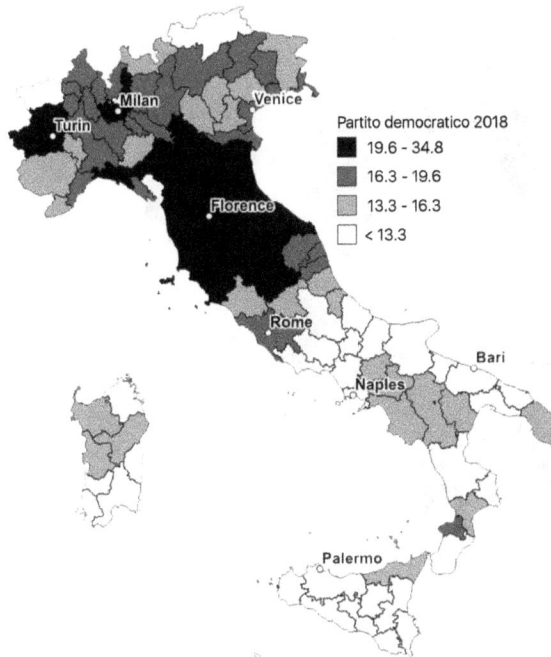

Map 6.1(b).   Geography of Democratic Party, 2018.
Source: Italian National Election Studies (ITANES).

multiple-member districts based on party/coalition lists (63 percent of seats), in fact it rewarded the M5S and above all the Center-Right while reducing the representation of the PD in its traditional areas of strength. If in the North the Center-Right stitched up almost all the single-member districts, in the South the M5S did so. In central Italy, though, the Center-Left was faced with competition that drastically reduced its yield of such seats. This was not the only factor in producing the overall electoral outcome (Pasquino 2018). The campaigns, the promise of the M5S to "clean house," and the unpopularity of the outgoing government all played a part. The 2018 election was the worst performance by Italian left-wing parties—PD and others (28 percent of total votes)—since World War II. The fact that the unpopular Matteo Renzi remained secretary of the PD, fueling suspicion that he might emerge to grasp the role of prime minister from the incumbent Paolo Gentiloni, probably also contributed (Pasquino 2018, 355).

Between the elections of 2013 and 2018, there was a sea change in the levels and geography of support for the various parties. The League went from 4 to 17.3 percent of the total national vote and M5S from 25.5 to 32.6 percent. Meanwhile, Forza

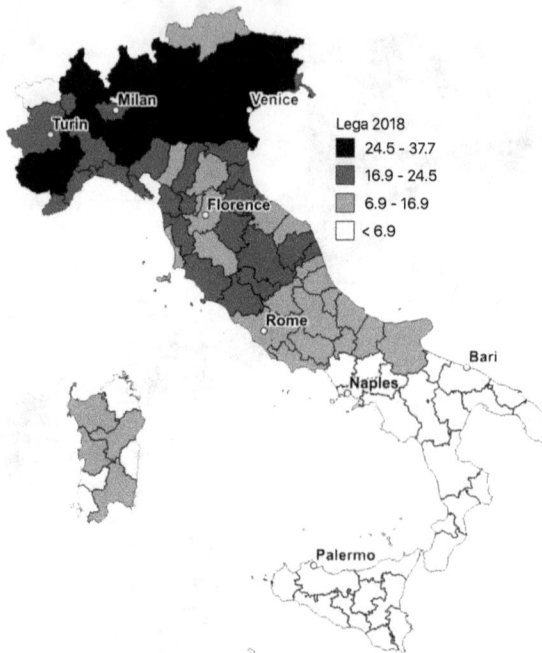

Map 6.1(c). Geography of League, 2018.
Source: Italian National Election Studies (ITANES).

Italia (Popolo della Libertà in 2013) declined from 21.5 to 13.9 percent and the PD from 25.4 to 18.7 percent. The two winners were obvious. If Matteo Salvini used immigration and fear of uncontrolled borders and the joint promise with his coalition partners to introduce a "flat tax" to create a League that went national rather than simply focusing on the North, Luigi Di Maio, the new *capo politico* of the M5S (as Beppe Grillo retreated into the shadows), advocated for a "citizen's income," criticized the corruption of professional politicians, and tried to appeal to the "average" Italian as opposed to the younger demographic the party had previously cultivated by emphasizing the novelty of his party and its commitments to Italians as opposed to the austerity policies mandated by the pro-EU Italian governments since 2011. Most clearly, in 2018 compared to 2013, this shows the League spreading out of its northern fastnesses, to which it had retreated in 2013, and the southernization of the M5S in contrast to a more homogeneous pattern in 2013 (Map 6.2). The League's success seems to have come mainly at the expense of Forza Italia, whereas the M5S was more omnivorous, drawing votes from the PD in the North, the South, and central Italy but also, because of limited competition from the League in the South,

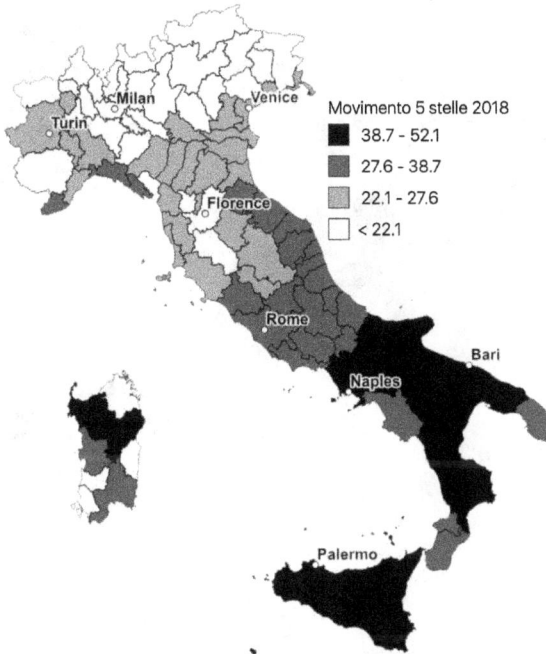

Map 6.1(d). Geography of Five Star Movement, 2018.
Source: Italian National Election Studies (ITANES).

attracting former center-right voters and prior abstainers (particularly again in the South) (Pritoni and Vignati 2018).

WHO SHOWED UP IN 2018?

Italy has long had among the highest electoral turnouts among European countries. Beginning in the late 1980s, however, turnouts began to decline. Some of this was due to declining party identifications, particularly among new younger voters, and the decreased efficacy of patronage voting, particularly in southern Italy. But from the 1990s, nonvoters seem to be less and less those on the margins of politics in terms of political interest and more and more well-educated voters abstaining because of disaffection from the political system (Tuorto 2006). As a result, the relative mobilization of voters in different places and among different demographic categories has become central to Italian electoral politics in a way it never was during the heyday of the party system based upon the Christian Democratic and Communist parties from

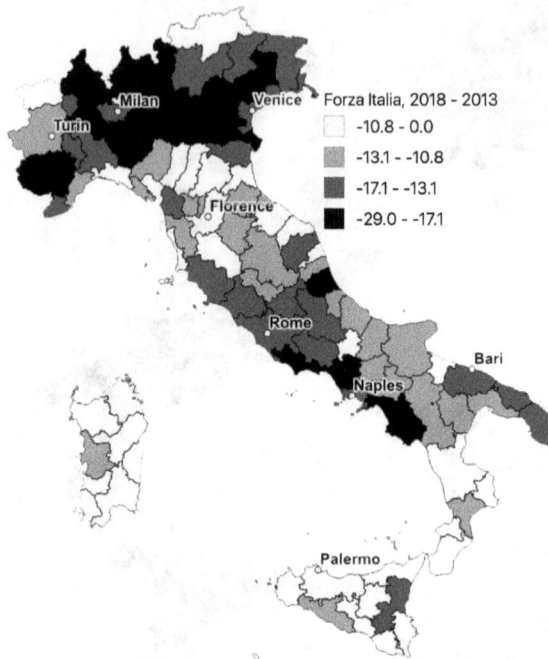

Map 6.2(a).   Change in Forza Italia, 2018–2013.
Source: Italian National Election Studies (ITANES).

the late 1940s until the late 1980s. This growing population was the hunting ground for the M5S and the League in the 2018 election. Of course, even the new populists cannot mobilize some voters who remain resolutely antiestablishment to the extent of refusing to participate in national elections (Pritoni and Vignati 2018, 384).

The 2018 election continued the long-term trend in declining turnout. At 72.9 percent this was the lowest since World War II. Perhaps most surprising, given the antisystem rhetoric of the two main populist protagonists in 2018, is that turnout did not decline that precipitately. Specifically, the M5S under the leadership of Luigi Di Maio managed to recruit voters in southern Italy and among those rejecting the historic parties (particularly the PD). The decision to focus the election campaign on proposals for helping the unemployed and marginalized by emphasizing a "citizen income" seemed to pay off in increased turnout. That said, the geography of turnout in 2018 is all too familiar to those who have studied previous Italian national elections. The highest turnouts across all demographic categories were in the Northeast and central Italy and the lowest were uniformly in the South and the islands (Sicily and Sardinia) (Map 6.3). This suggests that even if there was some switch in who

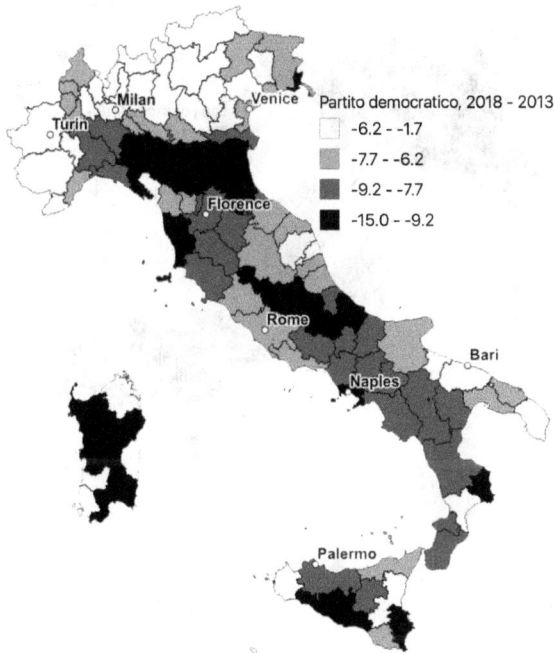

Map 6.2(b).   Change in Democratic Party, 2018–2013.
Source: Italian National Election Studies (ITANES).

voted in the South, it did not affect the overall levels of turnout there. Turnout was down everywhere in 2018 but more in some places than in others.

So, even if 2018 marked an overall national downturn in turnout, it was geographically differentiated. Interestingly, the difference between the North and the South was thus less than it had been in 2013, with the biggest decreases in Emilia-Romagna and around Rome, traditionally more left-wing areas, and the smallest decreases in the South, particularly in Basilicata and Calabria (Cavallaro et al. 2018, 84). The fading of the PD, the expansion of the League out of the "deep" North, and the rise of the M5S in the South are all related to the geography of turnout, with much of the success of the League in areas where it could mobilize pools of previous far-right voters (e.g., Mancosu and Landini 2018) and that of the M5S in places where unemployment, particularly of younger people, is extremely high and where there is a history of exchange or patronage voting in which voters are looking for specific government actions that will improve their lives (Cavallaro et al. 2018).

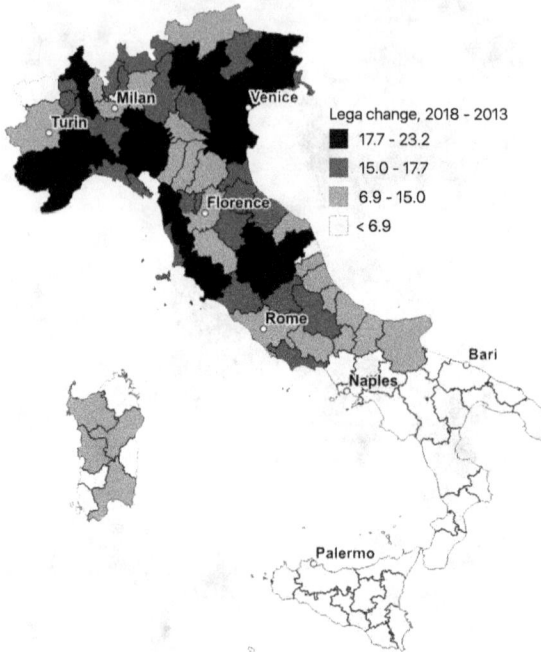

Map 6.2(c).   Change in League, 2018–2013.
Source: Italian National Election Studies (ITANES).

YOUTHFUL INNOCENCE VERSUS DARK CHARISMA?

Beppe Grillo, the main face of the M5S from its origins, was not able to run for election because of a long-ago conviction for vehicular homicide. But Grillo has for many years been congenitally hostile to the entire infrastructure of Italian politics, so his role was always more that of inciter or provocateur than plausible political leader. As a result the M5S had to run a neophyte as its main representative in the election. Luigi Di Maio was not just starting from scratch because the M5S had been the most important single party in 2013. Elected in the party's online primary by 82 percent of the vote in September 2017, he had a high degree of legitimacy as a result.

Under Di Maio's leadership, the party abandoned or mitigated some of its more radical positions, for example, advocating leaving the euro, attacking the European Union, and being antivaccination. This, along with the patronage appeal to voters looking for government income assistance, was directed at expanding the party's vote beyond that of 2013. In so doing, it was in practice abandoning the idea that what sold well in one part of Italy necessarily traveled well elsewhere. At the same time,

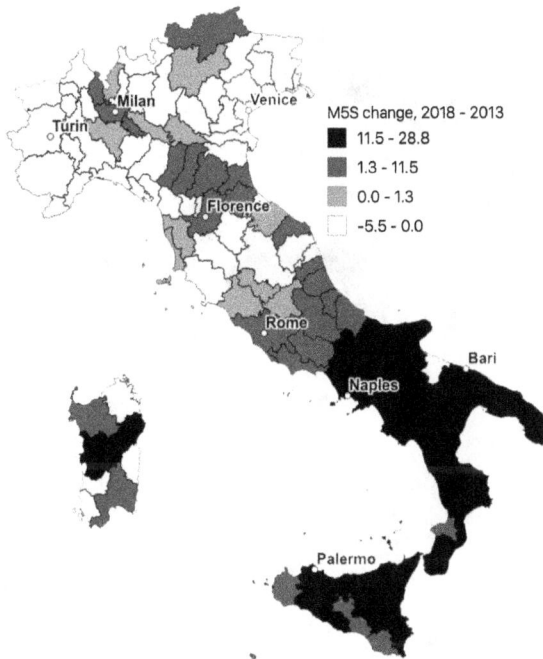

Map 6.2(d).   Change in Five Star Movement, 2018–2013.
Source: Italian National Election Studies (ITANES).

however, Alessandro Di Battisti, leader of the more radical side of the M5S, ran a parallel campaign to keep the more active voters in line. Perhaps Di Maio's main contribution to the populist element in the appeal was to "moderate" the image of the M5S and reassure voters at the same time that he also criticized the traditional parties. In the end, Di Maio can hardly be seen as a satisfactory stand-in for Grillo, with Di Battisti waiting in the wings if he founders, even if his ranking in polls has been higher than that of Grillo (Cavallaro et al. 2018, 42–43). His youthfulness is both an attraction and a defect in that he can be seen as both a new face and also as so inexperienced that he can be outmaneuvered by more skilled politicians. It is not Grillo but Matteo Salvini of the League who was (and is) the main challenger (Pucciarelli 2016).

Indeed, the challenge for the M5S is no longer from the "mainstream" parties but from its much more established populist far-right competitor, the League (renamed from the Northern League). This has been much more consistently right-wing in its electorate and its policy menu. It has become rabidly nationalist under the leadership of Matteo Salvini, demeaning of immigrants, and pro-Putin but still devoted to the reduction of taxes on northern small business (symbolized by positions in favor of a

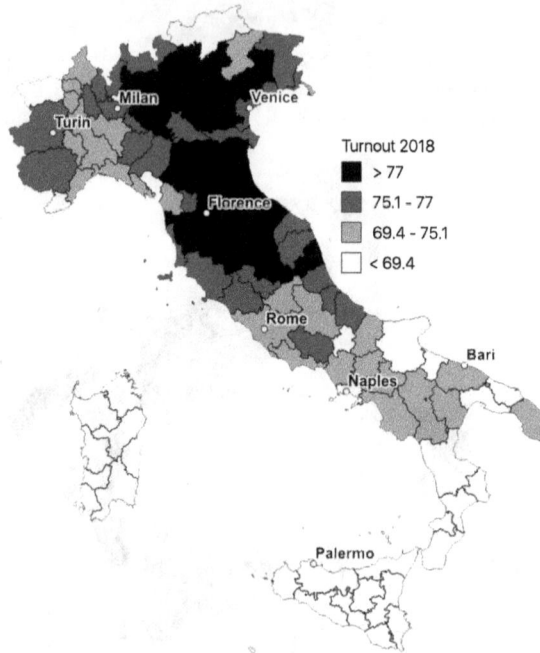

Map 6.3. Geography of 2018 voter turnout.
Source: Italian National Election Studies (ITANES).

"flat tax" and tax amnesties for previous evaders) and as skeptical of Roman bureaucracy as its precursor, the Northern League. Salvini sees himself as both a disciple of the Le Pens and of Donald Trump. His personal leadership or dark charisma, as we would term it, has enabled the League to engage in a complete makeover from a regionalist/separatist party before 2012 devoted now to building an Italy-wide constituency on anti-immigrant and anti-EU messages. Salvini, like Trump, is good at keeping himself in the news and thus using the main newspapers and TV news programs, including those that disapprove of him, as agents of his messaging. He dresses up as a policeman or firefighter to project the image of both an everyman and an agent of the state, even as he uses Facebook to humanize himself (selfies with fans) and identify himself as the quintessential Italian (Nutella on toast for breakfast, immense bowls of pasta for lunch) (Horowitz 2019; Marchetti 2019). He represents an Italian version of the national-identity politics that has taken off across Europe (e.g., Camus and Lebourg 2017; Zuquete 2018). Whether the nationalization of the League can be maintained while there is still memory of the antisouthern and anti-Rome messages of the Northern League and while many northern supporters of the League still see it as a northern localist/regionalist party remains to be seen (Albertazzi et al. 2018; D'Alimonte 2018; Bevilacqua 2019).

In the meantime, however, the M5S has become more like the League in a number of respects. Over time, from 2013 to 2018, those stating a preference for M5S have increasingly identified as on the right rather than on the left (Analisi Politica 2018). If in 2013 and 2017 those stating they were on the left completely outweighed those saying they were on the right, by 2018 there was almost parity between the two sides. So the shift happened rapidly in the lead-up to the March 2018 national election. What had once appeared to be perhaps a new center-left movement had lost its singular complexion. This seemed to be driven by the reformulation of its electorate as discussed earlier. But it has also reflected the competition with the other populist grouping, the League. They were competitors around the same issues and slogans more than rivals with absolutely distinctive visions and programs to match. Can Italy support two competing right-wing populisms based around mobilizing national identity?

In the final analysis, in appointing as its leader the youthful and baby-faced Luigi Di Maio, someone with little political and no administrative experience, the M5S has put itself at a net disadvantage in the leadership stakes to the League, with its bombastic and attention-seeking leader, Matteo Salvini. Di Maio was a compromise candidate who does not provide the kind of charismatic leadership that the M5S needs to compete nationally with the League. Absent the comic leader Grillo, the movement's core tenet of horizontal organization also works against the typical populist model of leadership. Grillo remains in the background. This means, of course, that it is something of a two-headed movement. Grillo is the "'guarantor' of the movement's overall direction. He retains ownership of the 5Star copyright, which he has used in recent years to excommunicate political opponents by denying them the right to use the symbol. When M5S activists or elected officials have criticized Grillo or seemed to violate the party's core tenets, they have been banished" (Stille 2018, 42–43). Di Maio, however, seems to favor a loosening of the rules to reflect the relative youthfulness and exuberance of its members. Much of the potential tension reflects the difficulty of turning a protest movement into a political party without sacrificing its commitment to technopopulism (Manucci and Amsler 2018). The reversals of established positions and the ascendancy of Salvini at the expense of Di Maio and the M5S since going into coalition with the League suggest limits to the M5S as a truly national movement. The League too has not yet transcended its original contradiction: which "people" does it represent, its northern constituency or a xenophobic bloc scattered across the country?

THE INTERNET VERSUS RETAIL POLITICS

Of course, what still sets the M5S apart from the League (and the other parties) is its organizational model based on the internet and social media. As in other countries, newspapers and television are of decreased importance in political communication compared to more recent technological innovations, although television news is probably still more important in Italy than say in the United Kingdom or France. As with television but more interactively, the internet does offer a different range of information sources and cross-place mobilizing opportunities than existing mass media such as newspapers and magazines. But much of the newness associated with the technologies is simply a matter of fingertip delivery and timeliness more than a qualitative break with past modes of information dissemination and mobilization. Even as the new technologies have expanded the total amount of communication, data from the United States suggest that some other modes of communication, such as print and interpersonal of all types, have retained their importance, while radio and television have declined (*Economist* 2012).

More interestingly in terms of the presumed political effects of the new technologies, numerous studies of social networking show that geographic constraints still exercise a strong influence over all social media. The probability of having social ties still decreases as a function of distance, suggesting strongly that social media tend to facilitate flows among existing social networks rather than to create them (e.g., Onnela et al. 2011). Indeed, there is evidence from survey data that the success of the party in 2013 owed much to voters' exposure to discussion networks among friends and acquaintances of those more tied into internet sources (Vezzoni and Mancosu 2015). In 2018 the geography of the M5S vote strongly suggests how much the internet was not that important in mobilizing voters. Beyond its success in the metropolitan hinterlands of such cities as Milan, Rome, and Naples, its levels of support were highest in many of those regions and localities with the lowest levels of internet penetration and use, such as Puglia and Sicily.

In fact, some polling data suggest that irrespective of how they have been mobilized, the supporters of M5S differ little in fact from other voters in terms of their expectations of how future Italian governments should be formed, and they can be found in some places much more than in others (lower-religiosity and higher-income areas, in particular) (Nasi 2012). Indeed, there is some evidence that the League and particularly its leader, Matteo Salvini, were better at exploiting social media such as Facebook than was the M5S (Kalia et al. 2018). This notwithstanding, the overall penetration of the internet (63 percent) and social media such as Facebook (21 percent) and Twitter (12 percent) is much lower in Italy than in countries such as France (83 percent internet penetration) and much the same as in Morocco (61 percent internet penetration) (Nasi 2016; Saporiti 2018; Trovati 2018). In 2013 Beppe Grillo himself took to traveling around Italy by bus to give his movement the "ground game" that retail politics still requires (Diamanti 2012c). The "party" was the primary party in votes cast in 50 provinces out of 108 in 2013 but achieved its greatest successes in Sicily, where the internet is not that widely used, and in Lazio and Lombardia, where a better case for the internet's role can be made but which are also the seats of Italy's largest metropolitan areas and plausibly the largest concentrations of those most disillusioned with the existing party system (Diamanti 2014). It achieved success at the local level overwhelmingly in northern Italy and Rome, thus justifying its claim to being a "civic" force for improving local public services and encouraging greater transparency in public administration. It had, then, what has been called a "double identity" (Vampa 2015, 245). By 2018 this was much less the case. M5S had southernized to the extent that its leader, his policies on income support, and popular support for the party no longer had the northern/metropolitan cast of the early years. If the League dominated in the North, the M5S had conquered the South.

Nationally the M5S has come to represent many of those protesting against the overall condition of national politics, particularly the austerity policies pursued by Italian governments since 2008. So the geography of its electoral support relates much more to patterns of social capital, exchange voting, and unemployment. The 2018 vote for the M5S maps much more onto lower levels of social capital and exchange voting (e.g., Cartocci 2007) and unemployment (Map 6.4) than it does onto access to and use of the internet. But locally in parts of Italy, it has also become a potential force for better municipal governance. This tension is apparent in the contrasts between Grillo and other national leaders, stressing the protest dimension,

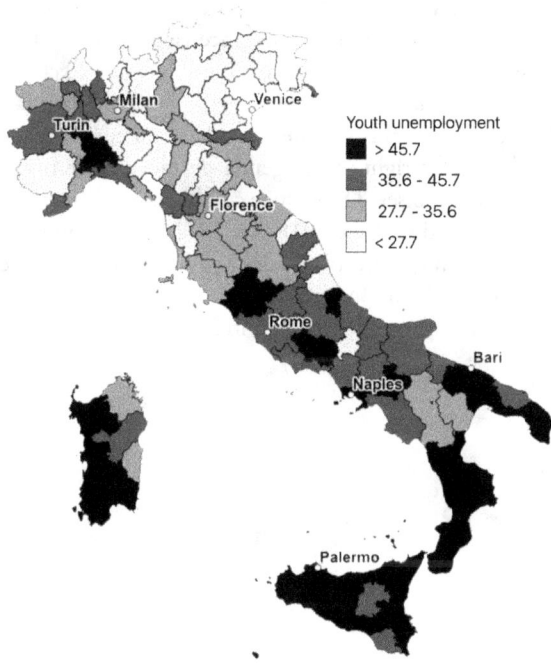

Map 6.4.   Geography of youth unemployment, 2016.
Source: Italian National Institute of Statistics (ISTAT).

and many local/municipal leaders, emphasizing the civic purposes of the movement. Either way, a placeless politics in which social media and mass communication completely replace face-to-face social interaction and the vagaries of everyday life grounded in particular places is clearly not on the immediate political horizon.

CONCLUSION

In the aftermath of the 2018 election, the M5S and the League formed a national coalition government with Di Maio and Salvini as presumably "matching" deputy prime ministers. Ironically, given the pretension of populists that they represent a phenomenon "beyond" conventional party politics, party affiliations and arrangement of a tit-for-tat "contract" between them, rather than online procedural democracy or coherent policy positions, were at the forefront in negotiations between the League and the M5S. As Aldo Schiavone (2013, 66) reminds us about the old party system of pre-1992, "It was the parties that managed the parliamentary groups, determined the duration of government cabinets, selected the political class and that of the government." From this viewpoint, today only the identity of the actors has changed, not the way they work. *Popolocrazia* isn't so different from *partitocrazia*. Only if a movement obtains totalistic dominance can the ideal of moving beyond normal politics be realized. In Italy this possibility looks unlikely, particularly for the M5S, which appears increasingly on the back foot in relation to Salvini and the League. What seems crucial is whether the M5S will continue to compete with the League on Salvini's far right-wing agenda or move back toward its original environmentalist-leftist impulses. The strange combination of internet populism and patronage politics that produced the 2018 vote for M5S does not encourage confidence. It would require a more effective leader and a return to its more participatory and localist imperatives to do so. But the League's clearly "illiberal" democracy would then at least have a challenger rather than an imitator.

7

Conclusion

Going to the people is much easier said than done. For one thing, the people must be identified and mobilized. This is becoming increasingly difficult with more socially and culturally heterogeneous electorates, on the one hand, and the weakening of states as autonomous actors because of the increased powers of global capitalism, on the other (Wolin 2004, 585–90). Mainstream parties are often seen to have become the agents of the latter. Populist movements aim to turn back the clock and reinvigorate the role of governments in the lives of "the people" through more direct representation of the popular interest and the "common sense" on which it relies (Sylvers 2018). The promise of populism is of politics without mediation, either institutional or geographical.

But who votes and for whom is not the same everywhere: in other words "the people" varies from place to place. Even powerful tycoons need political alliances to knit together political coalitions that produce an uneven spatial distribution of support for the leader's guidance of the people, and an internet-based movement still needs to adapt politically as it travels across the country and gains support for what become increasingly contradictory goals of popular protest and civic governance. There is also evidence that selective domestic migration and foreign immigration are producing more politically homogeneous neighborhoods and localities (e.g., Johnston et al. 2016). As a result, in appealing to very specific popular constituencies (white men, former Communist voters, those nostalgic for times when more people looked alike, and so on), populist movements are deeply polarizing of electorates, as we have seen in the accounts offered in previous chapters. They appeal much more in some places than they do in others because those places differ profoundly in terms of their sociodemographic and geographical characteristics.

Mapping populism as we have done for the four cases allows us to say something about the three features of populism that we have claimed are crucial to its recent efflorescence. These are its demographic basis regarding relative turnout in elections and previous nonvoters, the role of the charismatic leader as an alternative to the complexities of party rule, and the significance of shifts in the landscape of political communication for the spread of populist narratives. After surveying some general points drawn from comparisons across the four chapters, we turn briefly to several overarching themes that emerge from this discussion. These are, respectively, the importance of electoral systems to the nature and trajectories of populist groups, the increased geographical polarization of electorates prior to the recent growth of populism, and the hollowing out of liberal democracy because of its inability to ensure that political representation produces responses to the expressed needs of significant segments of national populations. We end with some pointers toward the future of populism and how it might be channeled and challenged.

POPULISM WITHIN FOUR COUNTRIES

Our approach rests on three elements that we claim are central to the genesis and mobilization of populist movements. The first of these is the demography of turnout and nonvoting. This refers to the availability of voters with loose ties to established parties who can then move into the electorate and shift its orientation toward populism. An important aspect of this, given the importance of early adulthood for political socialization, is the role of different political generations in facilitating this movement. In the Italian case it seems clear that on the whole younger first-time voters have played a significant part in the electoral success of the Five Star Movement, particularly in southern Italy and in the suburbs of the largest cities. At the same time, the League, the hard-right populist movement, has tended to rely much more on older voters in its northern Italian heartland. The other three cases reveal a different pattern. In the case of the Brexit and Trump votes, it was older, less educated rather than younger voters whose choices proved determining of outcomes. Crucial in the former case was the recruitment of enough older former Labour voters to supplement the overriding majority of former United Kingdom Independence Party (UKIP) and Conservative voters who voted leave. Insufficient younger voters showed up to balance what the opinion polls showed was a significant majority in favor of remain. For Trump a little over eighty thousand voters in three states, Pennsylvania, Michigan, and Wisconsin, proved critical to his victory in the electoral college. A sizeable number of these were probably older voters who had voted for Barack Obama in 2008 and 2012. Many younger and black voters stayed home in those states. At the same time, Trump was able to capture much of the right-wing base that had become increasingly dominant within the Republican Party since the 1990s in the so-called red states. For the French National Front, the demography of its support was a mix of its traditional middle-class base in southern and southeastern France and disillusioned working-class voters in the North. Overwhelmingly, however, these are aging cohorts. Given the centrist bias of the French electoral system, this proved of overriding importance in the defeat of Marine Le Pen in the second round of the 2017 presidential election.

The role of putative leader cum rabble-rouser was also important in all of the cases at hand, as it seems to be more generally with populist movements today. Part of this is due to the importance of "celebrity" in focusing attention on the movement in the context of an increasingly fragmented media environment and the need to replace the established party elites with new "outsider" cadres in tune with the "common sense" of the people. We live in the age of celebrity and the "society of the spectacle" (Debord 1983). In the French case, the most notable feature was a transfer of leadership from father to daughter, as the latter sought to move the party first established in 1972 into a more competitive position within the political system. There is little doubt that her role was vital not least in opening up the National Front to potential voters put off by Jean-Marie Le Pen's anti-Semitism, racism, and neoliberalism. Marine Le Pen's formulation of cultural conservatism and economic nationalism proved more appealing in the context of 2017 than her father's would ever have been. In the twin cases of Brexit and Donald Trump new figures essentially colonized existing parties to pursue electoral success. The Euroskeptics within the Conservative Party, including last-minute ones like Boris Johnson and Michael Gove, engineered a campaign that relied first and foremost on dramatic oversimplification and mendacity in equal degrees. Recall the ridiculous claim about rerouting funds from the European Union to the British National Health Service. This boldness paid dividends. Likewise with Trump: his opening salvo of attacks on immigrants and refugees from Mexico and Muslim-majority countries (except favored ones such as Saudi Arabia, from which most of the 9/11 terrorists came, suggesting how little the ban related to the real issue of terrorism but was a PR exercise geared to people who either knew nothing or chose to forget about where the 9/11 terrorists originated) was central to his campaign. It symbolized the extent to which existing political elites had sacrificed control over borders and the economic welfare of deserving Americans to foreigners. This would be the basis on which he promised to single-handedly "Make America Great Again." Finally, the Italian case is more complex. Before the 2018 election, the éminence grise of the Five Star Movement, the comedian Beppe Grillo, selected a surrogate, Luigi Di Maio, as the potential prime minister in government. Grillo was not eligible for office himself, having a manslaughter conviction on his record. But behind the scenes it is still Grillo, however much he claims to have receded from a central role, who calls the shots. Di Maio comes across more as a "friend down at the bar" than as a charismatic leader (Picone 2017). In rejecting the idea of "the leader" as a charismatic figure (Casaleggio and Grillo 2011), the dilemma for Grillo and the Five Star Movement is that they have been outflanked successfully by the more bombastic and vulgar Matteo Salvini, leader of the resurrected League (formerly Northern League), a now nationalist rather than separatist movement mixing anti-EU sentiment and xenophobia in equal measure. Whether the League's checkered history will affect its nationwide prospects remains to be seen.

What most sets the current era of populism apart from previous ones is the changed nature of political communication. Local newspapers are in total eclipse across the countries we have examined. They used to provide a modicum of "common" news shared locally that can refocus partisanship away from total polarization (Sullivan 2018; Darr et al. 2018; Benson 2018; Thompson 2018). When they do show signs of life, they are often viciously attacked by populist politicians who resent the very idea of independent journalism (e.g., Baron 2018). Along with the decline in popular patronage of national news outlets, including newspapers and an increasingly polarized menu of television-news options, this signals the decline of what can be called organized "public opinion" of which the "fading figure of the journalist is only an epiphenomenon" (D'Eramo 2018, 126; also see Starr 2019). The sort of celebrity gossip and farfetched stories found in tabloids like the *National Enquirer* in the United States and the *Sun* in the United Kingdom softened up large audiences of the barely literate for what came next. The increased importance of the internet today has been particularly obvious in the rise of the Five Star Movement in Italy, organized as it is around the website of Beppe Grillo and his coterie (e.g., Dal Lago 2017). But in every one of the cases we have examined, social media such as Twitter and Facebook have been of significance in polarizing electorates and in creating what Jared Kelley (2018) calls the "epistemic confusion" on which populism tends to feed. A strong case can be made that even without Russian trolls interfering in the 2016 election, Trump won in part because of his campaign's systematic use of biased news and misinformation on Facebook (Halpern 2018a). In the face of large-scale distrust of political institutions and the so-called mainstream media, such as television news and newspapers, people turn to sources that are congenial to their existing prejudices (e.g., Roberts 2017). If this does not so much create polarization as reflect its existence, it is still not very encouraging (Boxell et al. 2017). This was not what its early apologists told us the internet would engender (Tufekci 2018). It has "brutalized" political debate much more than stimulated rational communication between politicians and the public (Badouard 2018).

Leaders contribute to the echo-chamber effect by casting doubt on conventional narratives about the honesty of bureaucracy, the disinterestedness of the courts, and even the existence of "truth" itself. This is the essence of postmodern populism. Donald Trump is the master of the emphasis on what he calls "fake news," which comes down to anything that casts him in a bad light. Twitter has become his very modus operandi. But his use of it is not simply propagandistic. He combines a high level of mendacity and open lying about facts with a questioning of the "patriotism" and sanity of his critics. The leave campaign in the UK Brexit referendum also relied heavily on the use and manipulation of social media to sow disinformation and create doubts about the reliability of current government data concerning the pros and cons of the country's leaving the European Union. In Italy and France the populist parties have also used misleading information about immigration and its impacts, among other things, to also call into question "official stories" that conflict with the current goals of their movements. Social media have been crucial in offering the promise of unmediated access to information, sadly at the expense of much of its accuracy. As we have seen, however, the relative success of populist campaigns and leaders has been deeply polarizing socially and geographically rather than successful in gluing together disparate people and places into the singular whole that claims to represent "the people" might seem to suggest.

OVERARCHING THEMES

Much more could be said about the four cases we have examined in some detail. In brief compass we would simply draw attention to three overarching themes that our cases illustrate to one degree or another. The first of these is the clear importance of electoral systems for the specific forms of and prospects for populism. The lack of a history of referendums probably affected that on Brexit in that it allowed voters scope to exercise more general frustrations rather than to simply express a singular opinion about leaving or remaining in the European Union. They were not going to miss this chance to send a message! Beyond that specificity, in the UK and US cases, the majoritarian and heavily geographical character of their electoral systems encourage the "capture" of existing parties for populist goals more than the establishment of new ones. When new parties do emerge, as with UKIP, they tend to suffer in regular national elections from the sense that a vote for them is a "wasted" one. The French electoral system under the Fifth Republic with its two rounds of voting is rather less based on simple bipolarity between long-standing parties than on institutionalizing more centrist parties and presidential candidates because of the mobilization of bias on their behalf built into the second-round contests. The Italian electoral systems since the 1990s with their mix of majoritarian and proportional elements have been more open to new movements/parties. Given the increased lability of attachment to existing parties and their overall lack of staying power compared to, say, the Christian Democrats and Communists who dominated electoral politics before 1992, the relative success of populist movements in elections compared to those in the other cases is not that surprising.

These differences, important as they are, can disguise two vital similarities. The second theme, then, is that polarization of electorates in all the cases long predated the recent populist explosion. The third is that liberal democracy based on the politics of accommodation is everywhere in trouble. Long-term trends in electoral polarization lie beyond the recent expansion in support for populist groups and for votes such as that in the United Kingdom to leave the European Union. This is often put down to culture wars, demographic fears of majority racial groups that their time is running out, the left-behind working class suffering from the downside of neoliberal globalization, and so on. There is presumed to be a single explanation. In fact, it all seems more complicated. Our cases all suggest that since the 1970s, a number of trends have together brought about a transition away from the dominant model of party rule that prevailed in all these countries for much of the post–World

War II period to produce a polarization that has mutated into populism (including competing varieties, as in the United States, Italy, and France).

One of these, ironically, and most visibly in the United States, has been the collapse of party bosses as parties opened up under pressure to organize primary elections, allow massive infusions of campaign funds into elections, and facilitate insurgent candidates running against "Washington" or wherever (e.g., Sanders 2017). In the United States this started with Jimmy Carter in 1976 but was also characteristic of the candidacies of Bill Clinton and Barack Obama. The collapse of the old parties in Italy from 1992 to 1994 with the ending of the Cold War and a massive corruption inquiry also led to open season for new parties often of an openly "personal" quality, such as Silvio Berlusconi's Forza Italia. In the United Kingdom and France, the older parties retained much of their grip down until the recent past but slowly followed the same path as that blazed in the United States. Party leaders were now elected by members and not by representatives, and they became more important than the organizations they led. Fringe parties like UKIP and the National Front gingered up the mainstream center-right parties to move further to the right on issues like the EU and immigration (e.g., Bale 2018). A figure like Trump does not come out of nowhere.

A second factor relating to polarization per se has been an increased tendency for parties, particularly on the right, to become more openly ideological. This began in the 1980s with Ronald Reagan in the United States and Margaret Thatcher in the United Kingdom, but it has been encouraged in the United States by primary elections that mobilize only the more extreme voters and by the southernization of the Republican Party, making it both more racist and more nationalist (e.g., Hopkins 2017). Elsewhere, immigration and open trade have become the bogies on which much of the rightward trend has rested. Electorates that may be still largely "moderate" are faced with parties that have become more polarized. Many of these voters then stay home on Election Day. This thereby produces a more polarized electorate. Populism feeds off this polarization. Even though Trump did antagonize parts of the Republican electorate in 2016 because of his radical rightist views on immigration and trade, with many leading figures opposing his nomination as a capture of the party by an outsider, in the end his constituency of conservative religious voters, business owners, and white nationalists proved to be a winning combination. It is worth remembering that "time for a change" sentiment was also on Trump's side after eight years of a presidency held by the other party (Jacobson 2017). The National Front in France, the League in Italy, and the Conservative Party in the United Kingdom have all also encouraged the ideological polarization of electorates on issues like immigration and the EU as a strategy in itself presuming that they then would be its beneficiaries. Concurrently, putative center-left parties such as Tony Blair's Labour Party in the United Kingdom or the US Democratic Party have been increasingly and successfully portrayed as defenders of the neoliberal political-economic status quo and thus vulnerable to the charge that they represent the "globalist elites" against which the populists can then direct their anger. These are all instances of what Dani

Rodrik (2013) calls the "inescapable trilemma of the world economy" today: in a globalized world, a country can have economic integration, the nation-state, or democratic politics but not all three at once. Something has to give.

Finally, as a consequence of polarization, the decreased legitimacy of parties and other governing institutions, and increased doubt that national governments anywhere are up to the job of protecting their populations from the rigors of the contemporary world economy, liberal democracy is itself in question across each and every one of the countries we have examined. Aldo Schiavone (2013, 91) puts the issue succinctly: "Life is fast, democracy is slow." This is not so much a critique of liberal democracy in the sense that populations are radically inadequate in processing information and making decisions (e.g., Crain 2016) or even that popular sovereignty, in the sense loved by populists, is entirely a chimera. It is more that, as Sheldon Wolin (2008, 259) wrote at the onset of the financial crisis in 2008 and looking back at the US invasion of Iraq in 2003, "at a critical moment when a volatile economy and widening class disparities require a government responsive to popular needs, government has become increasingly unresponsive; and, conversely, when an aggressive state stands most in need of being restrained, democracy provided an ineffectual check." From this viewpoint, democracy is failing to provide the joint institutional balance and sense of collective purpose that leads to its normative elevation over other forms of government. Yet, without some constitutional division of authority, abuses of arbitrary power are without checks and balances (Runciman 2018). From the elective monarchy now occupied by Emmanuel Macron in France and the failed administrative response to a bridge collapse in Italy to the ill-conceived and mismanaged Brexit process in the United Kingdom and the government by whim and Tweet of Donald Trump, elective democracy in the presence of populism continues to disappoint. Whether this inevitably leads down the path to autocracy is the question of the day.

POPULISM'S FUTURE PROSPECTS

As we see it, the problem for contemporary populism in Europe and the United States, but possibly more generally, is threefold. First of all, "the people" is an eighteenth-century ideal that probably makes little sense today as a stand-in for a national population. The tension between the centripetal forces of a shrinking globe and the centrifugal tendencies of an increasing range of political identities (class, religious, regional, sexual, and so on) makes the search for "the people" increasingly one of finding a residual and declining founding group upon which to project the concept. Across Europe, for example, representation has splintered across an array of parties not just organized on a Left-Right spectrum but also by center-periphery, inside-outside, pro- and anti-EU, and other differences. This makes forming governing coalitions harder, creates political instability, and makes for some difficulty in identifying a clear "core" group that corresponds to "the people" (e.g., Abou-Chadi and Orlowski 2016; Hall 2019). In modern nation-states "the people" is divided against itself. It is difficult to find a single enemy any more against whom to mobilize when the "nation" itself does not correspond to a people in the singular. "Populism" as a term thereby reaches its limit.

At the same time, it is increasingly clear from electoral studies that "group and partisan loyalties, not policy preferences or ideologies, are fundamental in democratic politics. . . . [H]uman life is group life" (Achen and Bartels 2016, 375). Lurking behind apparent ideological preferences, such as those often associated with US Republicans for example, on tax cuts and so on are ethnic or racial loyalties about which groups should and should not, but currently do, benefit from government largesse. The possibility of populists critical of the status quo but without animosity toward "others," such as immigrants, coming together with anti-immigrant movements—for example, La France Insoumise getting together with the French National Front—needs to be balanced against the sociological and not simply the ideological character of their differences (e.g., Formenti 2018a; Oliver and Rahn 2016; *Economist* 2018e; Terracciano 2018). Even if such movements could combine economic nationalism with cultural conservatism, they would still be left with fundamentally different conceptions of both capitalism and democracy. In particular, they have fundamentally incompatible views on the central question of an insider "us" versus an outsider "them" (e.g., Fassin 2017; 2018). More likely is that such movements can potentially remake democracy by establishing new parties that reinvigorate democratic politics by competing with one another (Müller 2018). A case can still be made for "returning" to the "golden age" of the postwar period in which incomes for ordinary people tended to increase monotonically and welfare states were embedded institutionally (Formenti 2018b). But this would mean trying to define "the people" as distinct from "the nation," yet still territorializing the state as the premier agent of the economy in a world in which the economic train has left the national station, so to speak (Sylvers 2018; Gallo and Biava 2019).

For a while, however, all of this speculation may prove to be wishful thinking. The proportion of electorates in Europe and the United States alone voting for predominantly right-wing populist candidates such as the ones we have focused on in this book is around 35 percent and shows no sign as yet of declining. It was only around 10 percent in the 1990s and early 2000s. The recent levels have not been seen since the 1930s. Although the 2007–2008 financial crisis and subsequent austerity measures can receive some credit for this expansion, the years since have seen economic growth rather than massive depression across many of the countries with increased support for populists (except for Italy). This is very different from the unremitting economic gloom of the 1930s. What is different now is the combination of the discrediting of established political parties, epistemic chaos or lack of common narratives about contemporary events brought on in particular by social media and the polarization of opinions on ideological grounds, the fragmentation of electorates, and the widespread sense of enmity toward "elites" and foreigners in equal measure. A key issue such as immigration, even though absolute numbers of immigrants and refugees are down compared to ten years ago in all the countries we have examined, needs addressing if it is not going to be continually exploited by right-wing populists (e.g., *Economist* 2018a). As Gillian Tett (2018) says, "We still haven't reached peak populism." This is why it remains important to understand its various manifestations in all their complexity. As long as a sense of crisis can be created and sustained, populists will prosper (Fisher 2019; Da Empoli 2019).

Second, populism denies the inevitability of politics as a means of managing the interface between the centripetal and centrifugal tendencies everywhere at work economically and politically. The singular sovereignty claimed by populism is a delusion (Feltri 2018; Agnew 2018a). There is no single solution at a single geographical scale to the dilemmas of modern life. At the same time, politics is messy, difficult, patronage ridden, and sometimes corrupt. There is no denying it. As a result, as Gerry Stoker (2006) says, "The real problem with politics is that it is inevitably destined to disappoint because it is about the tough process of squeezing collective decisions out of competing interests and opinions." Myriam Revault d'Allonnes (2010, 9) makes the point in a more Gallic formulation: "Democratic power is without any transcendental guarantee." As a result, populism is often about giving up on politics, not putting new energy into it. Promises such as flat taxes and guaranteed incomes can enliven election campaigns, but their introduction mandates serious discussion of redistributive consequences completely missing from populist messaging (e.g., Carlini 2018). "Trade wars are easy to win," says Donald Trump, but governing by whim and sound bite turns out to be less successful than a policy based on thorough public debate about tariff policy might have been. Different regions and localities with different industries and population-age structures face different patterns of costs and benefits. Indeed, as was also apparent with the referendum on Britain's leaving the European Union, it reduced a complex question requiring expertise about likely costs and benefits on either side to an exercise in generational identity politics.

Finally, instead of looking to a singular national populism for a reinvigoration of democracy, this is one positive lesson from the Five Star Movement in Italy: we should recognize that we are all citizens not only of nations but also of neighborhoods, cities, and regions. "They are fundamental to perpetuating democracy. Not only do they provide the means for effecting the aims of the demos and translating them into laws and policies, but they are the 'the schools of democracy' (Tocqueville) where ordinary citizens learn the practices and values of being political" (Wolin 2004, 603). It is precisely the "intermediate institutions" locally and regionally that act as buffers between people and the state and as schools of democracy that provide a check on the excesses of the often fictive "majorities" (bare pluralities, electoral college majorities, and so on) that give populism its dangerous overreliance on majoritarianism and oppositionalism rather than leading toward increased self-government (Urbinati 2015; Pettersson 2019).

We need to take political geography more seriously in this normative sense. The emphasis on the national populist leader who will sort everything out and lack of self-reflection on one's own "common sense" are exactly what reduces politics to spectatorship rather than the active struggle that Bernard Crick has identified as central to democratic politics. Crick (1992, 18) writes that politics involves "at least some tolerance of differing truths, some recognition that government is possible, indeed best conducted, amid the open canvassing of rival interests." Alas, this must be learned; it is not inherited. That does not happen over the internet or at rallies idolizing the leader. We develop it by sitting on school boards, by petitioning and demonstrating, by running for local elections, and by turning up to vote for parties and candidates who actively and responsively solicit our votes.

In the end, this means denying that there is always one "simple" people. "Democracy" has been sold as being primarily about national elections that produce representatives who then rule on behalf of "the people." A self-evident "patriotism" exercised solely in relation to the nation-state thus underwrites much of what goes for populism and its presumption of what democracy is necessarily all about (e.g., Kateb 2006; Johnston 2007). Its recent political and intellectual revival provides the "scaffolding" for much of what goes for populism (Schneider 2019). During the Cold War, successive US governments tended to equate national elections, even crookedly administered ones, with democracy. It was part of the overarching conflict of the time. But absent political norms and practices that institutionalize political responsibility, the danger is that bureaucracy and self-serving behavior on behalf of private and party interests capture those who are elected. Elections in the absence of enforced constitutional and political norms cannot produce real democracy. In the face of perceived corruption and self-serving behavior, many people then turn to the movement (and leader) that promises to turn the system on its head and to lead them to the Promised Land. Democracy then degenerates into authoritarianism. If real democracy is the goal, a different recipe is required. Rather, as Pierre Rosanvallon (2011) has argued, there should be a "polyphony," with the people as an electorate only one among several "peoples" involved in acts of collective self-rule: from juries and expressions of popular opinion to active involvement in various social communities. Populism, of course, will have none of this. In Nadia Urbinati's (2013, 147) prescient words,

> Populism . . . prizes polarization more than pluralism. Indeed, it uses political conflict and electoral procedures for the sake of an overwhelming victory and as instrumental to the mobilization of one part of the people against the other, in view of making the winner the catalyst of the many fractions or parties, whose endless litigiousness—it is thought—weakens social unity. Populism holds the multi-party system in great suspicion; hence, it is a denial of electoral representation, which is the main institution or set of institutions through which procedural democracy is implemented. It depicts and theorizes democracy as hegemonic conflict for the domination of the popular sentiment and opinion over its components. In Robert Dahl's words, it gives the demos "total" and "final control" over the political order, which means empirically the control of the majority.

References

Abou-Chadi, T., and Orlowski, M. 2016. "Moderate as necessary: the role of electoral competitiveness and party size in explaining parties' policy shifts," *Journal of Politics*, 78: 868–81.

Abromeit, J. 2017. "A critical review of recent literature on populism," *Politics and Governance*, 5: 177–86.

Acharya, A., et al. 2018. *Deep Roots: How Slavery Still Shapes Southern Politics*, Princeton NJ: Princeton University Press.

Achen, C. H., and Bartels, L. 2016. *Democracy for Realists: Why Elections Do Not Produce Responsive Governments*, Princeton NJ: Princeton University Press.

Agnew, H. 2017. "Fillon and Le Pen criticize French media over coverage," *Financial Times*, 23 March.

Agnew, J. 1987. *Place and Politics: The Geographical Mediation of State and Society*, London: Allen and Unwin.

———. 2002. *Place and Politics in Modern Italy*, Chicago: University of Chicago Press.

———. 2005. *Hegemony: The New Shape of Global Power*, Philadelphia: Temple University Press.

———. 2011. "The big seducer: Berlusconi's image and home and abroad and the future of Italian politics," *California Italian Studies*, 2.

———. 2017. "Working the margins: the geopolitical marking of Italian national identity," *Carte Italiane*, 2, 11, https://escholarship.org/uc/item/6vv5w0jz#main.

———. 2018a. *Globalization and Sovereignty: Beyond the Territorial Trap*, 2nd edition, Lanham MD: Rowman & Littlefield.

———. 2018b. "Too many Scotlands? Place, the SNP and the future of nationalist mobilization," *Scottish Geographical Journal*, 134: 5–23.

Agnew, J., and Shin, M. 2016. "Electoral dramaturgy: insights from Italian politics about Donald Trump's 2015–16 campaign strategy . . . and beyond," *Southeastern Geographer*, 56: 265–72.

———. 2017. "Spatializing populism: taking politics to the people in Italy," *Annals of the American Association of Geographers*, 107: 915–33.

Albertazzi, D., et al. 2018. "'No regionalism please, we are *Leghisti*!' The transformation of the Italian Lega Nord under the leadership of Matteo Salvini," *Regional and Federal Studies*, 28: 645–71.

Alduy, C. 2015. "Mots, mythes, medias. Mutations et invariants du discours frontiste," in S. Crépon et al. (eds.) *Les faux-semblants du Front National: Sociologie d'un parti politique*, Paris: Presses de Sciences Po, pp. 247–68.

Alessandretti, L., et al. 2018. "Evidence for a conserved quantity in human mobility," *Nature Human Behavior*, 2, https://www.nature.com/articles/s41562-018-0364-x.

Almagisti, M. 2016. *Una democrazia possibile. Politica e territorio nell'Italia contemporanea*, Rome: Carocci.

Amengay, A., and Stockemer, D. 2018. "The radical Right in western Europe: a meta-analysis of structural factors," *Political Studies Review*, 17, 1, https://journals.sagepub.com/doi/abs/10.1177/1478929918777975.

Analisi Politica. 2018. "Il vero perdente," *L'Indipendenza Nuova*, http://www.lindipendenza-nuova.com/analisipolitica-it-se-il-vero-perdente-delle-elezioni-e-il-centrodestra.

Anderson, P. 2017. "The French spring," *New Left Review*, 105: 5–27.

Angelos, J. 2017. "The prophet of Germany's new Right," *New York Times*, 10 October.

Anselmi, M. 2017. *Populismo. Teorie e problemi*, Milan: Mondadori.

Antonucci, L., et al. 2017. "The malaise of the squeezed middle: challenging the narrative of the 'left behind' Brexiter," *Competition and Change*, 21: 211–29.

Applebaum, A. 2019. "Is this the end of political parties?" *Washington Post*, 25 February.

Aslanidis, P. 2015. "Is populism an ideology? A refutation and a new perspective," *Political Studies*, 63: 1–17.

Badger, E. 2018. "The outsize hold of the word 'welfare' on the public imagination," *Washington Post*, 6 August.

Badiou, A., et al. 2016. *What Is a People?* New York: Columbia University Press.

Badouard, R. 2018. "Internet et la brutalisation du débat public," *La Vie des Idees*, 6 November.

Bale, T. 2018. "Who leads and who follows? The symbiotic relationship between UKIP and the Conservatives—and populism and Euroscepticism," *Politics*, 38: 263–77.

Barber, B. 2004. *Fear's Empire: War, Terrorism, and Democracy*, New York: Norton.

Baron, Z. 2018. "The Fresno Bee and the war on local news," *GQ*, 28 December.

Beard, M., et al. 2018. "Repeating history: to what extent is it helpful or accurate to describe President Trump as a fascist?" *Times Literary Supplement*, 13 November.

Beauchamp, Z. 2018. "A new study reveals the real reason Obama voters switched to Trump. Hint: it has to do with race," *Vox*, 16 October.

Becker, S. O., et al. 2016. *Who Voted for Brexit? A Comprehensive District-Level Analysis*, Warwick: University of Warwick, Department of Economics, Centre for Competitive Advantage in the Global Economy.

Belpolito, M. 2009. *Il corpo del capo*, Parma: Ugo Guanda.

———. 2012. *La canottiera di Bossi*, Parma: Ugo Guanda.

Benkler, Y., et al. 2018. *Network Propaganda: Manipulation, Disinformation, and Radicalization in American Politics*, New York: Oxford University Press.

Bennett, D. H. 1988. *The Party of Fear: The American Far Right from Nativism to the Militia Movement*, Chapel Hill: University of North Carolina Press.

Benson, E. 2018. "What you lose when you lose local news," *High Country News*, 50, 24 December.

Berezin, M. 2009. *Illiberal Politics in Neoliberal Times: Culture, Security and Populism in the New Europe*, New York: Cambridge University Press.

Berger, S. 2017. "Populism and the failures of representation," *French Politics, Culture and Society*, 36: 21–31.

Berry, M. 2016. "Understanding the role of the mass media in the EU referendum," *LSE Referendum Analysis Project*, 12 August.

Betz, H.-G. 2013. *The New National Front: Still a Master Case?* Working Paper 30, Augsburg: Recode.

———. 2018. "Everything that is wrong is the fault of '68: regaining cultural hegemony by trashing the Left," *Open Democracy*, 4 August, https://www.opendemocracy.net/can-europe-make-it/hans-georg-betz/everything-that-is-wrong-is-fault-of-68-regaining-cultural-hegemony-by-trashing-left.

Bevilacqua, P. 2019. "La resustibile ascesa della Lega nel Sud," *Il Manifesto*, 22 February.

Bickerton, C. J., and Accetti, C. I. 2018. "'Techno-populism' as a new party family: the case of the Five Star Movement and Podemos," *Contemporary Italian Politics*, 10: 132–50.

Biorcio, R., and Natale, P. 2013. *Politica a 5 Stelle. Idee, storia e strategie del movimento di Grillo*, Milan: Feltrinelli.

Blais, A. 2010. "Political participation," in L. Le Duc et al. (eds.) *Comparing Democracies: Elections and Voting in the Twenty-First Century*. London: Sage, pp. 165–83.

Blais, A., and Rubenson, D. 2013. "The source of turnout decline: new values or new contexts?" *Comparative Political Studies*, 46: 95–117.

Blyth, M. 2013. *Austerity: The History of a Dangerous Idea*, New York: Oxford University Press.

Bobba, G., and Legnante, G. 2016. "Italy: a breeding ground for populist political communication," in T. Aalborg et al. (eds.) *Populist Political Communication in Europe*, London: Routledge, pp. 222–34.

Bobbio, N. 1996. *Left and Right: The Significance of a Political Distinction*, Cambridge: Polity.

Bonikowski, B. 2017. "Ethno-nationalist populism and the mobilization of collective resentment," *British Journal of Sociology*, 68: S181–S213.

Bonomi, A. 2008. *Il rancore. Alle radici del malessere del Nord*, Milan: Feltrinelli.

Bordignan, F. 2017. "In and out: Emmanuel Macron's anti-populist populism," *EURROP Blog*, London School of Economics, 28 April, https://blogs.lse.ac.uk/europpblog/2017/04/28/macron-anti-populist-populism.

Boxell, L., et al. 2017. "Greater internet use is not associated with faster growth in political polarization among US demographic groups," *Proceedings of the National Academy of Sciences*, 114: 10612–17.

Boyadjian, J. 2015. "Les usages Frontistes du web," in S. Crépon et al. (eds.) *Les faux-semblants du Front National. Sociologie d'un parti politique*, Paris: Presses de Sciences Po, pp. 141–59.

Brandolini, A. L. 2009 [1492–1494]. *Republics and Kingdoms Compared*, Cambridge MA: Harvard University Press, trans by James Hankins.

Brubaker, R. 2017. "Why populism?" *Theory and Society*, 46: 357–85.

Brunazzo, M., and Gilbert, M. 2017. "Insurgents against Brussels: Euroscepticism and the right-wing populist turn of the Lega Nord since 2013," *Journal of Modern Italian Studies*, 22: 624–41.

Buck, T. 2017. "No right turn for Spanish politics," *Financial Times*, 17 January.

Buckledee, S. 2018. *The Language of Brexit: How Britain Talked Its Way Out of the European Union*, London: Bloomsbury.

Burn-Murdoch, J., et al. 2017. "French election results: Macron's victory in charts," *Financial Times*, 8 May.

Caciagli, M. 2010. *Fra Arlecchino e Pulcinella. La cultura politica degli italiani nell'Eta di Berlusconi*, Trapani: Di Girolamo.

Cagé, J. 2018. *Le prix de la démocratie*, Paris: Fayard.

Calise, M. 2016. *La democrazia del Leader*, Rome-Bari, Italy: Laterza.

Campbell, J. E. 2016. *Polarized: Making Sense of a Divided America*, Princeton NJ: Princeton University Press.

Camus, J.-Y. 1997. *Le Front National, histoire et analyses*, Paris: Laurens.

Camus, J.-Y., and Lebourg, N. 2017. *Far-Right Politics in Europe*, Cambridge MA: Belknap Press of Harvard University Press.

Canestrari, M., and Biondo, N. 2018. *Supernova: Com'è stato ucciso il MoVimento 5 Stelle*, Milan: StreetLib.

Canovan, M. 2002. "Taking politics to the people: populism as the ideology of democracy," in Y. Meny and Y. Surel (eds.) *Democracies and the Populist Challenge*, Basingstoke, UK: Palgrave, pp. 15–32.

Caramani, D. 2017. "Will vs. reason: the populist and technocratic forms of political representation and their critique of party government," *American Political Science Review*, 111: 54–67.

Carlini, R. 2018. "Il populismo? É roba da ricchi. La diagnosi di Branko Milanovic," *L'Espresso*, 12 July.

Cartocci, R. 2007. *Mappe del tesoro. Atlante del capital sociale in Italia*, Bologna: Il Mulino.

———. 2011. *Geografia dell'Italia cattolica*, Bologna: Il Mulino.

Caruso, L. 2015. "Il Movimento 5 Stelle e la fine della politica," *Rassegna Italiana di Sociologia*, 56: 315–40.

Casaleggio, G., and Grillo, B. 2011. *Siamo in guerra: Per una nuova politica*, Milan: Chiarelettere.

Cavallaro, M., et al. 2018. *Una nuova Italia. Dalla communicazione ai risultati. Un'analisi delle elezioni del 4 marzo*, Rome: Castelvecchi.

Chan, J. B. 2016. "Portrait of a Trump supporter," *Reveal: The Center for Investigative Reporting*, 1 February, http://revealnews.org/author/juliabchan.

Charlot, M. 1986. "L'emergence du Front National," *Revue Française de Science Politique*, 36: 30–45.

Chassany, A.-S. 2017. "The French town that shows how Marine Le Pen could win," *Financial Times*, 10 April.

Chou, M., et al. 2016. "Elections as theater," *PS: Political Science and Politics*, 49, 1: 43–47.

Clarke, H. D., et al. 2017. *Brexit: Why Britain Voted to Leave the European Union*, Cambridge: Cambridge University Press.

Cohen, R. 2017. "France in the end of days," *New York Times*, 14 April.

Cohn, N. 2015. "Donald Trump's strongest supporters: a certain kind of Democrat," *New York Times*, 31 December.

Confessore, N., and Yourish, K. 2016. "$2 Billion Worth of Free Media for Donald Trump," *New York Times*, 16 March.

Connolly, W. E. 2017. *Aspirational Fascism: The Struggle for Multifaceted Democracy under Trump*. Minneapolis: University of Minnesota Press.

Coppola, P. (ed.). 1997. *Geografia politica delle regioni italiane*, Turin: Einaudi.

Corbetta, P., and Gualmini, E. (eds.). 2013. *Il partito di Grillo*. Bologna: Il Mulino.

Cowie, J. 2010. *Stayin' Alive: The 1970s and the Last Days of the Working Class*, New York: New Press.

Cozzo, P. 2011. "Un paese all'ombra del campanile. Immagini del parocco nell'Italia unita," in S. Soldani (ed.) *L'Italia alla prova dell'Unita*, Milan: Franco Angeli, pp. 65–85.

Crain, C. 2016. "The case against democracy: if most voters are uninformed, who should make decisions about the public's welfare?" *New Yorker*, 7 November.

Cramer, K. J. 2016. *The Politics of Resentment: Rural Consciousness in Wisconsin and the Rise of Scott Walker*, Chicago: University of Chicago Press.

Crehan, K. 2016. *Gramsci's Common Sense: Inequality and Its Narratives*, Durham NC: Duke University Press.

Crépon, S. 2015. "La politique des moeurs au Front National," in S. Crépon et al. (eds.) *Les faux-semblants du Front National. Sociologie d'un parti politique*, Paris: Presses de Sciences Po, pp. 185–205.

Crick, B. 1994. *In Defence of Politics*, 4th edition, Chicago: University of Chicago Press.

Crouch, C. 2011. *The Strange Non-death of Neo-liberalism*, Cambridge: Polity.

Da Empoli, G. 2019. *Les ingénieurs du chaos*. Paris: JC Làttes.

D'Alimonte, R. 2018. "Contraddizioni di successo in casa Lega," *Il Sole 24 Ore*, 15 November.

D'Eramo, M. 2013. "Populism and the new oligarchy," *New Left Review*, 82: 5–28.

———. 2018. "Rise and fall of the daily paper," *New Left Review*, 111: 113–27.

Dal Lago, A. 2017. *Populismo digitale. La crisi, la rete e la nuova destra*, Milan: Cortina.

Darr, J. P., et al. 2018. "Newspaper closures polarize voting behavior," *Journal of Communication*, 68: 1007–28.

Davidson, T., and Berezin, M. 2018. "Britain First and the UK Independence Party: social media and movement-party dynamics," *Mobilization*, 23: 485–510.

Davies, P. J. 1986. "The drama of the campaign: theatre, production and style in American elections," *Parliamentary Affairs*, 39: 98–114.

Davies, W. 2018a. *Nervous States: How Feeling Took Over the World*, London: Jonathan Cape.

———. 2018b. "What are they after? The Tory Brexiteers," *London Review of Books*, 8 March: 3–5.

Debord, G. 1983. *Society of the Spectacle*, Detroit: Black and Red.

Dennison, J., and Carl, N. 2016. "The ultimate causes of Brexit: history, culture, and geography," *British Politics and Policy* (blog). London School of Economics, http://blogs.lse.ac.uk/politicsandpolicy/explaining-brexit.

Dézé, A. 2015. "La construction médiatique de la 'nouveauté' FN," in S. Crépon et al. (eds.) *Les faux-semblants du Front National. Sociologie d'un parti politique*, Paris: Presses de Sciences Po, pp. 455–504.

Diamanti, I. 2003. *Bianco, rosso, verde . . . e azzurro. Mappe e colori dell'Italia politica*, Bologna: Il Mulino.

———. 2011. "L'anima romana della Lega," *La Repubblica*, 7 February, 1.

———. 2012a. *Gramsci, Manzoni e mia suocera. Quando gli esperti sbagliano le previsioni politiche*, Bologna: Il Mulino.

———. 2012b "La dissociazione tra politica e democrazia rappresentiva," *La Repubblica*, 20 August.

———. 2012c. "L'autobus di Grillo nel paese della politica che-non-c'è," *La Repubblica*, 13 July: 2.

——. 2014. "The 5 Star Movement: a political laboratory," *Contemporary Italian Politics*, 6: 4–15.

——. 2016. "Grillo e Salvini. Antipolitici e contro il governo, nasce il Carroccio a 5 Stelle," *La Repubblica*, 9 June.

Diamanti, I., and Lazar, M. 2018. *Popolocrazia. La metamorfosi delle nostre democrazie*, Bari-Rome: Laterza.

Diamond, P. 2018. "Brexit and the Labour Party," in P. Diamond et al. (eds.) *Routledge Handbook of the Politics of Brexit*, London: Routledge, pp. 119–32.

Dionne, E. J., Jr. 2016. "How Dixie rules the GOP," *Washington Post*, 28 February.

Dittrich, P.-J. 2017. *Social Networks and Populism in the EU: Four Things You Should Know*, Policy Paper 192, Berlin: Jacques Delors Institute, 19 April.

Dochuk, D. 2006. "Revival on the right: making sense of the conservative movement in Post–World War II American history," *History Compass*, 4, 5: 975–99.

Dorling, D. 2016. "Brexit: the decision of a divided country," *British Medical Journal*, 6 July: 354.

Dorling, D., and Tomlinson, S. 2019. *Rule Britannia: Brexit and the End of Empire*, London: Biteback.

Dunbar, R. I. M. 2016. "Do online social media cut through the constraints that limit the size of offline social networks?" *Royal Society Open Science*, 3: 1–9.

Dunbar, R. I. M., et al. 2015. "The structure of social networks mirrors those in the offline world," *Social Networks*, 43: 39–47.

Eatwell, R., and Goodwin, M. 2018. *National Populism: The Revolt against Liberal Democracy*, London: Pelican.

Eco, U. 1995. "Ur-Fascism," *New York Review of Books*, 22 June.

Economist. 2012. "Wordy goods: Americans are exchanging ever more words," *Economist*, 27 August: 18.

——. 2017a. "Brexit: a solution in search of a problem," *Economist*, 3 April.

——. 2017b. "Fractured France: an unprecedented election, with unprecedented risks," *Economist*, 4 March.

——. 2017c. "It's not the economy, stupid: European voters no longer care much about growth," *Economist*, 12 April.

——. 2017d. "Millennials across the rich world are failing to vote," *Economist*, 4 February.

——. 2018a. "A way forward on immigration," *Economist*, 25 August.

——. 2018b. "Back from a brief 'kip': a populist party bounces back in an altogether nastier form," *Economist*, 21 July: 44.

——. 2018c. "The safety net: working for it," *Economist*, 20 January.

——. 2018d. "The Trump cult: Republican voters love the president for whom he hates," *Economist*, 1 November.

——. 2018e. "What the Far Left and Right have in common, in Germany and elsewhere," *Economist*, 9 August.

——. 2018f. "What populists and anti-vaxxers have in common," *Economist*, 15 August.

Eltchaninoff, M. 2018. *Inside the Mind of Marine Le Pen*, London: Hurst, trans. by James Ferguson.

Enten, H. 2016. "Americans' distaste for both Trump and Clinton is record-breaking," *FiveThirtyEight*, 2 November, https://fivethirtyeight.com/features/americans-distaste-for-both-trump-and-clinton-is-record-breaking.

——. 2017. "Macron won, but the polls were way off," *FiveThirtyEight*, 8 May.

Eribon, D. 2013. *Returning to Reims*, Cambridge MA: Semiotexte, trans. by Michael Lucey.

Errejón, I., and Mouffe, C. 2016. *PODEMOS: In the Name of the People*, London: Lawrence and Wishart.

Essletzbichler, J., et al. 2018. "The victims of neoliberal globalization and the rise of the populist vote: a comparative analysis of three recent electoral decisions," *Cambridge Journal of Regions, Economy and Society*, 11: 73–94.

Evans, R. J. 2018. "Conspiracy theories and anti-Semitism," *Conspiracy Theories* (blog), Conspiracy and Democracy, 22 June, http://conspiracyanddemocracy.org/blog/conspiracy-theories.

Fabbri, M., and Diani, M. 2015. "Social movement campaigns from global justice movements to Movimento Cinque Stelle," in A. Mammone et al. (eds.) *The Routledge Handbook of Contemporary Italy*, London: Routledge, pp. 225–36.

Farinelli, A., and Massetti, E. 2015. "Inexperienced, leftists, and grassroots democrats: a profile of the Five Star Movement's MPs," *Contemporary Italian Politics*, 7: 213–31.

Farrell, J., and Goldsmith, P. 2017. *How to Lose a Referendum: The Definitive Story of Why the UK Voted for Brexit*, London: Biteback.

Fassin, E. 2017. *Populisme: le grand ressentiment*, Paris: Textuel.

———. 2018. *Populism Left and Right*, Chicago: University of Chicago Press.

Feldman, G. 2013. *The Irony of the Solid South: Democrats, Republicans, and Race, 1865–1944*, Tuscaloosa: University of Alabama Press.

Feltri, S. 2018. *Populismo sovrano*, Turin: Einaudi.

Finchelstein, F. 2017. *From Fascism to Populism in History*, Berkeley: University of California Press.

Fisher, M. 2019. "After a rocky 2018, populism is down but not out in the West," *New York Times*, 5 January.

Flinders, M. 2018. "The (anti-) politics of Brexit," in P. Diamond et al. (eds.) *Routledge Handbook of the Politics of Brexit*, London: Routledge, pp. 179–83.

Flores d'Arcais, P. 2016. "Quando capirà la 'sinistra' d'establishment che Renzi è l'apoteosi del Berlusconismo?" *MicroMega*, 22 June.

Ford, R., and Goodwin, M. 2014. *Revolt on the Right: Explaining Public Support for the Radical Right in Britain*, London: Routledge.

———. 2017. "Britain after Brexit: a nation divided," *Journal of Democracy*, 28: 17–30.

Foreign Affairs. 2016. "France's next revolution? A conversation with Marine Le Pen," *Foreign Affairs*, 95 (November/December): 2–8.

Formenti, C. 2018a. "Populismo vs establishment, la diga é crollata," *MicroMega*, 7 March.

———. 2018b. "Quando sovranismo fa rima con socialismo," *MicroMega*, 8 November.

Fraga, B. L. 2018. *The Turnout Gap: Race, Ethnicity, and Political Inequality in a Diversifying America*, New York: Cambridge University Press.

Frank, T. 2009. *The Wrecking Crew: How Conservatives Ruined Government, Enriched Themselves, and Beggared the Nation*, New York: Holt.

Frankfurt, H. G. 2005. *On Bullshit*, Princeton NJ: Princeton University Press.

Franzosi, P., et al. 2015. "Populism and Euroscepticism in the Italian Five Star Movement," *International Spectator*, 50: 109–24.

Fraser, S., and Freeman, J. B. 2010. "In the rearview mirror: history's mad hatters, the strange career of Tea Party populism," *New Labor Forum*, 19, 3: 75–81.

Freeden, M. 2017. "After the Brexit referendum: revisiting populism as ideology," *Journal of Political Ideologies*, 22: 1–11.

Gallo, E., and Biava, G. 2019. "Towards right and left 2.0?" *Open Democracy*, 7 January.

Galston, W. A., and Hendrickson, C. 2016. "How millennials voted this election," Brookings Institution, 21 November, https://www.brookings.edu/blog/fixgov/2016/11/21/how-millennials-voted.

Ganesh, J. 2018. "Extremism rises as experience of its consequences fades," *Financial Times*, 5 December.

Garrahan, M. 2016. "Political advertising: an industry in peril. US election and Brexit vote have exposed waning power of TV ad campaigns and billboards," *Financial Times*, 28 October.

Gerbaudo, P. 2018. "Digital parties on the rise: a mass politics for the era of platforms," *Open Democracy*, 13 December.

Ghitza, Y., and Gelman, A. 2014. "The Great Society, Reagan's Revolution, and generations of presidential voting," working paper, Department of Statistics, Columbia University.

Gilli, F., et al. 2017. "Élections 2017: pourquoi l'opposition métropoles-périphéries n'est pas la clé," *Terra Nova*, 13 October.

Glencross, A. 2016. *Why the UK Voted for Brexit: David Cameron's Great Miscalculation*, London: Palgrave Macmillan.

Goffman, E. 1959. *The Presentation of Self in Everyday Life*, New York: Doubleday.

Goodhart, D. 2017. *The Road to Somewhere: The Populist Revolt and the Future of Politics*, London: Hurst.

Goodliffe, G. 2012. *The Resurgence of the Radical Right in France: From Boulangisme to the Front National*, New York: Cambridge University Press.

Goodwin, M., and Heath, O. 2016. "The 2016 referendum, Brexit and the left behind: an aggregate-level analysis of the result," *Political Quarterly*, 87: 323–34.

Gordon, I. R. 2018. "In what sense left behind by globalization? Looking for a less reductionist geography of the populist surge in Europe," *Cambridge Journal of Regions, Economy and Society*, 11: 95–113.

Gosling, T. 2018. "The nationalist internationale is crumbling," *Foreign Policy*, 20 July.

Gougou, F. 2015. "Les ouvriers et le vote Front National: les logiques d'un réalignement électoral," in S. Crépon et al. (eds.) *Les faux-semblants du Front National: Sociologie d'un parti politique*, Paris: Presses de Sciences Po, pp. 323–43.

Graphical Insight. 2018. "British Politics," *Financial Times*, 31 December: 10.

Grattan, L. 2016. *Populism's Power: Radical Grassroots Democracy in America*, New York: Oxford University Press.

Grčar, M., et al. 2017. "Stance and influence of Twitter users regarding the Brexit referendum," *Computational Social Networks*, 4: 6.

Green, E. 2017. "It was cultural anxiety that drove white, working-class voters to Trump," *Atlantic*, 9 May.

Grossman, M., and Hopkins, D. A. 2016. *Asymmetric Politics: Ideological Republicans and Group Interest Democrats*, New York: Oxford University Press.

Guess, A., et al. 2019. "Who was more likely to share fake news in 2016? Seniors," *Washington Post*, 9 January.

Guilluy, C. 2014. *La France périphérique. Comment on a sacrifié les classes populaires*, Paris: Flammarion.

Guiso, L., et al. 2017. "Populism supply and demand," working paper, EPRC, Bocconi University, Milan.

Gundle, S. 2010. "Berlusconi, il sesso e il mancato scandalo mediatico," in M. Giuliani and E. Jones (eds.) *Politica in Italia: Edizione 2010*, Bologna: Il Mulino, pp. 73–93.

Hall, B. 2018. "Macron v Salvini: the battle over Europe's political future," *Financial Times*, 27 December.

———. 2019. "Europe shaken by splintering of traditional political systems," *Financial Times*, 11 January.

Hall Jamieson, K. 2018. *Cyberwar: How Russian Hackers and Trolls Helped Elect a President. What We Don't, Can't, and Do Know*, New York: Oxford University Press.

Hall Jamieson, K., and Taussig, D. 2017. "Disruption, demonization, deliverance, and norm destruction: the rhetorical signature of Donald J. Trump," *Political Science Quarterly*, 132: 619–50.

Halpern, S. 2018a. "How he used Facebook to win," *New York Review of Books*, 8 June.

———. 2018b. "How Republicans became anti-choice," *New York Review of Books*, 8 November.

Harding, L. 2017. *Collusion: Secret Meetings, Dirty Money, and How Russia Helped Donald Trump Win*, New York: Vintage.

Haskell, T. L. 1998. *Objectivity Is Not Neutrality: Explanatory Schemes in History*, Baltimore: Johns Hopkins University Press.

Heathcote, E. 2016. "How Donald Trump's towers explain his politics," *Financial Times*, 17 February.

Heim, J. 2019. "Jerry Falwell Jr. 'can't imagine Trump doing anything that isn't good for the country,'" *Washington Post*, 1 January.

Hendrickson, C., and Galston, W. A. 2017. "Why are populists winning online? Social media reinforces their anti-establishment message," *TechTank* (blog), Brookings Institution, 28 April, https://www.brookings.edu/blog/techtank/2017/04/28/why-are-populists-winning-online-social-media-reinforces-their-anti-establishment-message.

Hobolt, S. B. 2016. "The Brexit vote: a divided nation, a divided continent," *Journal of European Public Policy*, 23: 1259–77.

Hochschild, A. R. 2016. *Strangers in Their Own Land: Anger and Mourning on the American Right*, New York: New Press.

Hopkins, D. A. 2017. *Red Fighting Blue: How Geography and Electoral Rules Polarize American Politics*, Cambridge: Cambridge University Press.

Horowitz, J. 2019. "Matteo Salvini likes Nutella and kittens. It's all part of a media strategy," *New York Times*, 4 January.

Howarth, D. 2015. *Ernesto Laclau: Post-Marxism, Populism and Critique*, London: Routledge.

Hubé, N., and Truan, N. 2017. "France: the reluctance to use the word *populism* as a concept," in T. Aalborg et al. (eds.) *Populist Political Communication in Europe*, London: Routledge, pp. 181–94.

Huc, A. 2017. *Les deux corps du Front National. Étude contextualisée du vote Front National dans quatre communes ouvrières du Pas-de-Calais et des Bouches-du-Rhône*, doctoral thesis in political science, University of Montpellier.

Hurst, A. 2018. "Escape from the Trump cult," *New Republic*, 13 December.

Inskeep, S. 2016. "Donald Trump's secret? Channeling Andrew Jackson," *New York Times*, 17 February.

Ivaldi, G. 2012. "Front National: une election presidentiélle de reconquête," *Revue Politique et Parlementaire*, 1063–64: 101–19.

———. 2015. "Du néolibéralisme au social-populisme? La transformation du programme économique du Front National (1986–2012)," in S. Crépon et al. (eds.) *Les faux-semblants du Front National: Sociologie d'un parti politique*, Paris: Presses de Sciences Po, pp. 163–83.

———. 2018. "Crowding the market: the dynamics of populist and mainstream competition in the 2017 French presidential elections," Birmingham UK: Workshop at Aston University, 22–23 January, unpublished paper.

Ivaldi, G., et al. 2017. "Varieties of populism across a left-right spectrum: the case of the Front National, the Northern League, Podemos, and Five Star Movement," *Swiss Political Science Review*, 23, 4: 354–76.

Jackson, D., et al. (eds.). 2016. *EU Referendum Analysis 2016: Media, Voters, and the Campaign*, Bournemouth, UK: Bournemouth University CSJCC.

Jacobson, G. C. 2017. "The triumph of polarized partisanship in 2016: Donald Trump's improbable victory," *Political Science Quarterly*, 132: 9–41.

Jardina, A. 2019. *White Identity Politics*, New York: Cambridge University Press.

Johnson, B., and Farrell, N. 2003. "Forza Berlusconi!" *Spectator*, 6 September, 12–13.

Johnston, R., et al. 2016. "Spatial polarization of presidential voting in the United States, 1992–2012: the 'Big Sort' revisited," *Annals of the American Association of Geographers*, 106: 1047–1062.

———. 2018. "Geographies of Brexit and its aftermath: voting in England at the 2016 referendum and the 2017 general election," *Space and Polity*, 22, 2: 162–87.

Johnston, S. 2007. *The Truth about Patriotism*, Durham NC: Duke University Press.

Jones, R. P. 2016. *The End of White Christian America*, New York: Simon and Schuster.

Judis, J. B. 2016. *The Populist Explosion: How the Great Recession Transformed American and European Politics*, New York: Columbia University Press.

Kalia, A., et al. 2018. "Revealed: how Italy's populists used Facebook to win power," *Guardian*, 17 December.

Kateb, G. 2006. *Patriotism and Other Mistakes*, New Haven CT: Yale University Press.

Kauffmann, G. 2016. *Le nouveau FN. Les vieux habits du populisme*, Paris: Seuil.

Keefe, P. R. 2019. "How Mark Burnett resurrected Donald Trump as an icon of American success," *New Yorker*, 7 January.

Kelley, J. 2018. "The goal of the 'fake news' canard isn't propaganda—it's epistemic chaos," *Pacific Standard*, 3 April.

King, A. A., and Anderson, D. F. 1971. "Nixon, Agnew, and the 'silent majority': a case study in the rhetoric of polarization," *Western Speech*, 35: 243–55.

King, C. 2017. "Hitler usually wins: on the return of individual authoritarianism," *Times Literary Supplement*, 15 December: 26–27.

Knight, P. (ed.). 2002. *Conspiracy Nation: The Politics of Paranoia in Postwar America*, New York: New York University Press.

Kornacki, S. 2018. *The Red and the Blue: The 1990s and the Birth of Political Tribalism*, New York: Ecco.

Kuruvilla, C. 2018. "New study reveals white evangelicals' troubling views on race and immigration," *Huffington Post*, 5 November.

Kuziemko, I., and Washington, E. 2018. "Why did the Democrats lose the South? Bringing new data to an old debate," *American Economic Review*, 108, 10: 2830–67.

Lanchester, J. 2018. "After the fall," *London Review of Books*, 5 July: 3–8.

Lazare, D. 1996. *The Frozen Republic: How the Constitution Is Paralyzing Democracy*, New York: Harcourt Brace.

Le Bras, H. 2015. *Le pari du FN*, Paris: Autrement.

Legorano, G. 2019. "Pledges made by Italy's populist government come up against economic reality," *Wall Street Journal*, 8 January.

Lengyel, B., et al. 2015. "Geographies of an online social network," *PLoS One*, 10, 9: 11 September.

Lepore, J. 2010. "Tea and sympathy: who owns the American Revolution?" *New Yorker*, 3 May.

———. 2011. *The Whites of Their Eyes: The Tea Party's Revolution and the Battle over American History*, Princeton NJ: Princeton University Press.

———. 2016. "The party crashers: is the new populism about the message or the medium?" *New Yorker*, 22 February.

Levitsky, S., and Ziblatt, D. 2018. *How Democracies Die*, New York: Crown.

Lévy, J. (ed.). 2017. *Atlas politique de la France*, Paris: Autrement.

Lewis, M. 2018. *The Fifth Risk: Undoing Democracy*, London: Allen Lane.

Lichtman, A. J. 2018. *The Embattled Vote in America: From the Founding to the Present*, Cambridge MA: Harvard University Press.

Lilla, M. 2018. "Two roads for the new French Right," *New York Review of Books*, 20 December.

Liogier, R. 2017. "France's neither-nor election," *New York Times*, 12 April.

Loucaides, D. 2019. "Careful what you wish for: the inside story of Italy's Five Star Movement and the cyberguru who dreamed it up," *Wired*, 27, 3: 80–95.

Louis, E. 2017. *The End of Eddy: A Novel*, New York: Farrar, Straus and Giroux, trans. by Michael Lucey.

Luce, E. 2016. "Trump's hostile takeover gains pace," *Financial Times*, 21 February.

Lynch, C. 2018. "Why is it so hard to vote in America?" *Foreign Policy*, 5 November, https://foreignpolicy.com/2018/11/05/why-is-it-so-hard-to-vote-in-america.

Mair, P. 2013. *Ruling the Void: The Hollowing-Out of Western Democracy*, London: Verso.

Mancosu, M. 2014. "Geographical context, interest in politics and voting behavior: the case of the Northern League in Italy," *Contemporary Italian Politics*, 6: 131–46.

Mancosu, M., and Landini, R. 2018. "The 'new' League success in the red belt and its post-fascist inheritance: evidence from the 2018 elections," unpublished paper, Collegio Carlo Alberto.

Mann, T. E., and Ornstein, N. J. 2012. *It's Even Worse Than It Looks: How the American Constitutional System Collided with the New Politics of Extremism*, New York: Basic Books.

Manucci, L., and Amsler, M. 2018. "Where the wind blows: Five Star Movement's populism, direct democracy and ideological flexibility," *Italian Political Science Review*, 48: 109–132.

Marchand-Lagier, C. 2017. *Le vote FN. Pour une sociologie localisée des électorats frontistes*, Louvain-la-Neuve: De Boeck.

Marchetti, L. 2019. "Il potere carismatico del corpo del capo," *Il Manifesto*, 7 January.

Massey, D. S. 2012. "Location matters," *Science*, 336: 35–36.

Matonti, F. 2013. "Paradoxes du stigmata: les représentations médiatiques de Marine Le Pen," *Genre, Sexualité et Société*, 2: 10–14.

Mayer, J. 2016. *Dark Money: The Hidden History of the Billionaires behind the Rise of the Radical Right*, New York: Anchor.

———. 2019. "Trump TV: Fox News has always been partisan. But has it become propaganda?" *New Yorker*, 11 March: 40–53.

McAuley, J. 2019a. "How to write about the Right: an exchange," *New York Review of Books*, 17 January.

———. 2019b. "Low visibility," *New York Review of Books*, 21 March.

McKenzie, L. 2017. "'It's not ideal': reconsidering 'anger' and 'apathy' in the Brexit vote among an invisible working class," *Competition and Change*, 21: 199–210.

McQuarrie, M. 2017. "The revolt of the Rust Belt: place and politics in the age of anger," *British Journal of Sociology*, 68, S1: S120–52.

Mellnik, T., et al. 2018. "The geography of voting—and not voting," *Washington Post*, 23 October.

Mettler, S. 2018. *The Citizen-Government Disconnect*, New York: Russell Sage Foundation.

Moffitt, B. 2015. "How to perform crisis: a model for understanding the key role of crisis in contemporary populism," *Government and Opposition*, 50: 189–217.

———. 2016. *The Global Rise of Populism: Performance, Political Style, and Representation*, Stanford CA: Stanford University Press.

Moffitt, B., and Tormey, S. 2014. "Rethinking populism: politics, mediatization and political style," *Political Studies*, 62: 381–97.

Moioli, V. 1990. *I nuovi razzismi. Miserie e fortune della Lega Lombarda*, Rome: Edizioni Associate.

Molinari, M. 2018. *Perché è successo qui. Viaggio all'origine del populismo italiano che scuote l'Europa*, Milan: La Nave di Teseo.

Mols, F., and Jetten, J. 2017. *The Wealth Paradox: Economic Prosperity and the Hardening of Attitudes*, Cambridge: Cambridge University Press.

Mounk, Y. 2018. *The People vs. Democracy: Why Our Freedom Is in Danger and How to Save It*, Cambridge MA: Harvard University Press.

Mount, F. 2018. "The seducer," *London Review of Books*, 2 August: 3–8.

Mount, H. 2017. *Summer Madness: How Brexit Split the Tories, Destroyed Labour and Divided the Country*, London: Biteback.

Mudde, C. 2004. "The populist Zeitgeist," *Government and Opposition*, 34: 541–63.

Müller, J.-W. 2016. *What Is Populism?* London: Penguin.

———. 2018. "Italy: the bright side of populism?" *New York Review of Books Daily*, 8 June.

Murray, P. 2016. "Clinton holds lead amid record high dislike of both nominees," Monmouth University Polling Institute, https://www.monmouth.edu/polling-institute/reports/monmouthpoll_us_082916.

Mutz, D. 2018. "Status threat, not economic hardship, explains the 2016 presidential vote," *Proceedings of the National Academy of Sciences*, April, https://www.pnas.org/content/115/19/E4330.

Nasi, A. F. 2012. "Padani, liberisti e non giustizialisti. I grillini non sono l'antipolitica," *Libero*, 3 May.

———. 2015. "L'elettorato del M5S si sposta a sinistra, che è di centrodestra non lo sceglie più," *Libero*, 22 September.

———. 2016. "Perchè I social network non spostano voti," *Libero*, 10 March.

Newburger, H. B., et al. (eds.). 2011. *Neighborhood and Life Chances: How Place Matters in Modern America*, Philadelphia: University of Pennsylvania Press.

Nicholls, W. 2009. "Place, networks, space: theorizing the geographies of social movements," *Transactions of the Institute of British Geographers*, 34: 78–93.

Nichols, T. 2017. *The Death of Expertise: The Campaign against Established Knowledge and Why It Matters*, New York: Oxford University Press.

Norris, P., and Inglehart, R. 2019. *Cultural Backlash: Trump, Brexit, and Authoritarian Populism*, Cambridge: Cambridge University Press.

Nossiter, A. 2018. "'Yellow Vests' riot in Paris, but their anger is rooted deep in France," *New York Times*, 2 December.

Ogden, E. 2018. "Donald Trump mesmerist," *New York Times*, 4 August.

Oliver, J. E., and Rahn, W. M. 2016. "Rise of the *Trumpenvolk*: populism in the 2016 election," *Annals of the American Academy*, 667: 189–206.

Olson, K. 2016. "Fragile collectivities, imagined sovereignties," in A. Badiou et al. (eds.) *What Is a People?* New York: Columbia University Press, pp. 107–31.

Onnela, J.-P., et al. 2011. "Geographic constraints on social network groups," *PLoS One*, 6, doi 10.1371/journal.pone.0016939.

Orsina, G. 2013. *Il berlusconismo nella storia dell'Italia*, Venice: Marsilio.

O'Toole, F. 2018. *Heroic Failure: Brexit and the Politics of Pain*, London: Head of Zeus.

Pajetta, G. 1994. *Il grande cameleonte. Episodi, passioni, avventure del leghismo*, Milan: Feltrinelli.

Paparo, A., and Cataldi, M. 2013. "Waves of support: M5S between 2010 and 2013," in L. De Sio et al. (eds.) *The Italian General Election of 2013: A Dangerous Stalemate?* Rome: CISE, pp. 131–34.

Pasquino, G. 2014. "The 2013 elections and the Italian political system," *Journal of Modern Italian Studies*, 19: 424–37.

———. 2018. "Not a normal election: roots and consequences," *Journal of Modern Italian Studies*, 23: 347–61.

Passarelli, G., and Tuorto, D. 2014. "Not with my vote: turnout and the economic crisis in Italy," *Contemporary Italian Politics*, 6: 147–58.

———. 2018. "The Five Star Movement: purely a matter of protest? The rise of a party between political discontent and reasoned voting," *Party Politics*, 24: 129–40.

Pennycook, G., and Rand, D. G. 2018. "Cognitive reflection and the 2016 US presidential election," *Personality and Social Psychology Bulletin*, 45, 2, https://journals.sagepub.com/doi/10.1177/0146167218783192.

Perrineau, P. 2017. *Cette France de gauche qui vote FN*, Paris: Seuil.

Pettersson, J. 2019. *The Question of Political Community: Sameness, Logos. Space*, Lanham MD: Rowman & Littlefield.

Pew Research Center. 2016. "In their own words: why voters support—and have concerns about—Clinton and Trump," Pew Research Center, September, http://www.people-press.org/2016/09/21/in-their-own-words-why-voters-support-and-have-concerns-about-clinton-and-trump.

Pianta, M. 2012. *Nove su dieci. Perche stiamo (quasi) tutti peggio di 10 anni fa*, Rome-Bari: Laterza.

Picone, P. 2017. *Di Maio chi? Vita, opera e missione del politico più 'bersagliato' d'Italia*, Reggio Emilia: Aliberti.

Piketty, T. 2018. *Brahmin Left vs Merchant Right: Rising Inequality and the Changing Structure of Political Conflict (Evidence from France, Britain and the United States, 1948–2017)*, Working Paper 2018/7, Paris: World Inequality Lab.

Polonski, V. 2016. "Analyzing the social media voices of the UK's EU referendum," *Medium*, https://medium.com/@drpolonski/social-media-voices-in-the-uks-eu-referendum-brexit-or-bremain-what-does-the-internet-say-about-ebbd7b27cf0f.

Pombeni, P. 1993. *Autorità sociale e potere politico nell'Italia contemporanea*, Venice: Marsilio.

Poniewozik, J. 2015. "What 'The Apprentice' taught Donald Trump about campaigning," *New York Times*, 9 October.

Porter, E. 2018. "Where government is a dirty word, but its checks pay the bills," *New York Times*, 21 December.

Poulantzas, N. 1979. "La crise des partis," *Le Monde Diplomatique*, September, 28–30.

Pritoni, A., and Vignati, R. 2018. "Winners and losers: Turnout, results and the flows of vote," *Journal of Modern Italian Studies*, 23: 381–99.

Pucciarelli, M. 2016. *Anatomia di un populista. La vera storia di Matteo Salvini*, Milan: Feltrinelli.

Putnam, R. 1993. *Making Democracy Work: Civic Traditions in Modern Italy*, Princeton NJ: Princeton University Press.

Rachman, G. 2018. "World leaders adapt to era of Trumpism," *Financial Times*, 7 November.

Ramiro, L., and Gomez, R. 2017. "Radical-Left populism during the Great Recession: *Podemos* and its competition with the established radical Left," *Political Studies*, 65: 108–26.

Repubblica, La. 2018. "L'Italia invecchia: per la prima volta gli over 60 superano gli under 30," *La Repubblica*, 22 October.

Reungoat, E. 2015. "Le Front National et l'Union Européene: le radicalization comme continuité," in S. Crépon et al. (eds.) *Les faux-semblants du Front National: Sociologie d'un parti politique*, Paris: Presses de Sciences Po, pp. 225–45.

Revault d'Allonnes, M. 2010. *Pourquoi nous n'aimons pas la démocratie*, Paris: Seuil.

Revelli, M. 2015. *Dentro e contro. Quando il populismo è di governo*, Rome-Bari: Laterza.

———. 2017. *Populismo 2.0*, Turin: Einaudi.

Reynié, D. 2016. "'Heritage populism' and France's National Front," *Journal of Democracy*, 27: 47–57.

Ricolfi, L. 2012. "Il sogno svanito del federalismo," *La Stampa*, 13 April: 1.

———. 2017. *Sinistra e popolo. Il conflitto politico nell'era dei populismi*, Milan: Longanesi.

Riera, P., and Russo, L. 2016. "Breaking the cartel: the geography of electoral support of new parties in Italy and Spain," *Italian Political Science Review*, 46: 219–41.

Riley, D. 2018. "What is Trump?" *New Left Review*, 114: 5–31.

Rizzo, S., and Stella, G. 2009. *La casta*, Milan: Rizzoli.

Roberts, A. 2010. *The Logic of Discipline: Global Capitalism and the Architecture of Government*, New York: Oxford University Press.

Roberts, D. 2017. "Donald Trump and the rise of tribal epistemology," *Vox*, 22 March.

Rodrik, D. 2013. "Who needs the nation-state?" *Economic Geography*, 89: 1–19.

Romm, T. 2018. "New report on Russian disinformation, prepared for the Senate, shows the operation's scale and sweep," *Washington Post*, 17 December.

Rooduijn, M. 2018. "What unites the voter bases of populist parties? Comparing the electorates of 15 populist parties," *European Political Science Review*, 10, 3: 351–68.

Rosanvallon, P. 1992. *La crise de l'État-providence*, Paris: Seuil.

———. 2011. "A reflection on populism," Booksandideas.net, 10 November, https://booksandideas.net/A-Reflection-on-Populism.html.

Rose, R. 2016. *The Rolling Path to Brexit*, Studies in Public Policy Number 522, Glasgow: University of Strathclyde, Centre for the Study of Public Policy.

Rousseau, J.-J. 2002 [1762]. *The Social Contract and the First and Second Discourses*, New Haven CT: Yale University Press, edited by Susan Dunn.

Rubin, J. 2019. "Trump's lock on the GOP matters less and less," *Washington Post*, 7 January.

Runciman, D. 2018. *How Democracy Ends*, London: Profile.

Russo, L., et al. 2017. "Tracing the electorate of the Movimento Cinque Stelle: an ecological inference analysis," *Italian Political Science Review*, 47: 45–62.

Rydgren, J. 2006. *From Tax Populism to Ethnic Nationalism: Radical Right-Wing Populism in Sweden*. Oxford: Bergahn.

Salam, R. 2012. "The missing middle in American politics: how moderate Republicans became extinct," *Foreign Affairs*, 91, 2: 148–55.

Salmon, C. 2014. *La politica nell'era dello storytelling*, Rome: Fazi.

Sampson, R. J. 2012. *Great American City: Chicago and the Enduring Neighborhood Effect*, Chicago: University of Chicago Press.

Sanders, E. 2017. "The meaning, causes, and possible results of the 2016 presidential election," *Forum*, 15: 711–40.

Sannino, C. 2018. "Cacciari: 'Divario crescente tra Sud e Nord, cosi l'Italia si spacca,'" *La Repubblica, Napoli*, 28 December.

Saporiti, R. 2018. "Social network e consenso: la politica può vivere senza giornali?" *Info Data, Il Sole 24 Ore*, 13 October.

Sargent, G. 2016. "Donald Trump explains American politics in a single sentence," *Washington Post*, 10 February.

Sartori, G. 1989. "Videopolitica," *Rivista Italiana di Scienza Politica*, 19: 185–98.

Sayer, D. 2017. "White riot—Brexit, Trump, and post-factual politics," *Journal of Historical Sociology*, 30: 92–106.

Schaul, K., and Uhrmacher, K. 2016. "Ted Cruz has an evangelical problem," *Washington Post*, 21 February.

Scheuermann, C. 2018. "The Stephen Bannon project: searching in Europe for glory days gone by," *Der Spiegel Online*, 29 October, http://m.spiegel.de/international.

Schiavone, A. 2013. *Non ti delego. Perché abbiamo smesso di credere nella lora politica*, Milan: Rizzoli.

Schneider, S. 2019. "Nationalists of the world unite! Yoram Hazony's work provides a global scaffolding for the new Far Right," *Foreign Policy*, 8 January.

Scott, D. 2018. "The biggest political problem in America, explained in one chart: Americans don't just disagree on the issues. They disagree on what the issues are," *Vox*, 15 October.

Seaton, J. 2016. "Brexit and the media," *Political Quarterly*, 87: 333–37.

Segal, D. 2018. "In Brexit vote, town's nostalgia for seafaring past muddied future," *New York Times*, 23 April.

Shea, D. M. 1999. "The passing of realignment and the advent of the 'base-less' party system," *American Politics Research*, 27: 33–57.

Shields, J. 2014. "The Front National: from systematic opposition to systemic integration?" *Modern and Contemporary France*, 22: 491–511.

Shin, M., and Agnew, J. 2008. *Berlusconi's Italy: Mapping Contemporary Italian Politics*, Philadelphia: Temple University Press.

Sides, J., et al. 2018. *Identity Crisis: The 2016 Presidential Campaign and the Battle for the Meaning of America*, Princeton NJ: Princeton University Press.

Simpson, E. 2016. "This is how the liberal world order ends: not with a bang but with a pair of defiant anti-establishment presidential candidates," *Foreign Policy*, 19 February, http://foreignpolicy.com/2016/02/19/this-is-how-the-liberal-world-orderends/?utm_source=Sailthru&utm_medium=email&utm_campaign=New%20Campaign&utm_term=%2AEditors%20Picks.

Sinha, M. 2018. "Today's eerie echoes of the Civil War," *Daily* (blog), *New York Review of Books*, 8 November.

Skocpol, T., and Williamson, V. 2016. *The Tea Party and the Remaking of Republican Conservatism*, updated edition, New York: Oxford University Press.

Slobodian, Q. 2018. *Globalists: The End of Empire and the Birth of Neoliberalism*, Cambridge, MA: Harvard University Press.

Smith, A. 2018. "Charts of the year: from polarized politics to damaging pollution," *Financial Times*, 29 December.

Spiro, E. S., et al. 2016. "The persistence of division: geography, institutions, and online friendship ties," *Socius*, 2: 1–15.

Spruyt, B., et al. 2016. "Who supports populism and what attracts people to it?" *Political Research Quarterly*, 69: 335–46.

Starr, P. 2019. "Fall from grace," *New York Review of Books*, 21 March.

Stavrakakis, Y. 2017. "How did populism become a pejorative concept?" Working Paper 6, POPULISMUS, April, http://www.populismus.gr/wp-content/uploads/2017/04/stavrakakis-populismus-wp-6-upload.pdf.

Stephens, B. 2018. "Why aren't the Democrats walking away with the midterms?" *New York Times*, 3 November.

Stephens, M., and Poorthuis, A. 2015. "Follow thy neighbor: connecting social and spatial networks," *Computers, Environment and Urban Systems*, 53: 87–95.

Stephens, P. 2018. "Nostalgia has stolen the future," *Financial Times*, 25 July.

Stewart, K. 2018. "Why Trump reigns as King Cyrus," *New York Times*, 31 December.

Stille, A. 2006. *The Sack of Rome*, New York: Penguin.

———. 2018. "Not so funny," *New York Review of Books*, 45, 10 May.

Stockemer, D. 2017. "What affects voter turnout? A review article/meta-analysis of aggregate research," *Government and Opposition*, 52: 698–722.

Stockemer, D., and Barisone, M. 2016. "The 'new' discourse of the Front National under Marine Le Pen: a slight change with a big impact," *European Journal of Communication*, 32: 100–15.

Stoker, G. 2006. *Why Politics Matters: Making Democracy Work*, Basingstoke, UK: Palgrave.

Stothard, M. 2017. "Le Pen's online army leads Far-Right fight for French presidency," *Financial Times*, 25 February.

———. 2018. "Spanish Far Right makes impact from fringes," *Financial Times*, 9 November.

Streeck, W. 2017. *Buying Time: The Delayed Crisis of Democratic Capitalism*, 2nd edition, London: Verso.

Sullivan, M. 2018. "The local-news crisis is destroying what a divided America desperately needs: common ground," *Washington Post*, 5 August.

Sylvers, E. 2018. "Europe's populist Left and Right share a common call: state intervention," *Wall Street Journal*, 14 December.

Szelenyi, I. 2015. "Capitalisms after communism," *New Left Review*, 96: 39–51.

Taguieff, P.-A. 2002. *L'illusion populiste*, Paris: Berg.

———. 2007. *L'illusion populiste. Essai sur les demagogies de l'âge démocratique*, Paris: Flammarion.

Tarchi, M. 2015. *Italia populista: Dal qualunquismo a Beppe Grillo*, Bologna: Il Mulino.

Tarragoni, F. 2017. "Le peuple selon Ernesto Laclau," *La Vie des Idées*, 3 November, https://laviedesidees.fr/Le-peuple-selon-Ernesto-Laclau.html.

Terracciano, T. 2018. "Esiste un volto buono del populismo?" *Econopoly, Il Sole 24 Ore*, 20 November.

Tett, G. 2018. "Why we still haven't reached peak populism," *Financial Times*, 2 August: 8.

Thompson, J. 2018. "News deserts of the West," *High Country News*, 50, 24 December.

Thornhill, J. 2018. "How to fix Facebook," *Financial Times*, 6 August: 9.

Tooze, A. 2018. *Crashed: How a Decade of Financial Crises Changed the World*, New York: Viking.

Trovati, G. 2018. "Il flop dell'Italia digitale: 25 su 28 Paesi. Speso solo il 3% dei fondi Ue," *Il Sole 24 Ore*, 16 December.

Tufekci, Z. 2018. "How social media took us from Tahrir Square to Donald Trump," *MIT Technology Review*, 14 August.

Tuorto, D. 2006. *Apatia or protesta? L'astensionismo elettorale in Italia*, Bologna: Il Mulino.

Urbinati, N. 2012. "La politica degli antipolitica," *MicroMega*, 10 May.

———. 2013. "The populist challenge," *Raisons Politiques*, 51: 137–54.

———. 2015. "A revolt against intermediary bodies," *Constellations*, 22: 477–86.

Vampa, D. 2015. "Local representative democracy and protest politics: the case of the Five-Star Movement," *Contemporary Italian Politics*, 7: 232–50.

Van Elsas, E. J., et al. 2016. "United against a common foe? The nature and origins of Euroscepticism among left-wing and right-wing citizens," *West European Politics*, 39: 1181–1204.

Van Reybrouck, D. 2015. *Contro le elezioni: Perche votare non e piu democratico* Milan: Feltrinelli.

Veltri, G. A. 2010. "Sulle spalle di nessuno. Il ruolo delle scienze sociali nel dibattito culturale e politico in Italia," in A. Mammone et al. (eds.) *Un paese normale? Saggi sull'Italia contemporanea*, Milan: Dalai, pp. 128–43.

Verbeek, B., and Zaslove, A. 2016. "Italy: a case of mutating populism?" *Democratization*, 23: 304–23.

Veronese, L. 2018. "Visegrad, I sovranisti che dipendono dall'economia europea," *Il Sole 24 Ore*, 18 November.

Vezzoni, C., and Mancosu, M. 2015. "Diffusion processes and discussion networks: an analysis of the propensity to vote for the 5 Star Movement in the 2013 Italian election," *Journal of Elections, Public Opinion and Parties*, 10: 21–45.

Viroli, M. 2012. *The Liberty of Servants: Berlusconi's Italy*, Princeton NJ: Princeton University Press.

Wallace-Wells, B. 2015. "Donald Trump vs. the modern political campaign," *New Yorker*, 11 December.

Warren, D. I. 1976. *The Radical Center: Middle Americans and the Politics of Alienation*, South Bend IN: University of Notre Dame Press.

Webber, M. J., and Rigby, D. L. 1996. *The Golden Age Illusion: Rethinking Postwar Capitalism*, New York: Guilford Press.

Weil, S. 2014. *On the Abolition of All Political Parties*, New York: New York Review Books, trans. by Simon Leys.

Wellings, B. 2018. "Brexit and English identity," in P. Diamond et al. (eds.) *Routledge Handbook of the Politics of Brexit*, London: Routledge, pp. 147–56.

Wendel, D. D. B. 2015. "Toward a spatial epistemology of politics," in D. D. B. Wendel and F. S. Aidoo (eds.) *Spatializing Politics: Essays on Power and Place*, Cambridge, MA: Harvard Design Studies, pp. 2–13.

Williams, M. H. 2011. "A new era for French Far Right politics? Comparing the FN under two Le Pens," *Analise Social*, 46: 679–95.

Williams, P. M. 1964. *Crisis and Compromise: Politics in the French Fourth Republic*, London: Longman.

Wills, G. 2016. "Disciples of distrust," *New York Review of Books Daily*, 5 November.

Wills, J. 2013. "Place and politics," in D. Featherstone and J. Painter (eds.) *Spatial Politics: Essays for Doreen Massey*, London: Wiley, pp. 135–45.

Winock, M. 1993. "L'action française," in M. Winock (ed.) *Histoire de l'extrême droit en France*, Paris: Seuil, pp. 50–81.

Wolin, S. S. 2004. *Politics and Vision: Expanded Edition*, Princeton NJ: Princeton University Press.

———. 2008. *Democracy Incorporated: Managed Democracy and the Specter of Inverted Totalitarianism*, Princeton NJ: Princeton University Press.

Wren-Lewis, S. 2018. *The Lies We Were Told: Politics, Economics, Austerity and Brexit*, Bristol, UK: University of Bristol Press.

Zagrebelsky, G. 2010. "La neolingua del Cavaliere," Gruppo Laico di Ricerca, 14 October, http://www.gruppolaico.it/2010/10/22/la-neolingua-del-cavaliere.

Zimring, F. E. 1996. "Populism, democratic government, and the decline of expert authority: some reflections on three strikes in California," *Pacific Law Journal*, 28: 243–56.

Zuckerman, A S. 2005. *The Social Logic of Politics: Personal Networks as Contexts for Political Behavior*, Philadelphia: Temple University Press.

Zuquete, J. P. 2018. *The Identitarians: The Movement against Globalism and Islam in Europe*, South Bend IN: Notre Dame University Press.

Index

abortion, 72
Action Française, 94
activism: for conservative ideology, 115; for populism, 109; for Republican Party, 74; on social media, 110; voters and, 122
advertising, 70
Affordable Care Act, 27
The Apprentice (TV show), 73
Austria, 28–29

The Bachelor (TV show), 117
Bannon, Steve, 7, 21–22
Barrès, Maurice, 96
Di Battisti, Alessandro, 130–31
Belgium, 28
Berlusconi, Silvio, 28, 39, 43, 115–20, 124, 142
bigotry, 28, 32–33, 34, 62
Black Lives Matter, 70
Blair, Tony, 36, 142
Bossi, Umberto, 115, 118–19
Brandolini, Aurelio Lippo, 11
Brexit: for EU, 141, 145; for Europe, 49; for people, 4–5; psychology of, 41–42, 60, 62–65, *63*, *65*; as referendum votes, 54–57; Trump and, 11, 31, 44, 93, 138; for UK, 1, 4–5, 11, 17, *51*, 51–54, *53*, 143

Britain. *See* United Kingdom
Buchanan, Pat, 26
Bush, George W., 67, 71, 72
Bush, Jeb, 83

Cambridge Analytica, 88
Cameron, David, 29, 48–49, 54–55, 62
capitalism, 6, 8, 137
Carter, Jimmy, 74, 142
Casaleggio, Gianroberto, 114, 120–21, 139
case studies, 137; for populism, 44–45, *45*, 97–102, *98–100*; scholarship and, 138–41
celebrities, 39
centrist parties, 92–93, 103–4
charisma, 10, 43, 60–61, 116–17
Chile, 95
China, 5
Chirac, Jacques, 28
Christian Democrats, 3
Civil Rights Act (1964), 13
Civil War (US), 72
class issues, 78
Clinton, Bill, 36, 74, 142
Clinton, Hillary, 31, 67–71; in elections, 81, *82*, 83; for media, 87–88; Trump and, *45*, 77–78, *79–81*, 80–81, 106; for voters, 77

Colbert, Stephen, 15

Cold War, 1–3, 28, 31, 46, 142, 146

communication: in politics, 145; in populism, 43–44, 86–89; sound bite politics, 62–65, *63*, *65*; technology for, 17; in US, 134

communism: centrist parties and, 92–93; after Cold War, 28, 31; Democratic Party and, 141; in France, 3, 13–14, 107–8; Gramsci for, 4; in Italy, 127–28; in Russia, 27; for voters, 94

conservative ideology: activism for, 115; democracy and, 21; liberal democracy and, 35–36, 50, 54–57, 65–66; NF, 91–94; Tea Party, 26–27, 72–73; in US, 40

consumerism, 107

contemporary populism: in elections, 5–6; globalization and, 143–46; history of, 4–5; political theory of, 15–16; scholarship on, 22–23, *24*; in US, 89–90

Corbyn, Jeremy, 61

Coughlin, Charles, 26

Cox, Jo, 62

Crick, Bernard, 145–56

crisis, psychology of, 3

Croix de Feu, 94

Cruz, Ted, 76, 83

cultural elites, 7

Daily Mail (tabloid), 10

de Gaulle, Charles, 48, 92

democracy: Civil Rights Act (1964) for, 13; conservative ideology and, 21; for elections, 5; electoral college for, 86, 106; in globalization, 44–45, 136; policy for, 36–37, 146; social democracy, 36, *37*, 38. *See also* liberal democracy

Democratic Party: Clinton, B., for, 74; communism and, 141; history of, 72; psychology of, 78, 81; Republican Party and, *75*; for voters, 76. *See also* liberal democracy

Dixiecrat movement, 72

economics: capitalism, 6, 8, 137; for China, 5; of Cold War, 46; consumerism, 107; in elections, *41*, 41–42, 76–77;

for EU, 93, 120, 123; in Europe, 56; globalization of, 13–14, 32, 36; in Italy, 28; of media, 88; neoliberal capitalism, 6, 8; New Deal, 25–26; for people, 12; in protectionism, 45; in Spain, 29; unemployment, 54, *135*, 135–36; for voters, 49–50, 71, 119

education, 58–59, 100–101

efflorescence, 29, *30*, 31–34

elections: bigotry in, 28; charisma in, 10; Clinton, H., in, 81, *82*, 83; contemporary populism in, 5–6; democracy for, 5; economics in, *41*, 41–42, 76–77; education in, 100–101; electoral demography, 57–60, *58–59*; in Europe, *45*; Facebook and, 44, 88; Fox News in, 89; in France, 91, 110–11; in Italy, 120–27, *124–27*; Le Pen, M., in, 94–95, 97–101, *98–99*; M5S in, 127–29, *128–30*; media in, 86–89; for policy, 31–32; propaganda in, 87; referendum votes, 14–15; Romney in, 78; Trump in, 1–2, 15, 17, 23, 67–69, 83–86, *84*, 89–90, 101–2; Twitter in, 68–69, 85; unemployment in, 54; in US, *79*, 142–43; voters in, 11; voter turnout, *58–59*, 58–60

electoral college, 67–68, *80*, 80–81, 86, 106. *See also* voters

elitism, 9, 22, 32–33, 85–86

England. *See* United Kingdom

En Marche (party), 97

epistemic confusion, 140

EU. *See* European Union

Europe: Brexit for, 49; economics in, 56; elections in, *45*; immigration in, 21, 47; media in, 63–64; nationalism in, 38, 40, 48; pluto-populism in, 27; politics in, 17, 27–29, 142–43; populism in, 48–51, 91, 94–95; psychology of, 48–49; religion in, 95–96; social media in, 100; Twitter in, 110; UK and, 29; US and, 34, 141–42

European Union (EU), *65*; Brexit for, 141, 145; economics for, 93, 120, 123; Great Recession for, 33; Greece and, 21; parties in, *30*; politics in, 20–21, 29,

51, 51–54, *53*, 97–98, 119; psychology of, 54–57; Putin and, 88; UK and, 1, 47–51, 57–60, *58–59*, 65–66, 139; US and, 5; for voters, 16. *See also* Brexit; European Union

Facebook, 140; Cambridge Analytica and, 88; elections and, 44, 88; politics on, 110; populism on, 64; psychology of, 132; as technology, 87; Twitter and, 4, 19–20, 39, 134. *See also* social media
fake news, 140–41
fame, 117
Farage, Nigel, 50, 56, 62–63, 65–66
fascism, 22, 42, 113–14, 117–18. *See also* Italy; populism
Fidesz, Orban, 29, 44–45
Fillon, François, 97–101, *98, 100, 104,* 109
Five Star Movement (M5S), 11, 16–17, 134–36, *135*; in elections, 127–29, *128–30*; Grillo for, 114, 116, 120–22, 130–31, 139–40; politics of, 113–14, 130–33, *131–32*; as populism, 120–27, *124–27*. *See also* Italy
Fortuyn, Pim, 28
Forza Italia, 115, 117, 121–26, *124, 128*. *See also* Berlusconi
Fox News, 10, 39, 73, 87, 89
France, 4, 28, 142; communism in, 3, 13–14, 107–8; elections in, 91, 110–11; En Marche (party), 97; history of, 94–97; Italy and, 19, 35–36; Le Pen, M., for, 110–11; Muslims for, 108; nationalism in, 6, 11, 17, 28; politics in, 2; Putin for, 110; socialism in, 92, 97–98; UK compared to, 134; voter turnout in, 100–103, *104–6,* 106. *See also* Europe; National Front
Freysinger, Oscar, 96

Gentiloni, Paolo, 125
Germany, 21, 34. *See also* Europe
Giannini, Guglielmo, 114–15
Gingrich, Newt, 72
globalization: of capitalism, 137; contemporary populism and, 143–46; democracy in, 44–45, 136; of

economics, 13–14, 32, 36; fascism in, 42; immigration and, 144–45; nationalism in, 51–52, 107; of neoliberal capitalism, 6; of opinion polarization, 140; of populism, 2–3; protectionism compared to, *24*; subcultures in, 31; of terrorism, 33–34; Twitter in, 44
Gove, Michael, 56, 61–62, 139
government, 88, 92, 146
Gramsci, Antonio, 4
Great Recession, 31–33
Greece, 5, 21. *See also* Europe
Grillo, Beppe, 7; for M5S, 114, 116, 120–22, 130–31, 139–40; for people, 43–44, 126, 134–35
Guggenheim, Charles, 73

Hague, William, 55
Hannity, Sean, 89
hegemony, 86
heritage populism, 95–96
history, 1; contemporary populism, 4–5; of Democratic Party, 72; of fascism, 113–14; of France, 94–97; of NF, 94–97; of populism, 16–17, 19, 25–29, 116–20, 143–46; of Republican Party, 71–72; of socialism, 114–15; of US, 13
Hollande, François, 97, 109
Hungary, 21, 29

ignorance, 23, 25
immigration: in Europe, 21, 47; globalization and, 144–45; ignorance and, 25; policy for, 33–34, 95; politics of, 19–20; refugees and, 21–22; in UK, 96–97; in US, 70, 74; for voters, 54, 97–102
Internet populism, 120–27, *124–27,* 133–36, *135*
Iraq, 31–32, 143
Islam, 5, 73, 108, 139
Italy, 4, 17; communism in, 127–28; economics in, 28; elections in, 120–27, *124–27*; Forza Italia, 115, 117, 121–26, *124, 128*; France and, 19, 35–36; Internet populism in, 120–27, *124–27,* 133–36, *135*; nationalism in, 44;

Northern League, 28, 115, 117–19, 121, 131–32, 139; populism in, 11, 113–16; religion in, 3, 13; unemployment in, *135*, 135–36; US and, 7; voter turnout in, 127–29, *128–30*. *See also* Europe

Jackson, Andrew, 25
Johnson, Boris, 50, 56, 61–62, 117, 139
Johnson, Gary, 68
Johnson, Lyndon, 13
Jones, Alex, 87
Jospin, Lionel, 28, 92

Kennedy, Robert, 73

Laclau, Ernesto, 6
Latin America, 6, 34
leadership: of Berlusconi, 115–20, 124, 142; communication technologies for, 17; for media, 10; for nationalism, 131–32; opinion polarization and, 146; of parties, 141–42; for people, 43–44, 85–86, 107; policy in, 135; in populism, 43, 60–62, 130–33, *131–32*; psychology of, 16, 69–70, 139; for Republican Party, 85; social media for, 11–12; terrorism and, 23. *See also specific leaders*
the leave vote. *See* Brexit
Le Pen, Jean-Marie, 28, 109, 139
Le Pen, Marine, 2, 34, 43, 102–3, 132, 139; in elections, 94–95, 97–101, *98–99*; for media, 109–10; NF and, 106–8; populism and, 93, 96–97, 110–11
liberal democracy, 1; conservative ideology and, 35–36, 50, 54–57, 65–66; neoliberal capitalism, 6, 8; in US, 17; for voters, 40
Libertarian party, 68
Limbaugh, Rush, 87
Lincoln, Abraham, 71–72
Lindsay, John, 71–72
Long, Huey, 26
lottizzazione, 114

M5S. *See* Five Star Movement
Macron, Emmanuel, 19, 36, 97–101, *98*, 103–4, 106, 109, 143

mainstream parties, 131–32, 137
Di Maio, Luigi, 126, 128, 130–31, 133, 136
Maurras, Charles, 96
McCain, John, 76
media: Clinton, H., for, 87–88; economics of, 88; in elections, 86–89; in Europe, 63–64; leadership for, 10; Le Pen, M., for, 109–10; NF for, 109–10; for opinion polarization, 38–39; politics for, 10–11, 43–44, 77–78; tabloid realism, 10, 64; television, 69–70, 108. *See also* social media
Medicaid, 85–86
Mélenchon, Jean-Luc, 97–103, *98*, 106, 111
Mexico, 27, 89, 139
minorities, 83, *84*
Mitterrand, François, 95, 97
Monti, Mario, 120
Murdoch, Rupert, 39, 63–64
Muslims, 5, 73, 108, 139

NAFTA. *See* North American Free Trade Agreement
National Front (NF), 111, 142; conservative ideology, 91–94; history of, 94–97; Le Pen, M., and, 106–8; for media, 109–10; for people, 138–39; for voters, 97–102, *98–100*
nationalism: in Europe, 38, 40, 48; in France, 6, 11, 17, 28; in globalization, 51–52, 107; in Italy, 44; in Latin America, 34; leadership for, 131–32; parties for, 27–28; politics and, 15, 123; populism as, 5–7, *45*; on social media, 33, 133–34; in Spain, 6, 19–20; for voters, 14
nativism, 25
NATO. *See* North Atlantic Treaty Organization
neocolonialism, 38
neoliberal capitalism, 6, 8
neo-Nazism, 62
the Netherlands, 28
New Deal, 25–26
NF. *See* National Front

Nixon, Richard, 25–26, 71–72
North American Free Trade Agreement
(NAFTA), 1
North Atlantic Treaty Organization
(NATO), 1
Northern Ireland. *See* United Kingdom
Northern League (Italy), 28, 115, 117–19,
121, 131–32, 139

Obama, Barack, 27, 67, 78, 142; politics of,
72–73, 83; Romney against, 69, *79*; for
voters, 78, 80
Occupy Wall Street, 27
opinion polarization, 40, 138, 142;
globalization of, 140; leadership and,
146; media for, 38–39; in US, 74, *75*,
76–77; for voters, *75*
oppositional demagoguery, 5–7
Orban, Victor, 21

Palin, Sarah, 73
parties: centrist parties, 92–93, 103–4;
in EU, *30*; leadership of, 141–42;
as mainstream, 131–32, 137; for
nationalism, 27–28; populism and,
34–36, *37*, 38–40, 92–93, 103–4;
psychology of, 46; in US, 40, 144. *See
also* Democratic Party; Republican Party
people: Brexit for, 4–5; economics for, 12;
elitism for, 22, 85–86; government for,
146; Grillo for, 43–44, 126, 134–35;
leadership for, 43–44, 85–86, 107; NF
for, 138–39; of populism, 8–11, 121–
22, 137–41; protectionism for, 32; social
spaces and, 11–13; sovereignty for, 8–9;
working class, 52
Peron, Juan, 39
Perot, Ross, 26
Phillips, Howard, 26
Pinochet, Augusto, 95
pluralism, 32
pluto-populism, 26–27
Podemos. *See* Spain
Poland, 29, 54
policy: for democracy, 36–37, 146; elections
for, 31–32; for immigration, 33–34,
95; in leadership, 135; oppositional

demagoguery as, 5–6; in Russia, 21;
sovereignty as, 7; in UK, 27–28;
vaccinations, 130
politics, 5, 12, 19; charisma in, 116–17;
communication in, 145; education and,
58–59; in EU, 20–21, 29, *51*, 51–54,
53, 97–98, 119; in Europe, 17, 27–29,
142–43; on Facebook, 110; in France,
2; of government, 92; of immigration,
19–20; in Latin America, 6; of M5S,
113–14, 130–33, *131–32*; for media,
10–11, 43–44, 77–78; of Mexico, 89;
nationalism and, 15, 123; of Obama,
72–73, 83; opinion polarization in, 39–
40; pluralism, 32; political harassment,
55; political narrative, 56–57; political
theory, 4, 14–16; psychology of, 13–15;
of religion, 40, 94, 127–28; retail
politics, 133–36, *135*; scholarship on,
35–36, *37*, 38–39; on social media, 65–
66; sound bite politics, 62–65, *63*, *65*;
television and, 69–70, 108; of Trump,
74, *75*, 76–77; trustworthiness in, *63*;
in UK, 38; in US, 1, 14–15, 25–27,
67–68; working class, 52
populism, 4, 12–13; activism for, 109;
case studies for, 44–45, *45*, 97–102,
98–100; communication in, 43–44,
86–89; efflorescence of, 29, *30*, 31–34;
electoral college for, 67–68; in Europe,
48–51, 91, 94–95; on Facebook, 64;
globalization of, 2–3; heritage populism,
95–96; history of, 16–17, 19, 25–29,
116–20, 143–46; Internet populism,
120–27, *124–27*, 133–36, *135*; in Italy,
11, 113–16; leadership in, 43, 60–62,
130–33, *131–32*; Le Pen, M., and, 93,
96–97, 110–11; M5S as, 120–27, *124–
27*; mapping of, 15–16; as nationalism,
5–7, *45*; organization of, 7–8; parties
and, 34–36, *37*, 38–40, 103–4; people
of, 8–11, 121–22, 137–41; pluto-
populism, 26–27; psychology of, 20–21,
84–85; religion and, 107; Republican
Party and, 89–90; scholarship on,
21–22, 46, 137–38, 141–43; in Spain,
97–98; on Twitter, 64; for voters, *41*,

41–42, 57–60, *58–59*; waves of, 1–2, 20. *See also* contemporary populism

Poujade, Pierre, 94

Poulantzas, Nicos, 36

propaganda, 87

protectionism, *24*, 32, 33–34, 45

psychology: of Brexit, 41–42, 60, 62–65, *63, 65*; of Cold War, 3; of crisis, 3; of Democratic Party, 78, 81; of elitism, 9; of EU, 54–57; of Europe, 48–49; of Facebook, 132; of fame, 117; of ignorance, 23; of leadership, 16, 69–70, 139; from mapping, 103; of oppositional demagoguery, 6–7; of parties, 46; of politics, 13–15; of populism, 20–21, 84–85; of Republican Party, 68, 83–84; social media and, 39–40; social psychology, 11–12; of Trump, 9–10; of voters, 31–32, 35, 57, 81–82, 137

Putin, Vladimir, 1, 21, 28, 110, 131; EU and, 88; for US, 33

racism. *See* bigotry

Reagan, Ronald, 25, 38, 71–72, 74, 85, 142

referendum votes, 14–15, 54–57

refugees, 21–22, 33–34

religion, 3, 13, 73, 76; in Europe, 95–96; politics of, 40, 94, 127–28; populism and, 107

Renzi, Matteo, 19, 36, 116, 120

Republican Party, 68, 71–74, 76, 83–85, 87; Democratic Party and, *75*; populism and, 89–90. *See also* conservative ideology

retail politics, 133–36, *135*

Rockefeller, Nelson, 71–72

Roe v. Wade, 72

Romney, Mitt, 69, 78, *79*

Rousseau, Jean-Jacques, 16, 116

Rove, Karl, 72

Rubio, Marco, 83

Russia, 10–11, 21, 27, 88

Salvini, Matteo, 115, 131–32, 134, 136, 139

Sanders, Bernie, 5, 26–27, 74

Sarkozy, Nicolas, 97

Saudi Arabia, 34, 139

scholarship: case studies and, 138–41; on contemporary populism, 22–23, *24*; on politics, 35–36, *37*, 38–39; on populism, 21–22, 46, 137–38, 141–43

Scotland. *See* United Kingdom

The Social Contract (Rousseau), 16

social democracy, 36, *37*, 38

socialism, 92, 97–98, 114–15, 117–18

social media: activism on, 110; celebrities on, 39; in Europe, 100; fake news on, 140–41; for leadership, 11–12; nationalism on, 33, 133–34; politics on, 65–66; psychology and, 39–40; as technology, 111. *See also* Facebook; Twitter

social psychology, 11–12

social spaces, 11–13

Soros, George, 21

sound bite politics, 62–65, *63, 65*

sovereignty, 7–9, 48

Soviet Union. *See* Russia

Spain, 5–6, 14, 19–20, 29, 97–98

subcultures, 31

Sun (tabloid), 10

Survivor (TV show), 117

Sweden, 21, 28. *See also* Europe

Switzerland, 28–29, 96

tabloid realism, 10, 64

Tea Party, 26–27, 72–73

technology, 17, 87, 111

television, 69–70, 73, 108, 117

terrorism, 5, 23, 33–34, 70–71

Thatcher, Margaret, 38, 142

Trump, Donald, 109, 132, 138–40, 142–43, 145; Berlusconi compared to, 43; bigotry for, 34; Brexit and, 11, 31, 44, 93, 138; Clinton, H., and, *45*, 77–78, *79–81*, 80–81, 106; in elections, 1–2, 15, 17, 23, 67–69, 83–86, *84*, 89–90, 101–2; politics of, 74, *75*, 76–77; psychology of, 9–10; Sanders and, 26–27; Twitter for, 86–89; for US, 6, 20–22; for voters, 69–73, 81, *82*, 83

trustworthiness, *63*

truthiness, 85–89

Tukey, John, 41, *41*
Turkey, 95
Twitter, 44, 64, 110, 143; in elections, 68–69, 85; Facebook and, 4, 19–20, 39, 134; for Trump, 86–89. *See also* social media

UDCA. *See* Union for the Defense of Tradesmen and Artisans
UK. *See* United Kingdom
UKIP. *See* Brexit; conservative ideology; United Kingdom
unemployment, 54, *135*, 135–36
Union for the Defense of Tradesmen and Artisans (UDCA), 94
United Kingdom (UK), 2–3, 34–35, 42; Brexit for, 1, 4–5, 11, 17, *51*, 51–54, *53*, 143; EU and, 1, 47–51, 57–60, *58–59*, 65–66, 139; Europe and, 29; France compared to, 134; immigration in, 96–97; policy in, 27–28; politics in, 38; Spain and, 14; tabloid realism in, 10; voters in, 52–53, *53*, 100. *See also* Europe
United States (US), 2–4, 35, 42; Civil War, 72; class issues in, 78; communication in, 134; conservative ideology in, 40; contemporary populism in, 89–90; elections in, *79*, 142–43; EU and, 5; Europe and, 34, 141–42; Fox News in, 10; Great Recession for, 31–32; hegemony for, 86; history of, 13; immigration in, 70, 74; Italy and, 7; liberal democracy in, 17; Medicaid in, 85–86; Mexico and, 27; minorities in, 83; Muslims in, 73; opinion polarization in, 74, *75*, 76–77; parties in, 40, 144; politics in, 1, 14–15, 25–27, 67–68;

Putin for, 33; *Roe v. Wade*, 72; Russia and, 10–11; terrorism for, 70–71; Trump for, 6, 20–22
Uomo Qualunque, 27, 114–15
US. *See* United States

vaccinations, 130
von Clausewitz, Carl, 119
voters: activism and, 122; advertising and, 70; charisma for, 43, 60–61; Clinton, H., for, 77; communism for, 94; Democratic Party for, 76; economics for, 49–50, 71, 119; in elections, 11; EU for, 16; immigration for, 54, 97–102; liberal democracy for, 40; nationalism for, 14; NF for, 97–102, *98–100*; Obama for, 78, 80; opinion polarization for, *75*; populism for, *41*, 41–42, 57–60, *58–59*; psychology of, 31–32, 35, 57, 81–82, 137; Sanders for, 74; sovereignty for, 48; Trump for, 69–73, 81, *82*, 83; truthiness for, 85–89; in UK, 52–53, *53*, 100; voter turnout, *58–59*, 58–60, 81, *82*, 83, *84*, 100–103, *104–6*, 106, 127–29, *128–30*

Wales. *See* United Kingdom
Wallace, George, 26, 72
waves, of populism, 1–2, 20
Wilders, Geert, 28, 34, 96
Wilson, Harold, 48–49
Wittgenstein, Ludwig, 22
working class, 52

xenophobia. *See* bigotry

Zirinovsky, Vladimir, 29